Stress and Burnout in the Human Service Professions

(PGPS-117)

Pergamon Titles of Related Interest

Felner/Jason/Moritsugu/Farber PREVENTIVE PSYCHOLOGY:
Theory, Research and Practice
Karoly/Kanfer SELF-MANAGEMENT AND BEHAVIOR CHANGE:
From Theory to Practice
O'Brien/Dickinson/Rosow INDUSTRIAL BEHAVIOR MODIFICATION:
A Management Handbook

Related Journals*

CLINICAL PSYCHOLOGY REVIEW
EVALUATION AND PROGRAM PLANNING
PERSONALITY AND INDIVIDUAL DIFFERENCES

*Free specimen copies available upon request.

PERGAMON GENERAL PSYCHOLOGY SERIES
EDITORS
Arnold P. Goldstein, *Syracuse University*
Leonard Krasner, *SUNY at Stony Brook*

Stress and Burnout in the Human Service Professions

edited by

Barry A. Farber
Teachers College, Columbia University

PERGAMON PRESS
New York   Oxford   Toronto   Sydney   Paris   Frankfurt

Pergamon Press Offices:

U.S.A.	Pergamon Press Inc., Maxwell House, Fairview Park, Elmsford, New York 10523, U.S.A.
U.K.	Pergamon Press Ltd., Headington Hill Hall, Oxford OX3 0BW, England
CANADA	Pergamon Press Canada Ltd., Suite 104, 150 Consumers Road, Willowdale, Ontario M2J 1P9, Canada
AUSTRALIA	Pergamon Press (Aust.) Pty. Ltd., P.O. Box 544, Potts Point, NSW 2011, Australia
FRANCE	Pergamon Press SARL, 24 rue des Ecoles, 75240 Paris, Cedex 05, France
FEDERAL REPUBLIC OF GERMANY	Pergamon Press GmbH, Hammerweg 6, D-6242 Kronberg-Taunus, Federal Republic of Germany

Copyright © 1983 Pergamon Press Inc.

Library of Congress Cataloging in Publication Data

Main entry under title:

Stress and Burnout in the Human Service Professions.

    (Pergamon general psychology series ; v. 117)
    Includes index.
    1. Burn out (Psychology) 2. Helping behavior.
I. Farber, Barry A. II. Series. [DNLM: 1. Job
satisfaction. 2. Stress, Psychological.
3. Social work--Manpower. WM 172 S9125]
BF481.S86   1983   158.7   82-16142
ISBN 0-08-028801-4

Printed in the United States of America

Contents

Foreword

I don't know about other countries, but in the United States certainly one of our national characteristics is that we come up with simple labels for complex social phenomena. Burnout is one of those labels. It conjures up vivid imagery of individual decline and decompensation at the same time that it pushes into the background the social contexts from which the fires of frustration and symbolic death arise. And by social contexts I mean not only the immediate work setting but also the larger systems that are related to or impinge upon the immediate one. Put more simply, burnout is never a characteristic of or within an individual but rather, it is a complex of psychological characteristics that reflect features of the larger society. But that statement is also an oversimplification because it too easily glosses over the fact that in the same society not all people who do the same work, even in the same work setting, experience burnout.

I attended the conference at which the papers that appear as chapters in this book were given. Frankly, I came to the conference with the fear that the primary emphasis of the papers would be on the psyches of individuals, making it a field day for clinicians. I had been to other conferences on stress and burnout and came away both bored and angry. Bored because everyone seemed to be saying much the same thing about individuals, and angry because of the galactic neglect of social contexts and social history. This conference was encouraging precisely because most of the authors of the papers were struggling to see a larger picture. As a result, the readers of this book, if they read its contents carefully, will gain an understanding that they will get no place else in the literature. At the very least, the reader will be prevented from deriving simple conclusions about a very complex individual-societal phenomena.

It is a cliché to say that ours is a very complex society but let us not forget that clichés contain kernels of truth. In the past decade and a half, when the idea of burnout became so popular, there was little evidence that burnout was being understood in terms of a complex society that has a complex social history. This book is a necessary and valuable corrective to past oversimplifications. Undoubtedly, as time goes on, some of the views and opinions expressed in this book will be found wrong or in need of revision. I venture the opinion that our views will change to the extent that we begin to see more clearly why and how burnout is a function of our particular society, a society that has a distinctive social history, political-economic structure and dynamic, and an explicit and implicit ideology. It is to be hoped that we will not make the mistake made after World War II when disorders in living were viewed as a problem of individuals, a problem that would be discernibly decreased in frequency and adverse consequences by the mass production of psychotherapists. We were wrong. This book encourages me to hope that we have learned something from our past.

Seymour B. Sarason

Preface

The concept of burnout was born in the early 1970s, its heritage embedded in the ideas and efforts of Herbert Freudenberger in New York and Christina Maslach and Ayala Pines in California. This volume presents a "state-of-the-art" look at burnout at the end of its first decade—a period in which this concept has made its way into the popular vocabulary and dramatically changed the ways in which human service professionals and the general public have thought about human service work.

There is some doubt regarding the true extent of the burnout syndrome, about how many workers have actually burned out. There can be no doubt, however, regarding the ubiquity of the word itself. Parents complain of burned out teachers, college students complain of burned out professors, legal aid lawyers and policemen complain of burned out judges. Government workers—from clerks to air traffic controllers—perceive themselves as burned out, as do many nurses, doctors, and psychotherapists. On the job and during coffee breaks and lunch hours, burned out teachers plan on opening up boutiques and restaurants, and burned out case workers plan on careers in publishing and public relations. Burnout is also used in an extraordinarily wide variety of contexts. It is used as an accusation against uncaring workers by underserved, frustrated clients. It is also used as an excuse by some professionals for half-hearted efforts, as an indication to others of the need for professional renewal, and as a motivation for still others to leave their field altogether. Burnout is used technically to describe a stress-related syndrome that has circumscribed causes and symptoms, but is also used colloquially to describe a transient state of fatigue. Burnout is said to be caused by stress, yet is often used as a synonym for stress. Burnout is said to afflict human service professionals, but has also been used at times to describe parents, students, blue-collar workers, and indeed, practically everyone.

In short, despite the widespread use of the term, there is a conspicuous lack of consensual understanding of what "burnout" actually is. In addition, despite a rapidly growing literature, there is still a notable lack of critical perspective on the field. Much of what is published is "standard fare," a rehashing of the usual causes and symptoms of burnout sandwiched around a good deal of case material. Because the field is new there have been relatively few opportunities for theorists, clinicians, researchers, and consultants to collaborate, exchange views, or critique each other's work. Moreover, progress in the field has been hindered by the burden of a "pop psychology," trendy image. Thus, theories have not been built upon the work of previous researchers, insights proposed a decade ago are constantly being "rediscovered," and the field in general often seems as if it is being consumed and trivialized by popular magazines and other news-hungry media.

The purpose of this volume is to offer a comprehensive and critical perspective on the phenomena of stress and burnout in the human service professions, to gather in one volume the views of virtually all major workers in the field. This volume has its immediate roots in a two-day conference on stress and burnout held at Teachers College, Columbia University, in the Fall of 1982. This conference, sponsored by the Clinical Psychology Program of Teachers College, and the New York State Psychological Association (NYSPA), was the first such event held on a nationwide scale and brought together the most prominent and provocative thinkers in the field. Experts on stress and burnout from the fields of clinical, community, and social psychology, social work, anthropology, medicine, nursing, and education were invited to present papers at the conference. The primary aim of the conference was to provide those in attendance with a particularly up-to-date understanding of the theories, symptoms, and treatment of stress and burnout; indeed, each of the 16 invited speakers agreed to present only previously unpublished research or new theoretical ideas. The conference focused on both personal and professional issues affecting human service workers—those individuals such as teachers, psychologists, social workers, child-care workers, medical personnel, and policemen whose work directly involves helping others and whose tools are often their own interpersonal skills.

This volume is based primarily, though not exclusively, on the papers presented at the conference. Several of the papers presented have not been included in the book; others have been extensively revised. In addition, new chapters, not based on conference proceedings, have been included. There are several, quite good, books available on the general subjects of stress and burnout; in fact, many of these have been written by contributors to the present volume. This book seeks not to offer another general overview of these subjects but rather to suggest the diversity and robustness of current thinking in the field. It is intended for those professionals and preprofessionals who wish to gain a serious understanding of the multitude of issues involved in the field, who wish to compare the latest views of many of the major figures in the field, and who wish to learn what they can do to alleviate stress and to prevent burnout in their own lives. It is also intended for students and researchers who are interested in new developments in these areas, and for those members of the general public who wish to learn more about these widely discussed, yet often poorly understood issues.

Burnout, as opposed to stress, is the more "popular" current concern. Nevertheless, this volume offers testimony to the fact that aversive working conditions may produce a variety of stressful reactions of which burnout is but one, albeit severe, form. Indeed, several chapters describe stress reactions of the nonburnout variety: Farber writing about dysfunctional aspects of the psychotherapeutic role; Mawardi discussing aspects of the impaired physician; and Fischer contrasting the "worn-out" worker from the truly "burned out" one.

The chapters on burnout offer new slants on theory, symptomatology, and treatment. In Part I (Theoretical Perspectives), Freudenberger reviews the current state of theory in the field and indicates several directions in which the field must move: toward greater uniformity in definition; toward increased input from a greater variety of disciplines; and toward greater awareness of ethical issues in consultation. Also in Part I, Harrison proposes a social competence model of burnout, focusing on the fundamental need of workers to perceive themselves as competent in their roles; Fischer employs a psycho-dynamic perspective to explain the burnout phenomenon, pointing out specific characterological structures, tendencies, and resistances of burned out (as opposed to worn out) workers; and Heifetz and Bersani suggest that burnout among human service workers is best conceptualized within a cybernetic model, emphasizing the critical role of feedback in professionals' pursuit of client growth and their own professional development.

In Part II (The Nature and Dimensions of Burnout in the Human Service Professions), the focus of the book shifts toward an examination of the determinants and manifestations of stress and burnout in a number of the helping professions. Sakharov and Farber use the perspective of critical theory to demonstrate the relationship between social and economic conditions and the propensity of teachers to become disillusioned and burned out. Ianni and Reuss-Ianni, based on their studies of teachers and policemen, argue that the burnout syndrome is more a function of the stress inherent in the person-organization relationship than it is a function of problems residing in the professional-client relationship. Farber reviews the variety of stress reactions that may occur as a consequence of psychotherapeutic work, emphasizing the relationship between therapists' personal histories and their current experience of work. Mawardi, drawing upon the results of 20 years of investigation of medical school graduates, describes the causes, symptoms, and consequences of physician impairment—a condition that may range in severity from slight distortions in judgment following a sleepless night, to major disabilities such as alcoholism or drug addiction. Jayaratne and Chess contrast the nature of job satisfaction and burnout in a large sample of social workers, suggesting that despite certain common defining factors, these two concepts are essentially orthogonal in nature. And, in a similar vein, Eisenstat and Felner demonstrate how the quality of relations between workers and clients in human service institutions is inextricably linked to both the presence of job motivators and the absence of job stressors.

The third part of this volume (Prevention and Treatment) suggests ways in which individuals and organizations can best cope with the problems of stress and burnout. Many of the chapters in this section emphasize the importance of social support as a buffer against burnout. Pines, for example, demonstrates the need for several types of social support, such as listening, technical support, and technical challenge. For Fibkins, social support is best provided through the establishment of institutional support systems, such as teacher centers, which serve to encourage individual growth and development and interpersonal support and collaboration. Scully, on the other hand, emphasizes the problem-solving function of support groups, suggesting that these groups should focus exclusively on professional rather than personal issues. Cherniss and Krantz suggest that "ideological communities" provide a particularly effective means of social support; the shared commitment and common belief system inherent in ideological communities may reduce the ambiguity and internal conflict that is so common to human service work. Aber takes a somewhat different approach to preventing burnout, emphasizing the need to understand the political system, and in particular the policy-making structure, under which workers function; only through such an understanding, suggests Aber, can systems be modified to better meet the needs of workers and prevent the occurrence of burnout. Finally, Shinn and Mørch propose a tripartite model of coping with stress and burnout, involving the use of individual, group, and organizational strategies.

My own initiation into the field of stress and burnout occurred when I began to teach elementary school in New York City back in 1968. I was assigned to a class of eight emotionally disturbed fourth and fifth graders and had one other young, inexperienced teacher as my partner. It wasn't long before we became a class of ten emotionally disturbed people. Although at the time I didn't label myself as burned out—the term had not yet been coined—my symptoms were, in fact, parallel to those of currently burned out teachers: physical and emotional exhaustion, detachment, and a strong desire to find an alternative career. Ultimately I overcame by burned out state and spent five gratifying though often frustrating years as a teacher. When I left teaching to pursue a career in clinical psychology I retained an interest in the areas of stress and burnout. Several individuals have been instrumental in encouraging this interest, in helping to organize the Stress and Burnout Conference at Teachers College, and in preparing this book. I wish to thank the following people: Lou Heifetz, Seymour Sarason, and Roşalea Schonbar for their support and interest over the years; Dean Michael Timpane and President Lawrence Cremin of Teachers College for the institutional, as well as personal, support they provided for the conference; Richard G. Kopff of NYSPA for his interest and help; Kirsten Anderson and Carole Sands for the long hours they spent in helping to plan the conference; Isabel Mount, Jane Saladorf, and Niname Parker for their efforts in publicizing the conference; Robert J. Schwarz, and his cadre of expert typists for their help with conference materials and with this manuscript; Beth King and Marcia Levine for their invaluable assistance in preparing this manuscript; Beth Marinelli and Amy Faust, my work-study students, for their months of helping out everywhere with everything; Sol and Nettie Farber, Neal and Varda Farber, Bernard, Muriel, and Wayne Forrest, and Sam and Sue Menahem for always caring; Jerry Frank, at Pergamon Press, for his faith, interest, and assistance; a generous, anonymous donor who made the conference possible; and, of course, the presenters at the conference and contributors to this book for their commitment to these projects, for their kind words, and for their dedication to helping others. Finally, I wish to thank my immediate family—April, Alissa, and David—for their patience, understanding, and love. Daddy's finally home, at least until the next book.

Stress and Burnout in the Human Service Professions

(PGPS-117)

Introduction:
A Critical Perspective on Burnout

Barry A. Farber

Since the mid-1970s interest in the phenomenon of professional burnout has grown enormously. Books, newspapers, magazines, professional journals, television, and radio have all helped popularize the topic; indeed, it sometimes appears as if each week the media identifies another group of workers as "burned out." The media, of course, have created as well as reflected an increased demand for stories, interviews, and data related to burnout; nevertheless, it is clear that vast numbers of people, especially those in the human service professions, have embraced the concept of burnout and integrated it within their collective self-image as workers. Teacher trainers, for example, report that burnout is often the highest-rated subject on needs assessment instruments designed to identify major teacher concerns (Shaw et al., 1979); in fact, the National Education Association (NEA) made burnout the central theme of their 1979 convention. In recent years, virtually all major professional organizations have included at least one symposium on burnout at their annual conventions. Burnout, it seems, may well become a "catch phrase" of the 1980s (Kennedy, 1979).

Burnout, though, is more than a "hot topic." It is a serious issue that affects the welfare of not only millions of human service workers but of their tens of millions of clients as well. Teachers and their students, psychotherapists and their patients, caseworkers and their clients are all potential victims of the attitudes and behaviors that are characteristic of burnout. As Sarason (1977) has noted, the detrimental implications of disillusionment in human service workers extend "far beyond the spheres of their individual existence" (p. 232).

What is burnout? And who "created" it? Freudenberger (1974, 1975) is usually given credit for first using the term in its present sense: to denote a state of physical and emotional depletion resulting from conditions of work: Freudenberger took a word that was used colloquially in the 1960s to refer to the effects of chronic drug abuse ("burned out" on drugs) and used it instead to characterize the psychological state of certain volunteers who worked with him in the late 1960s and early 1970s at alternative health care agencies. Within a few months of work, these young, idealistic men and women would begin to appear to Freudenberger as more tired, depressed, apathetic, and needy than the clients for whom they were ostensibly working. These symptoms were accompanied by guilt, paranoia, and a sense of omnipotence which made it difficult for these workers to cut back on their level of activity or involvement.

Even before Freudenberger, however, Graham Greene (1961), wrote a novel about "a burnt-out case." Greene's protagonist was a spiritually tormented, disillusioned, and despondent man who found an appropriate metaphor for his malaise in a leper colony; the symptoms of this fictional character fit the current descriptions of burned out individuals. While Greene's book was popular, it did not make burnout a household word in the 1960s. For the most part, it was Freudenberger, as well as Christina Maslach and Ayala Pines, colleagues at the University of California at Berkeley, who popularized the concept, pioneered its study, and legitimized its status as a critical social issue.

Freudenberger was trained as a psychoanalyst and is currently in private practice in New York. His model of burnout is based primarily on a paradigm that emphasizes the psychology of the individual. His work relies on a case-study approach and focuses on the psychological capabilities and vulnerabilities of individuals placed in stressful work situations. He has studied and described the individual dynamics of burnout: the psychological reasons why it occurs, and the process by which it occurs. Maslach and Pines, on the other hand, are both social psychologists by training. Maslach was influenced by Zimbardo's work in the early 1970s on dehumanization and depersonalization. Before coming to the United States, Pines did research on stress for the Israeli army. Their approach has been to study burnout from a more social psychological, research-oriented perspective with a heavier focus on the relationship between environmental and individual factors. Working individually as well as together, they have collected data on several thousand workers across many types of human service jobs, thus providing an empirical basis for the study of burnout. Using both questionnaires and interviews, they have systematically investigated the etiology, symptomatology, and treatment of burnout. For example, their early work documented the presence of three central factors within the burnout syndrome (emotional exhaustion, depersonalization, and personal accomplishment), and also explored the role of social support networks as potential mediators of job stress. Thus, their research examined not only helpers' reactions to their work but also situational factors that contribute to these reactions. As Maslach (1977) noted, the field had "reached the point at which the number of rotten apples in the barrel [warranted] examination of the barrel itself" (p. 14).

These two perspectives—the "clinical" approach of Freudenberger and the "empirical" approach of Maslach and Pines—have complemented each other well. For the most part, the findings based on each perspective have been mutually corroborative. Together, these approaches have generated a wealth of data and insights into the phenomenon of burnout.

THE PROBLEM OF DEFINITION

Burnout has been defined in a variety of ways in the nearly ten-year history of the field. Pines and Aronson (1981) note that burnout is "characterized by physical depletion, by feelings of helplessness and hopelessness, by emotional drain, and by the development of negative self-concept and negative attitudes toward work, life, and other people. . . . [It is a] sense of distress, discontent, and failure in the quest for ideals" (p. 15). Freudenberger and Richelson (1980) describe burnout as a "state of fatigue or frustration brought about by devotion to a cause, way of life, or relationship that failed to produce the expected reward" (p. 13). Edelwich and Brodsky (1980) define burnout as a "progressive loss of idealism, energy, purpose, and concern as a result of conditions of work" (p. 14). They note that "the seeds of burnout are contained in the assumption that the real world will be in harmony with [one's idealistic] dreams" (p. 16).

There is a general consensus that the symptoms of burnout include attitudinal, emotional, and physical components. As Maslach (1976) has noted, burned out professionals "lose all concern, all emotional feelings for the persons they work with and come to treat them in detached or even dehumanized ways" (p. 16). In addition, burned out professionals may become cynical toward clients, blaming them for creating their own difficulties or labeling them in derogatory or diagnostic terms. Burned out professionals are more frequently absent or late for work than their non-burned out colleagues; they become noticeably less idealistic and more rigid; their performance at work deteriorates markedly; and they may fantasize or actually plan on leaving the profession. Furthermore, the frustrations attendant to the phenomenon of burnout may lead to emotional stress (often manifest as anxiety, irritability, sadness, or lowered self-esteem), psychosomatic problems (insomnia, ulcers, headaches, backaches, fatigue, high blood pressure), and increased marital and family conflicts.

Despite the general unanimity of opinion regarding some of the characteristics of burnout, the determination of whether a worker is or is not burned out is not easily made. Burnout does not seem to lend itself to such clear dichotomies—in part, because burnout is a *process,* not an *event.* Nor is the process identical for each person. As Mattingly (1977) has observed, "burn-out . . . is a subtle pattern of symptoms, behaviors, and attitudes that are unique for each person" (p. 131). In general, burnout can be conceptualized as a function of the stresses engendered by individual, work-related, and societal factors.

INDIVIDUAL FACTORS IN BURNOUT

An understanding of the individual factors underlying burnout must include an assessment of individual personality variables, mediational processes (such as, cognitive appraisal of stressful events), and current life stresses and supports. For example, there is general agreement that burnout-prone individuals are empathic, sensitive, humane, dedicated, idealistic, and "people oriented," but also anxious, introverted, obsessional, overenthusiastic, and susceptible to overidentification with others (Bloch, 1977; Cherniss, 1980b; Edelwich & Brodsky, 1980; Freudenberger & Richelson, 1980; Pines & Aronson, 1981). People who go into human service work want to help others, sometimes desperately so. Some of these individuals may base their self-esteem too exclusively on the attainment of unrealistic, albeit humane, goals.

Recent studies have also suggested that "workaholic," Type A persons are particularly prone to developing physiological symptoms, including cardiac problems, as a consequence of stress (see Glass, 1977). Type A personalities are aggressive, competitive, intense, and moody. They are less able to tolerate frustration than their Type B counterparts, and are more likely to get angry and stressed when they perceive their efforts to be unsuccessful or unfairly compromised by others' interference. In general, how a person reacts to job stress is a function of both the stress encountered and individual personality type. It is the "goodness of fit" between job demands and personal abilities that determines the amount of stress experienced (French & Caplan, 1972). In this regard too, what complicates the measurement and definition of stress is that individual perception of, and reaction to, stress is a subjective matter and varies significantly from person to person. The idea that an individual can react dysfunctionally to the mere *perception* of stress, regardless of its objective existence, is generally agreed upon by researchers (see Cattell, 1972; Lazarus & Opton, 1966). Cognitive appraisal of stress involves a two-part sequence: primary appraisal used to determine *whether* an event is stressful, and secondary appraisal used to reduce or eliminate stress per se (Lazarus & Opton, 1966).

Life changes may make individuals especially susceptible to burnout. Consistent relationships have been found between the numbers and types of changes in a person's life and the onset of illness or disease within as little as one year (Holmes & Rahe, 1967). Both positive changes (such as marriage) and negative changes (such as death or divorce) are considered stressful, inasmuch as both types demand adjustments by the individual to new behavior patterns. Life changes may also be viewed from a developmental perspective. Theorists such as Erikson (1963, 1968), Levinson (1978), and Vaillant (1977) have all proposed models of adult development that include normative-crisis periods. These periods occur between each stage of adult development and may involve significant reevaluation of one's personal or professional life. As such, these periods may dramatically affect an individual's self-esteem, marital relationship, or faith and investment in work. Though "normative," these transitional periods are nonetheless stressful, and leave an individual with less capacity to cope successfully with other daily stresses. Thus, individuals who are undergoing significant changes in their lives may be particularly vulnerable to burnout.

The impact of significant events and transitional periods on an individual's capacity to withstand work-related stresses is obvious. Less obvious, but equally important, however, are the quality and tone of an individual's daily relationships with family and friends. Constant marital difficulties, for example, may make it more difficult for an individual to relax or feel comfortable at work, to fulfill responsibilities, to care for clients, and ultimately, to garner satisfaction from the job. Conversely, satisfying relationships with family and friends produce a support network that mitigates the impact of work-related stresses. The satisfactions and stresses of one's personal life and those of one's professional life are, therefore, mutually influential. Bhagat (1980) also suggests an interactive relationship between work-stress and life-stress, noting that high levels of such work-related stresses as role conflict tend to exacerbate the negative impact of life stress on individual work performance.

WORK-RELATED FACTORS

"The search for causes [of burnout]" states Maslach (1978), "is better directed away from identifying the bad people and toward uncovering the characteristics of the bad situations where many good people function" (p. 114). This viewpoint emphasizes the central role of work-related stresses, i.e., the nature of the work role and the nature of the work setting, in the etiology of burnout.

For any professional group, one could compile an almost endless list of work-related stresses, some common to all human services work, others unique to the specific field and work setting. For example, virtually all human service professionals complain of long hours, isolation, lack of autonomy, client "neediness," public misunderstanding of the nature of their work, insufficient resources, lack of criteria to measure accomplishments, excessive demands for productivity, inadequate job training, and administrative indifference to or interference with their work. In addition to these general stresses, teachers may complain of large class size, demanding parents, and disruptive students; psychotherapists may feel stressed by the nonreciprocated attentiveness, giving, and responsibility demanded by the therapeutic relationship as well as by the erratic pace of therapeutic progress; and policemen, legal aid attorneys, and judges may feel overwhelmed by the magnitude of the problems that they are charged with addressing.

Those who work in institutional rather than private settings are often faced with stresses endemic to organizational structures, most notably role ambiguity, role conflict, and role overload (Caplan & Jones, 1975; French & Caplan,

1972; Kahn, 1974; Tosi & Tosi, 1970). *Role ambiguity* is associated with a lack of clarity regarding a worker's rights, responsibilities, methods, goals, status, or accountability. According to Gowler and Legge (1975), individuals in organizations are likely to become stressed if, "on the one hand, they feel they must achieve, and on the other hand, the success criteria which define and evaluate their achievement are ambiguous" (p. 64). Other factors that may lead to role ambiguity include the increasing complexity of tasks and technology, the rapidity of organizational change, and the interconnectedness of organizational positions. *Role conflict* occurs when inconsistent, incompatible, or inappropriate demands are placed upon an individual. For example, an individual may experience role conflict when told to do things that he or she perceives as outside the domain of professional work (e.g., administrative duties, paperwork). Or role conflict may occur when an individual's values and ethics conflict with those of his or her supervisor or supervisee. Office politics, competition for status and promotion, and territorial disputes over roles and responsibilities (e.g., between nurses and doctors, or between social workers and psychologists) can all precipitate role conflict. *Role overload* is one of the most common complaints among those who work in organizations. In a study by Farber and Heifetz (1982), for example, a heterogeneous sample of psychotherapists reported "excessive workload" as the single most stressful aspect of their work. Moreover, this source of stress is likely to become more prevalent in the near future as a result of budget cutbacks and job freezes. Role overload has often been considered only in quantitative terms—that is, as a function of having too much to do. It appears clear, however, that there may be a qualitative aspect of role overload as well, when increasingly complex work requires skills or abilities that are beyond an individual's current level of functioning. In this context, then, role overload may lead to role ambiguity and role conflict.

The common element to most work-related stresses is that each promotes a feeling of *inconsequentiality,* a feeling on the part of professionals that no matter how hard they work, the payoffs in terms of accomplishment, recognition, advancement, or appreciation, are not there. This feeling is exemplified by the teacher who asks, "Why should I plan for my class for three hours, when one hour will produce the same (disappointing) results?" or, the mental health worker who asks, "Why should I keep up with advances in the field when my chronic patients aren't going to benefit anyway?" This sense of inconsequentiality is similar to Seligman's (1975) notion of "learned helplessness." Both concepts refer to a state in which individuals feel that their actions can no longer effect desired changes in the environment and that, therefore, there is no point in continuing to try.

Burnout, then, can be viewed as a process that occurs when workers perceive a discrepancy between their input and expected output. To balance the equation, burned out workers begin to give considerably less to their jobs. For example, teachers who become burned out may be less sympathetic toward students, may have a lower tolerance for frustration in the classroom, may plan for their classes less often or less carefully, and in general, may feel less committed and dedicated to their work (Farber & Miller, 1981).

SOCIAL, ECONOMIC, AND HISTORICAL FACTORS

Burnout is most often viewed in the context of the relationship between the individual and his or her work environment. But the kind of systematic frustration and disenchantment that many workers, both professional and nonprofessional, report with reference to their jobs suggests that burnout may also be a symptom of broader social concerns. Cherniss (1980a, 1980b) has, in fact, noted that there are sources of burnout at the individual, organizational, and societal levels.

Is burnout therefore no more than a current word for what used to be referred to as "worker alienation"? Marxist theory, of course, suggests that dissatisfaction and burnout in workers are inevitable outgrowths of capitalist societies. Marx first began exploring the question of work and its relationship to social structure in the mid-nineteenth century. He conceived of work, or productive activity, as the "organic" expression of humanness and he drew no distinctions between work, activity, and creativity in their pure or "unalienated" forms. Thus, for Marx, productive activity not only served as the principal *expression* of an individual's combined powers but also as the primary *catalyst* for the development of these powers (Ollman, 1971). Marx believed that people were inevitably alienated from their work (and thus, their essential natures) in any but a communist state. This alienation, he thought, was characterized by several "divisions": the division of people from products they make but cannot distribute; the division of people from each other as a result of class antagonisms; and the division of people from their work as a source of personal identity. According to Marxist thought, an individual's relationship to his or her mode of production affects the development of thoughts, attitudes, and behaviors. Thus, alienating work necessarily leads to alienated individuals. Indeed, in 1844, Marx wrote a description of the alienation of labor which sounds remarkably like current descriptions of burnout:

> [Because] labor is external to the worker . . . he does not affirm himself but denies himself, does not feel content but unhappy, does not develop freely his physical and mental energy but mortifies his body and ruins his mind. The worker therefore only feels himself outside his work, and in his work feels outside himself. [Cited in Ollman, 1971, p. 136.]

Capitalism in the United States is a relatively recent phenomenon. Braverman (1974) reports that at the beginning of the 19th century, four-fifths of the population of the United States was self-employed. That proportion dropped to one-third with the advent of the industrial revolution, was one-fifth by 1940, and by 1970, only one-tenth of the population of this country worked for themselves. Braverman notes too that as a result of capitalism, workers' skills have become fragmented and workers themselves have become increasingly objectified, that is, they are viewed as component parts of a nexus of human and inanimate machinery geared to the production of goods and services. As a result of these changes, tradition, sentiment, and pride in one's work have all been superseded by a devotion to self-interest.

While a Marxist analysis of society involves a deterministic stance which many find uncongenial, the insights of Marxist scholars can potentially be applied to the examination of the experiences of helping professionals. In terms of a Marxist model, professional dissatisfaction and burnout, as well as nonprofessional, blue-collar dissatisfaction and tedium, can be viewed as reactions to the fragmentation of work, to competition within the workplace, and to the loss of worker autonomy. In regard to this last point: although the public often assumes that professionals experience a high level of autonomy accompanied by relatively little tedium in their work lives, in fact, many of the privileges presumably accorded professionals are illusory. As Sarason (1977) has noted, "enhanced social status is a weak base for continued satisfaction when daily reality confirms that you are not in control over your destiny, that decisions affecting your work and life are made elsewhere, often by people and forces unknown and unknowable to you" (p. 223). And Cherniss (1980a) has noted that the loss of autonomy is particularly true for public-sector professionals who are subject to the constraints of large bureaucracies.

While insights into the impact of capitalism on the experience of work can prove useful in an explication of burnout in the helping professions, a class analysis of the role of professional workers is inadequate in and of itself. Human service work is, in many ways, unique and does not fit neatly into Marxist doctrine. First and foremost, human service professionals are exceptional in that they *are* their own "tools" and means of production. This situation, notes Cherniss (1980b), leaves helping professionals vulnerable to particular issues of competency, power, and control that are substantially unrelated to Marxist thought. For example, a professional's sense of his or her competence and success is, to a large extent, dependent upon the cooperation, involvement, and motivation of clients or patients rather than managers or entrepreneurs. A second, related issue lies in the nature of professional satisfactions. For many human service professionals, gratification at work—in the form of promoting growth and change or achieving a sense of intimate involvement in the lives of their clients—is an unpredictable yet profoundly moving experience. Satisfaction and fulfillment may occur suddenly in the midst of an otherwise chaotic day, week, or month and may provide instant affirmation of the wisdom of one's career choice. A teacher who is feeling burned out may be suddenly heartened by a sense of having finally reached a difficult child; a therapist who's been feeling "stuck" and somewhat disillusioned may become rejuvenated by the sudden progress of a long-term, resistant patient; a caseworker who is feeling overwhelmed and unsupported may reinvest time and energy in work after receiving a simple thank-you note from an appreciative client. Feeling that you've made a significant difference in the life of another human being is the *sine qua non* of human service work; such moments can provide an emotional "fix" that may last through months of doubt or disillusionment. A final indication that Marxist formulations regarding worker alienation are not entirely applicable to helping professionals lies in the small but consistent body of research findings that suggest that high levels of job satisfaction can, and do, coexist with high levels of stress and burnout (Cherniss & Egnatios, 1978; Cherniss & Kane, 1977; Eisenstat & Felner, 1981; Evans & Bartolomé, 1980). Indeed, a high level of commitment to one's work is often regarded as a prerequisite to burnout and is most likely to occur in the context of a relatively high level of job satisfaction. Bloch (1977), for example, has found that teachers who are obsessional, passionate, idealistic, and dedicated to their work are more prone to burnout. Being excellent in one's work is both gratifying and demanding; the balance between these two states is often, however, precarious. Burnout often affects the most caring and most involved workers; they are the ones for whom a discrepancy between effort and results matters the most.

In short, Marxist thought regarding worker alienation and job dissatisfaction, though provocative and of heuristic value, does not offer an entirely satisfactory understanding of the experiences of many human service professionals. Work, however, is not simply a "here and now" phenomenon unrooted in a perceived past and future (Sarason, 1977); alternative ways of thinking about burnout in a social and historical context must therefore be sought. Among others, Lasch (1979), Packard (1972), Sarason (1977), and Slater (1976) have all documented relatively recent and dramatic changes in family, work, and social structures within American society. Lasch (1979), for example, suggests that we are currently living in a "culture of narcissism," which has its roots in the "competitive individualism" of Western civilization. Our culture, according to Lasch, has been influenced by gradual changes in the structure of society: a shifting emphasis from production of commodities to consumption; the growth of large organizations and bureaucracies; the increasingly transient, unrewarding, and even combative nature of social relationships. The effects of these changes on individuals, notes Lasch, are best expressed in psychological rather than economic terms. Our present culture fosters the development of narcissistic, self-absorbed, manipulative individuals who demand immediate gratification but who live "in a state of restless, perpetually unsatisfied desire" (p. 23). The narcissist fears dependence, has difficulty in forming deep, personal attachments, experiences a sense of inner emptiness and isolation, and has a deep reservoir of repressed rage. Withdrawal, despair, anger, the ethic of self-preservation, and the "trappings" of success are thus common elements of both the narcissistic and the burned out individual. Indeed, Lasch suggests that "narcissism appears realistically to represent the best way of coping with the tensions and anxieties of modern life" (p. 101). Burnout, then, in Lasch's view, might constitute a particularly explicit articulation of a pervasive social pattern.

Lasch's views are shared in large measure by Slater (1976) and Packard (1972), both of whom contend that our commitment to individualism leads to a suppression of our needs for community, engagement, and dependency. Slater notes that as individuals learn to internalize needs and controls (partly in response to the increasing fluidity and complexity of American society), they experience life less intensely and are no longer able to "make strong responses to events in their lives" (p. 33). Indeed, comments Slater, as our society continues to move away from an "instinctive sense of community that villagers had in the past," we move with "dizzying speed toward greater anonymity, impersonality, and disconnectedness" (p. 128). Similarly, Packard (1972) has labeled post–World War II America, "a nation of strangers," pointing to such phenomena as high-rise apartments, "broken" families, urban renewal, the relocations of industry, and the general mobility of American citizens. The impact of such a fragmented society, claims Packard, results in indifference to community events, wariness to become involved in others' lives, an uncertain sense of self, and a resolve to "live for the moment." "Individualism," then, not only leads to general feelings of alienation and disconnectedness but also, by its very nature, impedes the formation of a psychological sense of community or even collegial support systems, either of which can mitigate stress and prevent burnout. Moreover, as a result of social fragmentation and uprootedness, each opportunity for gratification and fulfillment grows increasingly important to individuals. Work, then, especially work that holds the promise of a "noble calling," is invested with great meaning and expectations. It is the failure of these expectations that may catalyze the burnout process.

Finally, Sarason (1977) has focused specifically on the work-related consequences of rapid social change following World War II. According to Sarason, the aftermath of the war precipitated an era of general optimism based on the dual perceptions of unlimited national resources and unlimited individual potential. It was a time of rapidly rising expectations, and of hopes for economic success, social mobility, and personal growth. On the other hand, this new emphasis on individual needs helped to establish a mythology of the individual as separate from the community, and as unneedful of a network of mutually supportive, self-validating relationships. The value of a psychological sense of community in mitigating the impact of stress and loneliness at work was overlooked by individuals in their choice of a career and a work setting. It was only *after* dissatisfaction with work had set in that individuals began to recognize the effects of a psychological sense of community on their experience of work:

> After a person becomes aware that he cannot continue to make a strong commitment to work, that an impersonal society has rendered him impotent and dependent and has frustrated the desire for personal growth, the resulting alienation and loneliness bring to the fore the absence and need for a sense of community. [Sarason, 1977, p. 287.]

The need for a psychological sense of community, argues Sarason, is central to the positive experience of work and has become an ever stronger need as "the centrifugal forces in our society have whirled with increasing speed" (p. 283).

Taken together, the work of these four theorists (Lasch, Slater, Packard, and Sarason), along with the recent work of Yankelovich (1981), suggests that as a result of social changes, American workers have become increasingly disconnected and alienated from their communities, and increasingly insistent upon attaining personal fulfillment and gratification from their work. The combination of these two trends has produced workers with higher expectations of fulfillment and fewer resources to cope with frustrations—a perfect recipe for burnout. In addition, the present economic conditions in our society have made career shifts increasingly difficult. Burned out professionals, particularly those with many years of good experience, may find few, if any, economically comparable opportunities in other fields. Thus, they may feel "stuck," increasingly resentful at remaining in their present job. Their sense of frustration grows, and feelings of burnout increase. Perhaps the only sanguine note in this entire picture is Yankelovich's finding of a renewed concern in America, within the last few years, for "community and caring relationships." This trend may at least ameliorate the effects of stress on workers.

THE HUMAN SERVICES MOVEMENT

What remains in developing a social-historical context for understanding professional burnout is to take into account the history of the human service movement in this country. Levine and Levine (1970) and Sarason (1981) are informative regarding this issue. They have noted that the human services became a profession for the first time in the 1920s, in the post-settlement-house era. The small number of human service workers at this time were a close-knit group, possessed of a common "missionary zeal" to help others; for the most part they were uninfluenced by government policy or bureaucracy. According to Sarason, these individuals (most of whom were social workers) were in no way burned out. They had "the word," they had each other, and they did not have to worry about government funding. They also understood the disparity between what they wanted to do, what needed to be done, and their ability to do it.

In the 1930s, as a result of the depression, government unwillingly had to get into the business of supporting people. It was a decade when social work became important, and government projects and programs proliferated. Still, there was no burnout: a sense of opportunity and a sense of mission were still keenly felt by human service workers. The experience of human service work though began to change in the post–World War II era as the relationship between the government and human service workers grew closer. Although this connection was enthusiastically pursued by professional groups as a way of expanding their influence, it was not without its unintended consequences. Human service work, notes Sarason, became professionalized, bureaucratized, credentialized, and isolated. A growing sense of professionalism served to increase the distance between the helpers and the helped. Moreover, an increasing demand for services, coupled with government support for these services, created a widely held perception that the human services could solve all society's problems. The stage was now set for burnout: large numbers of relatively isolated human service workers with great expectations, and little autonomy, were working as part of an impersonal bureaucratized system of organizations and agencies where policies over which workers had no control were formulated (Sarason, 1981). As government interference increased (more paperwork, more cases, more agencies) and as clients became needier and more "entitled," the possibility for finding fulfillment in human service work grew markedly dimmer. Indeed, disillusionment and burnout is rife among those human service professionals who currently work in government agencies (see Cherniss, 1980a) and the situation may not be so dramatically different for those "independent practitioners" who still must contend with the myriad regulations of federal, state, and local agencies. What may be concluded then from Sarason's perspective on the helping services is that burnout becomes more prevalent as client-professional relationships become increasingly encumbered by institutional constraints or confounded by unrealistic expectations.

AN INTEGRATIVE MODEL OF BURNOUT

Models of burnout that attribute its occurrence solely to work-related stresses are still common in the popular press. For example, descriptions of teacher burnout in newspapers and magazines invariably fail to mention the role of personality variables, mediational processes, or social-historical factors in the burnout process. The professional literature has, however, offered increasingly complex etiological models of burnout, often emphasizing the interaction of individual, organizational, and societal factors. Illustrative of this trend is Cherniss's work on helping professionals in the public sector (Cherniss, 1980a, 1980b). Cherniss has examined the interaction of individual helpers' expectations and goals (their ideal notions of the helping relationship), the institutional constraints of working in and for large bureaucracies, and the public's perceptions of the nature of such work (the "professional mystique"). This professional mystique involves the public's belief that professionals experience a high level of autonomy and job satisfaction, are highly trained and competent, work with responsive clients, and are generally compassionate and caring (Cherniss, 1980a). Cherniss argues that this mystique is initially accepted by incoming public-sector professionals and serves to reinforce their unrealistically high expectations. Inevitably, though, this mystique clashes with the reality of bureaucratic constraints and work-related stresses, ultimately culminating in disillusionment and burnout. In short, Cherniss's model offers an unusually comprehensive understanding of the dynamics of the burnout process; its focus on specific factors occurring in specific work settings affecting a specific type of worker is a progressive step for the field.

PARAMETERS OF THE BURNOUT SYNDROME

To what range of phenomena does the concept of burnout extend? At times, burnout has been used in a very broad sense to describe dysphoric feelings that may occur in almost any setting. Freudenberger and Richelson (1980) talk of people burning out in relationships, Edelwich and Brodsky (1980) refer to burnout in artists and lovers, and Chance (1981) extends the concept to include runners. Other researchers though have supported a narrower definition of the term, applying it only to workers in the helping professions. Pines and Aronson (1981), for example, prefer to distinguish between burnout and "tedium," a similar constellation of feelings that affects workers in nonhuman-service jobs. Restricting the definition of burnout to human service workers acknowledges the unique pressures of utilizing one's self as the "tool" in face-to-face work with needy, demanding, and often troubled clients.

Perhaps in reaction to the currently ubiquitous use of the term in everyday speech, the concept of burnout has recently been criticized in the popular press for being a convenient explanation of individual malaise or lack of will. Paul Quinnett (1981), writing in *The New York Times*, contends that "we have stumbled upon a worthy and thoroughly modern concept with which to label our discontent. . . . [It] covers our personal failures much better than ordinary forms of irresponsibility to ourselves and others. It gives us, as I see it, the perfect out" (p. A-23). Similarly, Lance Morrow (1981) in *Time*, views burnout as a peculiarly American "hypochondria of the spirit," arguing that labeling oneself as burned out provides an easy escape from life's pressures. "The idea contains a sneaking self-aggrandizement tied to an elusive self-exoneration" (p. 84). In short, there are those who see burnout simply as a currently acceptable excuse for failure and who question whether the invocation of "burnout" as a description of behavior has any diagnostic, predictive, or therapeutic utility.

In professional circles, it has often been noted that the symptoms of burnout, in many ways, mirror those of depression: feelings of hopelessness, helplessness, emptiness, sadness; psychosomatic complaints; and neurovegetative signs (eating and sleeping disturbances, lack of energy). In response to the inference that burnout is essentially a reactive depression, Freudenberger (1981a) notes that depression is most often accompanied by guilt, whereas burnout generally occurs in the context of conscious anger. Moreover, the symptoms of burnout, at least initially, tend to be situation-specific rather than pervasive. In other words, a person may be burned out in one sphere of his or her life and functioning quite well in another. In classic depression, on the other hand, a person's symptoms tend to be manifest across all situations. It should be noted though that burnout, if continued unchecked, will invariably affect nonwork situations; for example, a husband who feels burned out from work may well have less energy and sympathy for his wife or children; nevertheless, that same husband may be generally more optimistic, loving, and future-oriented than the person suffering from depression. Most importantly, the focus of intervention in burnout is on work conditions rather than on intrapsychic factors. Whether one elects to conceptualize burnout as a particular form of depression or as an independent (though possibly related) syndrome does not abnegate the fact that environmental factors play a critical role in the creation, exacerbation, and amelioration of its symptomatology.

Finally, it should be noted that both the popular press and the professional literature have often confused or equated "stress" with "burnout." Though these two concepts are similar, they are not identical. Burnout is more often the result not of stress per se (which may be inevitable in the helping professions) but of *unmediated stress*—of being stressed and having no "out," no buffers, no support system (Farber, 1982). What is often overlooked is that stress can have both positive and negative effects—a fact that Selye (1956) noted over 25 years ago. Stress occurs when there is a substantial imbalance (perceived or real) between environmental demands and the response capability of the individual. As the environmental demands increase or the response capability of the individual decreases, the likelihood of stress becoming a negative experience—and ultimately effecting a burned out state—becomes more probable.

It is no wonder though that the two concepts get confused. In several theories, certain stress reactions are referred to in terms that are quite similar to those used in the description of burnout. For example, Hackman (1970), has noted four general types of strategy for coping with stress: (1) explicit movement against the stressful situation or its agent, such as agression, attack, or hostility; (2) movement away from the source of stress, such as avoidance, withdrawal, resignation, inaction, or escape; (3) submission, or collaborative movement toward the source of stress, such as ingratiation or undue cooperation; and (4) distortion of the situation through traditional psychological mechanisms such as denial, displacement, reaction formation, or intellectualization. In this context, burnout may be seen as the final step in the progression from active problem solving to submission and distortion (strategies three and four, above), to anger and depletion (strategies one and two, above). When earlier steps in this progression fail to alleviate stress, more severe reactions (i.e., those seen commonly as part of the burnout syndrome) become manifest. In a similar vein, Lazarus (1966) has noted that efforts to reduce stress can take the form of active problem solving (for example, increased information seeking), psychological defense, or withdrawal. Finally, Selye (1956, 1976) has proposed a stage theory of stress which he terms "The General Adaptation Syndrome." In stage one, "Alarm Reaction," the body mobilizes forces to defend itself against stresses. In stage two, "Resistance," a person is able to function in what appears to be a normal fashion. But in stage three, "Exhaustion," the cumulative effects of damaging stress have become too severe to allow for adaptation. The symptoms noted in this last stage are, again, similar in many respects to the symptoms of burnout. In short then, burnout can be regarded as the final step in a progression of unsuccessful attempts to cope with a variety of negative stress conditions.

PREVENTION AND TREATMENT

Efforts to formulate and validate treatment approaches to burnout have been hindered by several factors, including: the continued confusion in the field between the concepts of stress and burnout; the tendency to focus treatment on a limited number of discrete, observable, etiological variables; the lack of a commonly accepted etiological model; and a general paucity of empirical investigation of the efficacy of established programs of prevention and treatment.

A number of approaches to treating burnout have been employed, with the specific choice of treatment varying most often as a function of the training and orientation of the burnout consultant. Thus, those trained in a clinical, psychotherapeutic model have proposed individual or group psychotherapy for burned out professionals. For example, Freudenberger (1981b) has had success with a short-term, goal-limited approach, and Edelwich and Brodsky (1980) have touted the use of "Reality Therapy" (Glasser, 1975). Stress management consultants, some of whom have had training in cognitive-behavioral psychology, have suggested stress-reduction techniques such as systematic desensitization, relaxation training, biofeedback, meditation, and yoga. Organizational and social psychologists have recommended structural changes in the work setting: reducing client-staff ratios, shortening work hours, sensitizing administrators to the problems and stresses of staff, offering staff members more flexibility in their schedules and more autonomy in their work, and improving pre- and in-service training programs. And community psychologists have often argued for a primary preventive approach to burnout, stressing the need for a "psychological sense of community" in which workers' needs for collaboration, support and comraderie are fulfilled on a daily basis. According to this viewpoint, work settings should be organized to meet the needs not only of clients, but of workers as well. A psychological sense of community, it is suggested, can mitigate workers' feelings of isolation and inconsequentiality, and thus improve morale and productivity (Farber & Miller, 1981; Sarason, 1977).

Other suggestions for dealing with burnout have come from the colleagues, friends, and families of burned out professionals. These common-sense, often effective solutions include the need for a burned out professional to discuss problems with others (rather than withdraw), to organize and set priorities, to become involved in social and recreational activities, to attend to his or her physical well-being through exercise, dieting, and vacations, and to give serious consideration to a career change if feelings of stress or burnout continue unabated.

Among the most promising new approaches to treating burnout is the development of strong social support systems. On a personal basis, social support usually involves a network of family and friends who provide the validation of a professional's self-worth that may be lacking at work. Strong personal support systems buffer the impact of work-related stress and lessen the probability or severity of burnout. Thus, Maslach and Jackson (1981) found that married workers exhibit less "emotional exhaustion" (one of three symptomatic components of burnout) than their unmarried colleagues.

More typically, however, the burnout consultant recommends the establishment and maintenance of social supports at work. In some instances these groups represent self-help programs that workers have organized for themselves; in other cases employers have established the groups in response to employee needs. Both groups fall into two general categories: those designed to provide increased stimulation and learning as a means of making jobs more fulfilling, and those where the primary goal is to provide peer support and permit discharge of feelings evoked in daily human service work. In the former category, Fibkins (1974, 1980a, 1980b) has written extensively on the value of Teacher Centers that use a peer education-skills exchange model in an effort to enhance teachers' work lives; in these settings, the primary goal is professional renewal rather than ventilation of feelings or the acquisition of specific techniques for dealing with stress. On the other hand, Walley and Stokes (1981) have described the training of volunteer Chicago Public School teachers to act as consultants to support groups geared to the amelioration of teacher stress. Similarly, Scully (1981) has discussed the functions of support groups for nurses, emphasizing the value of such groups in effecting stress reduction and conflict resolution.

Evidence of the efficacy of social support is beginning to accumulate. Brownell and Dooley (1981), for example, found that social support lessened the psychological effects of physical stress. Farber (1982) found that while suburban teachers do not generally experience a psychological sense of community (that is, they do not often have rewarding contact with parents or administrators), they do experience and benefit from rewarding contact with selected colleagues in their school. However, while social support is obviously of value, it cannot be regarded as a panacea. To begin with, the establishment of a social support network within a chaotic work setting may be quite difficult. As Edelwich and Brodsky (1980) have noted, this process tends to be frustrated by the fact that "the very conditions that create conflicts on the job act to prevent one from building up the reciprocal emotional ties with other people . . . that would give one greater strength for coping with those conflicts" (p. 85). In addition, it must be recognized that while social support can attenuate the impact of stress, it usually cannot alter the conditions of work that created the stress initially. Thus, as Farber and Miller (1981) have remarked, social support is essentially a "first-order" change strategy (see Watzlawick, Weakland, & Fisch, 1974)—that is, it does not alter the nature of the malfunctioning system and, in fact, may serve to perpetuate current misconceptions regarding the nature and treatment of the problem. Effective remediation of burnout, according to Farber and Miller, requires second-order change strategies—a reconceptualization of the problem in a different manner and subsequent modification of the *system's* functioning.

TOWARD A BETTER UNDERSTANDING OF THE BURNOUT PHENOMENON

This introduction, an attempt to place the concepts of stress and burnout within a critical perspective, has reviewed the theories, research, and controversies that have marked the field's first ten years (1973–1982). It is apparent that the concept of burnout has had a major impact, in American society at least, on professionals' assumptions and expectations regarding work. Indeed, to the extent that burnout has become "legitimized" and even *expected* of certain workers (notably teachers), it has surely affected some workers' motivation to continue to work hard at their jobs.

It is a critical time for the concept of burnout. Will burnout prove to be a concept of enduring value, useful in understanding and treating a class of work-related symptoms? Or will the concept itself "burn out" from overuse, overextension, and lack of new direction? The present volume offers affirmative testimony to the first proposition—that burnout has become an integral part of our society's self-image and that new theories, research, and treatment approaches are essential and forthcoming.

This book is divided into three sections. The first section ("Theoretical Perspectives") includes chapters that question and challenge established views of burnout, as well as those that offer provocative new models to explain its occurrence. The second section ("The Nature and Dimensions of Burnout in the Human Service Professions") contains chapters that describe the various forms that stress and burnout may take in a number of the helping professions: social work, teaching, psychotherapy, medicine, and police work. And finally, the last section ("Prevention and Treatment") consists of chapters that offer a range of solutions to the burnout problem.

REFERENCES

Bhagat, R. S. *Effects of stressful life events upon individual performance effectiveness and work adjustment processes within organizational settings: A research model.* Paper presented at the 88th Annual Convention of the American Psychological Association, Montreal, Canada, 1980.

Bloch, A. The battered teacher. *Today's Education,* 1977, **66**, 58–62.

Braverman, H. *Labor and monopoly capital: The depradation of work in the twentieth century.* New York: Monthly Review Press, 1974.

Brownell, A. & Dooley, D. *Perceived social support: A moderator of health-related stress.* Paper presented at the Annual Convention of the American Psychological Association, Los Angeles, August 1981.

Caplan, R. D. & Jones, K. W. Effects of workload, role ambiguity, and Type A personality on anxiety, depression and heart rate. *Journal of Applied Psychology,* 1975, **60**, 713–719.

Cattell, R. B. Anxiety and motivation: Theory and crucial experiments. In C. D. Speilberger (Ed.), *Anxiety and behavior.* Vol. 2. New York: Academic Press, 1972.

Chance, P. That drained-out, used-up feeling. *Psychology Today,* 1981, **15**, 88–92.

Cherniss, C. *Professional burnout in human service organizations.* New York: Praeger, 1980. (a)

Cherniss, C. *Staff burnout: Job stress in the human services.* Sage Studies in Community Mental Health. Beverly Hills, Ca.: Sage Publications, 1980. (b)

Cherniss, C. & Egnatios, E. Is there job satisfaction in community mental health? *Community Mental Health Journal,* 1978, **14**, 309–318.

Cherniss, C. & Kane, J. S. *Public sector professionals: Satisfied but alienated from work.* (Unpublished paper) Ann Arbor: University of Michigan, 1977.

Edelwich, J. & Brodsky, A. *Burnout: Stages of disillusionment in the helping professions.* New York: Human Sciences Press, 1980.

Eisenstat, R. A. & Felner, R. D. *The relationship between job characteristics, work attitudes and human service workers' perceptions of end behavior towards clients.* (Unpublished paper) New Haven: Yale University, 1981.

Erikson, E. H. *Childhood and society.* 2nd ed. New York: Norton, 1963.

Erikson, E. H. *Identity: Youth and crisis.* New York: Norton, 1968.

Evans, P. A. & Bartolomé, F. The relationship between professional life and private life. In C. B. Dean (Ed.), *Work, family, and career.* New York: Praeger, 1980.

Farber, B. A. *Stress and burnout: Implications for teacher motivation.* Paper presented at Annual Meeting of the American Educational Research Association, New York, 1982.

Farber, B. A. & Heifetz, L. J. The process and dimensions of burnout in psychotherapists. *Professional Psychology,* 1982, **13** (2), 293-301.

Farber, B. A. & Miller, J. Teacher burnout: A psycho-educational perspective. *Teachers College Record,* 1981, **83** (2), 235-243.

Fibkins, W. The whys and hows of teachers' centers. *Phi Delta Kappan,* 1974, **55** (8), 567-569.

Fibkins, W. Teacher centering to reduce burnout and isolation. *Action in Teacher Education,* Spring 1980, 31-36. (a)

Fibkins, W. *The work experience of teachers and professional burnout.* Fairfield, Conn.: Teacher Center, Inc., 1980. (b)

French, J. R., Jr., & Caplan, R. D. Organizational stress and individual strain. In Marrow, A. J. (Ed.), *The failure of success.* New York: AMACOM, 1972.

Freudenberger, H. J. Staff burnout. *Journal of Social Issues,* 1974, **30,** 159-165.

Freudenberger, H. J. The staff burnout syndrome in alternative institutions. *Psychotherapy: Theory, Research, and Practice,* 1975, **12,** 73-82.

Freudenberger, H. J. Burnout: Contemporary issues and trends. Paper presented at The National Conference on Stress and Burnout, New York, 1981. (a)

Freudenberger, H. J. *The burned out professional: What kind of help?* Paper presented at the First National Conference on Burnout, Philadelphia, November, 1981. (b)

Freudenberger, H. J. with Richelson, G. *Burnout: The high cost of high achievement.* Garden City, N.Y.: Anchor Press, 1980.

Glass, D. C. *Behavior patterns, stress and coronary disease.* Hillsdale, N.J.: Erlbaum, 1977.

Glasser, W. *Reality therapy.* New York: Harper Colophon Books, 1975.

Gowler, D. & Legge, K. *Managerial stress.* New York: Wiley & Sons, 1975.

Greene, G. *A burnt-out case.* New York: Viking Press, 1961.

Hackman, J. R. Tasks and task performance in research on stress. In J. E. McGrath (Ed.), *Social and psychological factors in stress.* New York: Holt, Rinehart, & Winston, 1970.

Holmes, T. H. & Rahe, R. H. The social readjustment scale. *Journal of Psychosomatic Research,* 1967, **11,** 213-218.

Kahn, R. L. Conflict, ambiguity, and overload: Three elements in job stress. In McLean, A. (Ed.), *Occupational stress.* Springfield, Ill.: C.C. Thomas, 1974.

Kennedy, E. The looming 80's. *The New York Times Magazine,* December 2, 1979, pp. 68-69, 110-120.

Lasch, C. *The culture of narcissism: American life in an age of diminishing returns.* New York: Norton, 1979.

Lazarus, R. S. *Psychological stress and the coping process.* New York: McGraw-Hill, 1966.

Lazarus, R. S. & Opton, E. M. The study of psychological stress: A summary of theoretical formulations and experimental findings. In C. D. Speilberger (Ed.), *Anxiety and behavior.* Vol. 1. New York: Academic Press, 1966.

Levine, M. & Levine, A. *A social history of helping services.* New York: Appleton-Century-Crofts, 1970.

Levinson, D. *The seasons of a man's life.* New York: Knopf, 1978.

Maslach, C. Burned out. *Human Behavior,* 1976, **5,** 16-22.

Maslach, C. *Burnout: A social psychological analysis.* Paper presented at the Annual Convention of the American Psychological Association, 1977.

Maslach, C. Job burnout: How people cope. *Public Welfare,* 1978, **36,** 56-58.

Maslach, C. & Jackson, S. E. The measurement of experienced burnout. *Journal of Occupational Behavior,* 1981, **2,** 99-113.

Mattingly, M. A. Sources of stress and burnout in professional child care work. *Child Care Quarterly,* 1977, **6,** 127-137.

Morrow, L. The burnout of almost everyone. *Time*, September 21, 1981, p. 84.

Ollman, B. *Alienation: Marx's conception of man in capitalist society.* Cambridge, England: Cambridge University Press, 1971.

Packard, V. *A nation of strangers.* New York: McKay, 1972.

Pines, A. & Aronson, E., with Kafry, D. *Burnout: From tedium to personal growth.* New York: Free Press, 1981.

Quinnett, P. The perfect out. *The New York Times*, August 26, 1981, p. A23.

Sarason, S. *Work, aging, and social change.* New York: Free Press, 1977.

Sarason, S. *Opening address.* Presented at The National Conference on Stress and Burnout in the Human Service Professions, New York, 1981.

Scully, R. Staff support groups: Helping nurses to help themselves. *The Journal of Nursing Administration*, March 1981, 48–51.

Seligman, M. E. P. *Helplessness.* San Francisco: W. H. Freeman, 1975.

Selye, H. *The stress of life.* New York: McGraw-Hill, 1956.

Selye, H. *The stress of life.* Rev. ed. New York: McGraw-Hill, 1976.

Shaw, S.; Bensky, J. M.; Dixon, B.; & Bonneau, R. *Burnout among special educators: Causes and coping strategies.* Paper presented at The 95th Annual Invitational Conference on Leadership in Special Education Programs, Minneapolis, November 1979.

Slater, P. *The pursuit of loneliness.* Rev. ed. Boston: Beacon, 1976.

Tosi, H. & Tosi, D. Some correlates of role conflict and role ambiguity among public school teachers. *Journal of Human Relations*, 1970, **18**, 1068–1076.

Vaillant, G. *Adaptation to life.* Boston: Little, Brown, 1977.

Walley, W. & Stokes, J. *Self-help support groups for teachers under stress.* Paper presented at the Annual Convention of the American Psychological Association, Los Angeles, August 1981.

Watzlawick, P., Weakland, J., & Fisch, R. *Change: Principles of problem formation and problem resolution.* New York: Norton, 1974.

Yankelovich, D. *New rules: Searching for self-fulfillment in a world turned upside down.* New York: Random House, 1981.

Part I:

Theoretical Perspectives

1

Burnout: Contemporary Issues, Trends, and Concerns

Herbert J. Freudenberger

The rapidity with which the term and the concept of burnout have been incorporated into the daily argot of our society is astonishing. Over the last few years, burnout has become a "buzz word" used to convey an almost unlimited variety of social and personal problems. The field itself is approximately eight years old, essentially brought to public awareness by this author's initial papers on burnout in 1974 and 1975. The newness of the field compels our attention to certain theoretical, practical, and social pitfalls that often beset the evolution of a concept. For example, out of needs to be accepted and legitimized, proponents of a new concept may promise more than they can deliver. One corporate consultant talks of burnout as the cause of alcohol and drug abuse, thus assuming that if the dynamics of burnout were understood, substance abuse in industry would decline. Another suggests that the elimination of *one* burned out person could improve the productivity of an entire organizational unit. Still others talk of burnout as essentially an organizational problem, assuming that if the structure of an organization were altered then the tendency of individuals to burn out would be significantly reduced. These idealistic notions, unfortunately, may only serve to confuse the public, and in time may lead to a significant diminution of the usefulness of burnout as a concept.

PROBLEMS WITH DEFINITION AND CONCEPTUALIZATION

Several other difficulties of the field have recently become apparent. For example, among the most vexing of theoretical problems is one of definition: what is it we mean by the term "burnout"? Some current definitions are vague, contradictory, or overly inclusive. For example, some theorists refer to burnout as a loss of will, or as an inability to martial one's forces to get going. Others

23

imply that burnout is essentially a pervasive mood of anxiety which ultimately manifests itself in depression and giving up. Still others refer to burnout as if it was simply an adjustment technique used (unsuccessfully) to cope with stress. We also find that burnout is equated with alienation, depression, anxiety, loss of idealism, and loss of spirit. These conflicting and idiosyncratic ways of referring to the term can only serve to confuse those who are seeking to clarify the dimensions of the burnout phenomenon.

Overusage and overextension tend to make the term meaningless. We cannot insist that the term "burnout" fit all the ills of society. We need to derive some basic commonalities of definition and application; we need to develop a basic theoretical framework. As Maslach (1981) has noted, not only do the definitions of any single stress-related disorder (such as burnout) vary from each other, but similar definitions are sometimes applied to different concepts. We also need, however, to prevent premature closure in our thinking; that is, we need to avoid becoming rigid or inflexible in our thinking as a defense against our anxieties or felt lack of knowledge. It is far too easy to reify our definitions of burnout and close ourselves off to potentially useful ideas from other professionals and other fields. Indeed, there is a need for a diversity of professional perspectives in understanding the phenomenon of burnout. Historically, burnout has been explored and investigated in the social service areas. Consequently, it has primarily attracted psychologists, social workers, and educators as its main proponents and early researchers. But if we perceive burnout to be a reflection of and response to a broad range of social conditions, then we need to encourage sociologists, biologists, economists, psychiatrists, political scientists, industrial engineers, and business people to assist us in our explorations.

Another "definitional" problem is the tendency to conceptualize burnout within a medical model framework. Historically, the medical model is one that has had its widest applications in dealing with individuals who are physically ill or suffer from maladaptive behavior; in using the medical model we refer to symptoms, signs, and disease. Intrinsic to this type of formulation is the thought that the maladaptive behavior is a function of something observably wrong within the person. As this author has previously suggested (Freudenberger, 1973), when we use the medical approach in investigating and explaining burnout, we significantly limit our visions and applications of burnout. A comprehensive understanding of burnout requires a framework within which antecedent variables, of both a personal and a social nature, are explored in terms of how they impact on the present of a person, and in turn change the individual's view of the future. In short, there is a need to understand the psychosocial context in which burnout occurs—to think in terms of process, values, and social systems. Process refers to the changing, interactive nature of psychological variables within the individual as well as the dynamic interchange between the person and his or her environment. An awareness of process is essential to understanding the individual psychological dimensions of burnout. In addition, the values of individuals, as well as the systems within which they work, must be viewed from a historical perspective in order to understand the psychosocial context of the current concern with burnout. Finally, we cannot disregard the impact of significant transformations in our society, or the effects of these changes on our thinking and behavior. For example, there have been dramatic shifts in our family units, as evidenced by the increased incidence of divorce and single-parent families. The continued shifts of families from one location to another, for economic and climatic reasons, have produced a group of families lacking a substantial support network. In addition, the emergence of women's liberation, has required shifts in both women's and men's roles; sexual values and traditions have also been challenged and questioned. Still another cultural shift concerns our religious observances and rituals. On the one hand, we have seen a resurgence in religious fundamentalism and participation in cult movements; on the other hand, we note, too, that a significant number of nuns, priests, ministers, and rabbis have left their religious positions to seek other fields of work. Each of these value shifts in our society has contributed to the ambiguity in our lives, which, in turn, has created a fertile ground for the growth of burnout (Freudenberger, 1981).

Our initial conceptions of burnout were based on clinical observation. Research has finally begun to augment, as well as to challenge, our first assumptions by measuring and quantifying the process of burnout. Important questions, though, remain to be investigated. Does the process of burnout recur intermittently throughout individuals' lives? Does it affect only specific individuals, and if so, what "types"? Is the process specific or contiguous to a particular period of life or age group? Can we talk of childhood or adolescent burnout? What childhood and adult dynamics render individuals vulnerable to burnout? And what characteristics of individuals render them relatively invulnerable to stress and burnout? Similar questions need to be directed to organizations as well. For example, what variables within an organization serve to induce burnout? Is burnout a function of the nature of leadership in organizations, or the absence or presence of competition and cooperation among workers? Is burnout best treated by changing the individual or by changing the system? How does the phenomenology of burnout differ among human service workers? Is teacher burnout different from burnout in social workers, psychologists, or alcohol counselors? In general, there is a need for specificity in regard to identifying the etiology, symptoms, and effective treatment of burnout in any given individual or system.

Burnout has most often been conceptualized in the literature as an expression of negative adaptation to stress. Theoretical formulations and empirical investigations have tended to focus on the detrimental effects of burnout in human service workers in a wide variety of settings (see Bramhall & Ezell, 1981;

Freudenberger, 1977, 1982; Freudenberger & Richelson, 1980; Maslach, 1976; Pines & Maslach, 1978; White, 1978). It may also be useful, however, to consider the homeostatic function of burnout, that is, to consider how the process of burnout provides signals for us to monitor and alter maladaptive personal and social systems. An awareness of the health-endangering symptoms of burnout (e.g., physical or emotional depletion) may enable us to recognize our stress points and consequently to shift our goals, limit our activities, and rethink our life styles. Viewed from this perspective, burnout provides data that can be used effectively to make positive, health-promoting changes in our lives.

ORGANIZATIONAL ISSUES

In recent years industry has become increasingly aware of the problem of burnout, and as a consequence, many individuals have been called upon to act as consultants. Burnout consultants who operate within an industrial setting need to be aware of the "values" of the setting, most importantly the fact that industry operates on the profit-loss motive. Consultants need to be aware too of the politics of a setting, the formal and informal power structure, and the importance management places on employee performance and production. Consultants also need to anticipate management demands for immediate and dramatic results. Management may want a consultant to improve efficiency and productivity, decrease absenteeism, heighten the spirit of cooperativeness, and improve worker morale. The consultant, therefore, needs to make it clear that "results" may be neither immediate nor directly in accordance with management's needs, and that "time" and ongoing cooperation among management, union, and employees are essential for fruitful outcome.

Another critical issue is that of confidentiality. How much of what we learn as consultants is to be shared with an employer who is usually paying our fee? We need to establish, from the outset, clear boundaries for both the employee and the employer regarding what we can and cannot keep confidential. In addition, we need to be aware of our own values in regard to management-employee relationships. For example, is it within our domain to insist that certain humane criteria be met within an organization? Moreover, how realistic and ultimately productive is it for us to help employees "actualize" themselves when the nature of that actualizing may be significantly counterproductive to the individual and/or to the value system of the corporation? Supporting appropriate peer groups or closer interpersonal relations between supervisory personnel and staff are appealing options, but these changes may also cause a significant shift from a concern with productivity to a concern with interpersonal relations—a shift that may inhibit productivity. In this regard, Golembiewski (1981) notes that the typical stress-management workshop emphasizes individual change far more than organizational development. What he suggests, therefore, is that consultants should assist both workers and management in developing compromises between humanitarian aims and the values and priorities of the corporation. Similarly, Minnehan and Paine (1981) have proposed that workshops and training sessions should help individuals to assess their own needs while providing an orientation to the resources available both within and outside an organization. In short, burnout consultants in industry must be realistic regarding goals and short-term changes, and must tailor their interventions to the specific setting within which their work is taking place.

THE FUTURE

Several critical tasks face the field in the coming years. For those in academia who are interested in burnout, the task ahead will be to convince colleagues of the seriousness of the phenomenon, and to support students' desires to do research in the area. For the clinician or consultant, the major task will be to develop preventive strategies for use in agencies, corporations, schools, hospitals, and private practice settings. Perhaps too, in time, we will have amassed sufficient data regarding the process of burnout to be able to teach young people how to develop values and life styles that reduce the risk of burning out. And for the burnout researcher, the future may well lie in further study of how behavior at work relates to behavior at home. An individual who feels powerless, dulled, deadened, overburdened, bored, and driven at work often displaces these attitudes onto his or her family. Ultimately, the home becomes replete with stress, strife, and declining physical and mental health, which, in turn, further promotes alienation, family abuse, urban nomadism, and burnout. Only through studies that deal with the direct relationships between attitudes at work and attitudes in the home, can we hope to gain the understanding necessary to bring about the changes that are so desperately needed in our society.

Finally, there is a political problem that "burnout professionals" must confront. Given our government's continued concern with productivity, cost efficiency, and budget balancing, professionals in the field must loudly insist that the economic health and productivity of our nation cannot be based on the neglect of its most valuable resource—its human beings. We, as professionals, must convince our government that technological advancements that fail to recognize human needs can only lead to increased burnout, anxiety, alcoholism, drug abuse, and maladjustment in our society (Freudenberger & North, 1982).

REFERENCES

Bramhall, M. & Ezell, S. How burned out are you? *Public Welfare,* Winter 1981, 23–27.

Freudenberger, H. J. Departure from medical model oriented psychotherapies. *Journal of Clinical Issues in Psychology,* 1973, **1** (2), 10–15.

Freudenberger, H. J. Staff burnout. *Journal of Social Issues,* 1974, **30**, 159–165.

Freudenberger, H. J. The staff burnout syndrome in alternative institutions. *Psychotherapy: Theory, Research and Practice*, 1975, **12** (1), 73–82.

Freudenberger, H. J. Burnout: Occupational hazard of the child care worker. *Child Care Quarterly,* 1977, **6** (2), 90–99.

Freudenberger, H. J. *Executive burnout.* Paper presented at The Harvard Business Club. Cambridge, Mass., October 1981.

Freudenberger, H. J. Coping with job burnout as a law enforcement officer. *Law and Order,* 1982, **30** (5), 64–67.

Freudenberger, H. J. & North, G. *Situational anxiety—Coping with everyday anxious moments.* New York: Doubleday, 1982.

Freudenberger, H. J. & Richelson, G. Burnout: The high cost of high achievement. New York: Anchor Press, 1980.

Golembiewski, R. T. *Organization development interventions: Limiting burnout through changes in interaction, structure and politics.* Paper presented at The First National Conference on Burnout, Philadelphia, November 1981.

Maslach, C. Burned out. *Human Behavior,* 1976, **5**, 16–22.

Maslach, C. *Understanding burnout: Problems, progress and promise.* Paper presented at the First National Conference on Burnout, Philadelphia, November 1981.

Minnehan, F. & Paine, S. *Burning money: Analyzing some basic economic and legal consequences of burnout.* Paper presented at the First National Conference on Burnout, Philadelphia, November 1981.

Pines, A. & Maslach, C. Characteristics of staff burnout in mental health settings. *Hospital and Community Psychiatry,* 1978, **29**, 233–237.

White, A. L. *Incest in the organizational family: The unspoken issue in staff and program burnout.* Rockville, Md.: HCS, 1978.

2

A Social Competence Model of Burnout

W. David Harrison

Burnout is one of the most fashionable, though real and tragic afflictions of workers in the postindustrial age. Two different tasks face practitioners and researchers who are interested in burnout. The first is to determine the nature of the phenomenon, in particular to determine whether or not it is a discrete entity. The second task is to make conceptual order out of the diversity of ideas and theories. A number of theories and models offer plausible explanations of how burnout develops, and some may offer a measure of predictive power. Practitioners and researchers must decide which dimensions of the burnout phenomenon warrant further investigation. In this chapter I will first briefly review some examples of theoretical perspectives that could be applied to burnout, and then present what I have come to call a social competence approach. This viewpoint proposes that burnout results from ineffective efforts to help. Finally, I will use the model to speculate about the future of burnout.

The following three examples illustrate the range of theoretical perspectives on burnout. Karger (1981) has argued that burnout, as described by other writers, is the same phenomenon that Marx called "alienation." He asserts that burnout is a cluster of anomic symptoms. Most importantly, Karger says that studies of burnout have looked at the wrong problem: they have focused on the condition itself, rather than on the dehumanizing process that affects workers in both industrial and human service settings.

Another example comes from the study of stress. Although not referring specifically to burnout, Jenkins (1979) has described a similar concept, referring to such "pathological end states" of stress as exhaustion, despair, apathy, psychopathology, meaninglessness, victimization, and disruption of interpersonal ties. They sound familiar to those of us who have listened to a number of "self-certified" burnouts. This example is important for present purposes in that Jenkins proposes a logical and sensible system that describes and explains the consequences of stress without invoking the "burnout" label.

The concepts of alienation and stress provide alternative ways to look at burnout, but we could also return to freshman psychology texts and assess burnout from Erikson's (1959) epigenetic viewpoint. Many developmental struggles occur on the job in our postindustrial society. Erikson's psychosocial stages (e.g., intimacy versus isolation, generativity versus stagnation, and integrity versus despair) are not typically invoked in discussions of burnout, yet we might be wise to examine how the struggle to master these crises has led people into the helping occupations. It would also be of interest to know how these crises are encountered on the job, and how they are related to burnout. From this perspective, burnout can be seen as an amalgam of the untoward components of adult developmental crises, and labeled the "isolation-stagnation-despair and disgust syndrome."

Each of these perspectives—Marxist, social psychological, and developmental—offers a plausible starting point for understanding burnout. Many others could be added. They range from the broad social perspectives of "future shock" and postindustrialism through viewpoints about politics, organizations, and management, down to the individual helping relationship and personality level (Harrison, in press). A social competence model of burnout offers a logical framework for integrating these multiple viewpoints.

A SOCIAL COMPETENCE MODEL

The helping professions are conducted in a seemingly endless variety of environments. Some are supportive, others oppressive, and the resources needed to do the tasks at hand may or may not be present at either type of setting. Moreover, workers themselves come in all varieties. Generalizing, therefore, about worker's transactions and interactions, as well as the effects of work upon them, can be particularly difficult. Faced with this complexity of data, many research efforts have attempted in-depth investigations of selective variables (e.g., lack of supportive colleagues, presence of role conflict). In looking at burnout from this perspective, however, we risk losing common sense for some sort of social science fiction. What is called for instead is a comprehensive, multifaceted model of burnout that seeks to approximate the real world more closely.

The first step in developing a comprehensive model of burnout was to search for recurrent themes in professional literature and clinical "folklore." One such theme appearing in the recent literature is the proposal that burnout is inversely related to perceived competence and effectiveness: "a sense of competence and a feeling of efficacy are the results of being able to affect the environment and meet its challenges. . . . workers are able to develop positive affective responses to their jobs only if there is some certainty that what they do is valuable and makes a difference in the lives of clients" (Harrison, 1980, p. 42). Cherniss

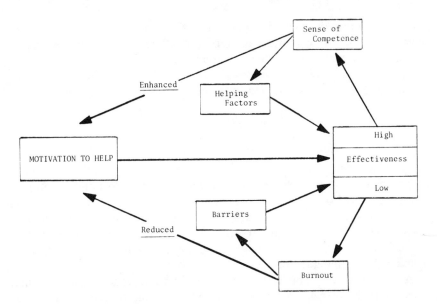

Figure 2.1.   A social competence model of burnout. Adapted from "Burnout: The case of the helpless helper," by W. David Harrison. In *Social Service Practice Relationships,* by T. Keefe and D. Maypole. Copyright © 1983 by Wadsworth, Inc. Reprinted by permission of Brooks/Cole Publishing Company, Monterey, California.

(1980) also referred to the quest for competence and the crisis of competence as crucial antecedents of burnout, and Pines and Aronson (1981) discussed the process by which idealistic, sensitive beginning practitioners lose their commitment in situations in which they lack autonomy, control, a "sense of completion," and rewards. Human service professionals often highlight these same themes when they speak of their work, discussing burnout in terms of their exasperation of being unable to see changes, and at the many ways in which "the system" stymies their efforts toward competence and efficiency. When one assumes a competence-oriented viewpoint in reading the burnout literature and listening to practitioners, one is impressed by the frequency with which this concept surfaces as an explanation. Yet a model that focuses on competence and relates burnout to the larger body of competence theory has not been previously developed.

From the assumption that burnout is primarily a function of perceived competence, a composite model was constructed (See Figure 2.1). It begins with the assumption that burnout is not an inevitable consequence of certain kinds of work. Not everyone in tough, demanding, or unpleasant jobs burns out. However, burnout *may* be inevitable for some people in some jobs.

The overwhelming majority of people who enter the social services are highly motivated to do something good *for,* and sometimes *with,* other people.

Practically all beginners are in some sense "fired up" with motivation. Being helpful is a state that they see as important. Freudenberger and Richelson (1980) have succinctly described this situation:

> The helper has come to his profession with visions of a supportive institution peopled with wise superiors and co-operative patients, students, or clients. He has contemplated results and tangible proof of his ability to create a difference in people's lives. What he finds instead is red tape, harried administrators, intractable cases. No one has prepared him for this. [p. 154]

The most important determinants of the helping professional's ability to achieve the goal of helpfulness are the severity of the problems that clients present; the specific environmental resources and barriers that are present; and the worker's skill, including techniques, judgment, and the ability to use him or herself effectively. These determinants can be classified as either "barriers to helping" or "helping factors."

A number of new applications of the competence concept are emerging, particularly in the helping practice. Most recent applications can be traced to Robert White's (1959, 1963, 1979) work on competence motivation. In White's view, people seek environmental interactions that allow them to feel that they are the cause of observable effects. Competence is, in White's words (1963), "a person's existing capacity to interact effectively with his environment. . . . Competence, in other words, is a cumulative result of the whole history of transactions with the environment no matter how they were motivated" (p. 39). Although this was not a new idea, White's innovation was in linking it to developments in ego psychology and laying a foundation for further conceptualizations of competence in operant and cognitive-behavioral terms. White's ideas about person-environment transactions are also compatible with contemporary ecological and systems metaphors for helping practice. The work of Deci (1975, 1980), Goldfried and D'Zurilla (1969), Harter (1978), and Maluccio (1981) represent particularly valuable applications and expansions of competence ideas into the developmental and intervention areas.

I have used the term "social competence" to distinguish those interactions that are principally interpersonal from those that involve mastery of the physical environment (e.g., driving a car). In the helping fields, the pursuit of social competence can be thought of as a special case of what White referred to as competence motivation. White proposed that people strive to interact competently with the environment; would-be helpers can be thought of as channeling this motivating force into helping relationships. The possibility of achieving competence as a helper—that is, knowing that one is having beneficial effects in a selected part of the social environment—seems to be the predominant motivation for helpers. It is also the most important reward or reinforcement. When this sense of having valued effects is absent, or when hope of achieving it is lost, burnout is the likely result. The situation is particularly problematic when there are concomitant unrealistic expectations for rapid improvement of client problems. The social competence model allows us to look systematically at some of the most important ways in which high hopes for helping may lead either to increased competence and achievement motivation or to burnout and its characteristic reorientation of motivational patterns.

Workers are generally striving for competence in regard to certain goals. Competence, power, perceived control, and one's expectations regarding the attainment of these goals are of crucial importance in determining how one feels about one's efforts. In recent years, as the United States has emerged as a reluctant welfare state, opportunities have arisen for many of the most idealistic to seek personal fulfillment through helping others. The idealism of the beginning worker has been cited frequently as a major factor in the development of burnout (see, for example, Cherniss, 1980; Horejsi, Walz, & Connolly, 1977; Freudenberger, 1974, 1975; Pines & Aronson, 1981). In the two decades prior to the labeling of the burnout phenomenon in the mid-1970s, there was major expansion of governmental responsibility for social welfare and social action. The notion of professional helping was accepted to a greater degree than ever before. Many new socially sanctioned jobs and occupations developed as a result. Given these opportunities, idealistic individuals sought meaningful employment in the human services. The values of the postindustrial era also encouraged people to expect increasing control over their jobs. Workers have also grown to expect their work to be creative and even uplifting. The channeling of competence motivation into helping fields has set the stage for the emergence of burnout as a pressing professional concern (Harrison, in press).

The social competence model is extremely applicable to practitioners who hold high expectations for the achievement of good works. In attempting to help people in serious trouble, however, more than high motivation is required. Certain environmental conditions have to be present, and certain worker characteristics are required in order for reliably effective helping to occur. The first part of the model might be thought of as an equation in which burnout is a function of expectation and actual experience.

The "work experience" portion of the equation consists of several factors. If the worker's valued goal of helping is to be attained regularly, the first requirement is that the milieu or environment must support the helping role by providing unambiguous expectations of role functioning. This is not always the case, as is clearly revealed in fields such as child-protective services where the worker's role shifts from police officer, to chauffeur, to medical assistant, to expert witness, and so on. Nurses, to cite another example, are tantalized by the possibilities of helping through exercise of professional autonomy and teamwork, only to be frequently deprived of both by physicians, administrators, and others who see nursing roles less imaginatively.

Helping in a complex society also requires that certain resources be made available. An example of this second environmental condition can be seen in practice with the aged. When one's approach to helping presupposes the desirability of in-home care for those who want it, plans will inevitably require the availability of resources to support life at home. Work milieux are often deficient in the provision of requisite resources.

The third environmental necessity is information. The practitioner needs data on his or her performance of the task. Isolated workers, lacking the evaluation of others, need particularly well developed skills of self-evaluation and monitoring of the helping process. They are forced to abstract indirect information from the environment and to process it into a form that relates to their competence in goal attainment.

To this point, environmental factors contributing to perceived competence have been emphasized. The practitioner also contributes to the helping situation. While practitioner abilities may be developed on the job, this is frequently an arduous task that is never quite accomplished. Skills are obviously essential. Many workers, though, are lacking in skills and are therefore likely to have trouble achieving goals. There have been many efforts to improve the situation. Marshall, Charping, and Bell, (1979) for example, found 122 studies of "interpersonal skills training" in the human services within a ten-year period. But skills alone do not ensure competence. While an individual's ability to differentiate between open-ended and closed-ended questions or to practice "attending" behavior may improve, the quality of his or her judgment may not. Professional judgment usually comes from knowledge of useful practice theories, articulated value systems, and trial and error. For example, beginning clinicians are often so busy gathering data for their diagnostic formulations that they may alienate clients who urgently want relief of "symptomatic" problems. Knowing how to arrive at a focus with a client also requires considerable judgment. Similarly, there are frequently rival prescriptions for what the practitioner "ought" to do, coming from such varied sources as supervisors, judges, or other clinicians. In addition, practitioners' judgments may be influenced by often unexamined, or even unconscious, beliefs and attitudes; for example, the worker who systematically avoids discussion of racial issues with clients who are of a different race, or the welfare commissioner who initiates programs to control teen-age pregnancy as his two daughters enter adolescence. Finally, workers' values may change over the years—some workers "have solved their own problems and have forgotten what it cost them" (Keith-Lucas, 1972, p. 89).

Despite the individual variations that workers bring to human service jobs, the crux of the social competence model is the payoff to the worker that comes from helping clients attain desired goals. As noted previously, this process may be frustrated because the practitioner may have his or her own agenda to pursue. But regardless of the specifics of motivation, of practitioner qualities and values, and of institutional characteristics, the objective reality of the client's problem has to be included in the burnout equation. Cherniss (1980) has discussed the worker's reaction to these situational realities as a matter of "coming to terms with clients" (p. 38). It matters greatly, as a student recently informed me, "whether they'll come to an office or not." Not everyone wants the proferred help that appears so logical to the beginner. It is also important to weigh the nature of transactions that are so readily identified as evidence of "resistance" or "motivation." Certain client systems are nearly impossible to change according to the rules we play by and the ethics we believe in. This ordinarily leads to a state of frustration and ultimately to burnout, as unrealistic goals are not attained. In other settings and for other practitioners, the probability of defining and achieving realistic goals is much higher. Unfortunately, we often see the least equipped workers working in the least supportive settings on the hardest problems with the least help in determining what realistic successful outcomes might be.

Social competence refers to how one feels about one's capacity to interact with, and therefore to influence the social environment. But the feelings should be shaped by the most complete information possible about the effects of efforts, and determining one's degree of effectiveness is a very difficult task. Since the perception of competence is of such crucial importance in this model, I would suggest that we pay even more attention to it as we teach and learn about helping. Trying to use the "scientific method" to document what we are doing and how well we are doing it offers one important avenue. But we also have to face the fact that many of the phenomena that are of particular interest and concern to us are not easily quantifiable. They will remain largely matters of feeling and intuition.

Often there are individual differences of opinion regarding goals and criteria of effectiveness. In addition, organizational goals and policies may differ dramatically from those of workers. And, there may be built-in organizational obstacles to what seem to be plausible and practical plans. I recall, for example, a British social service department that required the approval of the county council before a foster child could visit his or her natural parents. The problem was not that the counselors were unreasonable; they usually were cooperative. But the amount of paperwork needed to make such a visit discouraged social workers and parents alike. Moreover, the goals of the social service department were child care and safety; psychological and family system values were, for the most part, ignored. Most professionals in social work, education, nursing, psychology, and other burnout-prone helping fields operate in similar public or semipublic bureaucracies, and they highly value whatever autonomy they can claim. The loss of autonomy, particularly in goal setting, is discouraging.

Other environmental factors may also influence achievement. These factors include the influence of other people on one's client, the availability or lack of social welfare resources, and the spectrum of opportunities and deprivations that affect one personally. Barriers in the environment that are constantly changing and are outside the influence of the practitioner and client impede the practitioner's task of monitoring effectiveness and developing a sense of competence. For many, the greatest such barrier is simply the size of the caseload. Competent workers with large caseloads will almost always have learned to focus on small, feasible goals that they can achieve regularly.

Practitioners, of course, are not the only ones who are monitoring and attempting to evaluate their performance. Co-workers, supervisors, clients, and others also provide information. Each of these sources of information may have different degrees of credibility for the individual worker. For some, client reports of improvement have a very high value in the development of competence. For others, supervisory input is most important. Supervisors may even provide a good deal of criticism, but will do it in such a way that the practitioner makes effective use of it to increase his or her competence. We vary considerably in what we need from others and how we can best receive and process it. One of the most exasperating conditions for most workers is the lack of comprehensible feedback from others who know or should know about their efforts. It may be that progress in clinical research will offer a future avenue for the individual practitioner to develop a more reliable information-gathering system. For the present, most professionals will rely on subjective and impressionistic accounts, often filtered through the sieve of negativism that burnout usually engenders.

Suppose that a worker learns that many clients are doing reasonably well, and that evaluations and general feedback are positive. Before a sense of competence can develop, an attribution process occurs in which the worker evaluates the information and interprets it in causal terms. Is progress an effect that the worker causes? Would it have occurred anyway? The same applies when progress is lacking and clients develop more problems. "Am I to blame?" "Was it inevitable?" The worker ponders these questions, and ultimately develops some beliefs about causation. Figure 2.2 shows how this situation can be thought of as a two-by-two matrix with dimensions of success and failure partitioned by worker-caused and other-caused. All workers will have a distribution of efforts in the four cells of the matrix, and competent workers would have most cases in the "worker-caused/successful" cell. This is the condition that leads to continued motivation and enhanced ability. When the practitioner seldom sees success, and particularly when failure is seen as a result of his or her efforts, burnout is likely. The situation of misperceptions of success, that is, erroneously calling a case successful due to worker efforts, is likely to cause long-range difficulties because sooner or later the evidence will emerge to indicate that the worker really was not a significant factor in goal attainment in a given helping case or episode. Meanwhile, the worker has felt fairly good about it, and has thereby reinforced and perpetuated maladaptive efforts that will later fail to achieve desired results and ultimately precipitate long-term problems.

Typical Perceived Outcome of Practice

	Successful	Unsuccessful
Worker-caused	Sense of competence	Burnout
Other-caused	May enhance or detract from sense of competence	Burnout-vulnerable

Attributed Cause of Outcome

Figure 2.2.   Matrix of perceived outcome of practice, attributed causal agent, and worker response. Adapted from "Burnout: The case of the helpless helper," by W. David Harrison. In *Social Service Practice Relationships,* by T. Keefe and D. Maypole. Copyright © 1983 by Wadsworth, Inc. Reprinted by permission of Brooks/Cole Publishing Company, Monterey, California.

Pines and Aronson (1981), who have made proposals for building accurate attributions into efforts to remedy burnout, note that "attributions can have a great effect on interpersonal relations, particularly because there are usually few opportunities to correct wrong attributions once they have been made" (p. 139). What I have called "worker-caused" and "other-caused" attributions can be thought of as specific cases of what Pines and Aronson refer to as dispositional and situational attributions, respectively. Attribution is important because of its relationship to the self-rewarding nature of competence. When I have asked social workers and other helping professionals to list the positive and negative aspects of their jobs, I have usually received at least a two-to-one ratio of negatives to positives. "Why do you keep at it?" I ask. And the most common response is that certain positives are very highly valued. The fact that people actually do feel helpful fairly often, even in desperately difficult lines of work, is certainly an important reality in the burnout picture. Feeling helpful is feeling competent. Feeling competent is a necessary part of helping. This feeling state apparently represents an intrinsic reward for a great many workers who maintain the motivations I mentioned as a starting point in this model. The absence of competence among workers who seek it is directly related to burnout. Likewise, competence nourishes itself and leads to both enhanced practice and more competence motivation.

While the feeling of doing well at one's valued activity is very important, the material rewards are also significant. Their importance varies considerably from worker to worker and setting to setting, but in times we think of as economically tight, small differentials in salary and other types of extrinsic reward that are ostensibly tied to competence may take on great significance. Where material rewards are absent or inadequate, the path to burnout is considerably facilitated.

I started by noting the difficulty of grasping the essence of burnout. A great deal of effort on the part of a number of scholars has gone into describing and defining it. Burnout is a loose term for a collection of specific states and feelings that vary from person to person. To me, burnout is the loss of motivation and expectation to do very well at doing good. When one highly values one's work but is unable to achieve the desired goals, perceptions of social competence will not develop. Burnout will. Burnout is alienation from one's initial reasons for being in a helping role.

WHITHER BURNOUT?

What will become of burnout? In a time of economic uncertainty and hardship, more people will need human services, and fewer services will be available than in recent years. The burnout phenomenon, then, is not likely to subside greatly. However, attention to the phenomenon may well subside as widespread client needs and calls for new services emerge and move to the forefront of public and professional concern.

Indeed, practitioners may be more overwhelmed than ever over the next few years. All the situational elements that make competence difficult to achieve are likely to intensify. We are in for difficult times for the sick, the aged, the poor, and, among others, public employees. But there may also be cause for a degree of optimism. In the face of mounting client need and reduced services, practitioners may be forced to adapt their goals and methods toward a more practical and somewhat less idealistic approach to helping than many workers have used in recent times. Models that are reality-based, goal-directed, and client-oriented rather than professional-oriented may be strengthened. By focusing more clearly on the client and less on the trappings of professionalism, practitioners may enhance their perceived competence. Cherniss (1980) and Karger (1981) have argued that major social and cultural forces must change in order for the burnout phenomenon to change significantly. Ironically, the wholesale human service program reductions and lowered public expectations of government assistance may be just the necessary changes. To the extent that experienced and beginning practitioners modify their expectations and use practice principles that lead to effectiveness, they will experience competence and avoid burnout. The fundamental task for all of us is to achieve these changes without reducing our commitment to and compassion for the vulnerable, the distressed, and the dispossessed.

REFERENCES

Cherniss, C. *Professional burnout in human service organizations.* New York: Praeger, 1980.

Deci, E. L. *Intrinsic motivation.* New York: Plenum Press, 1975.

Deci, E. L. *The psychology of self-determination.* Lexington, Mass.: Heath, 1980.

Erickson, E. H. Identity and the life cycle. *Psychological issues.* Vol. 1. New York: International Universities Press, 1959.

Freudenberger, H. J. Staff burnout. *Journal of Social Issues,* 1974, **30**, 159–165.

Freudenberger, H. J. The staff burnout syndrome in alternative institutions. *Psychotherapy: Theory, Research and Practice,* 1975, **12**, 73–82.

Freudenberger, H. J. & Richelson, G. *Burnout: How to beat the cost of success.* New York: Bantam/Doubleday, 1980.

Goldfried, M. R. & D'Zurilla, T. J. A behavioral-analytical model for assessing competence. In Spielberger, C. D. (Ed.), *Current topics in clinical and community psychology.* Vol. 1. New York: Academic Press, 1969.

Harrison, W. D. Role strain and burnout in child-protective service workers. *Social Service Review,* 1980, **54**, 31–44.

Harrison, W. D. Burnout: The case of the helpless helper. In Keefe, T. & Maypole, D. (Eds.), *Social service practice relationships.* Monterey, Calif.: Brooks-Cole, in press.

Harter, S. E. Effectance motivation reconsidered—Toward a developmental model. *Human Development,* 1978, **21**, 34–64.

Horejsi, J. E., Walz, T., & Connolly, P. R. *Working in welfare.* Iowa City: University of Iowa School of Social Work, 1977.

Jenkins, C. D. Psychosocial modifiers of response to stress. *Journal of Human Stress,* 1979, **5** (4), 3–15.

Karger, H. J. Burnout as alienation. *Social Service Review,* 1981, **55**, 270–283.

Keith-Lucas, A. *Giving and taking help.* Chapel Hill: University of North Carolina, 1972.

Maluccio, A. N. *Promoting competence in clients.* New York: Free Press, 1981.

Marshall, E. K., Charping, J. W., & Bell, W. J. Interpersonal skills training: A review of the research. *Social Work Research and Abstracts,* 1979, **15**, 10–16.

Pines, A. M. & Aronson, E. *Burnout: From tedium to personal growth.* New York: Free Press, 1981.

White, R. W. Motivation reconsidered: The concept of competence. *Psychological Review,* 1959, **66**, 297–333.

White, R. W. Ego and reality in psychoanalytic theory. *Psychological Issues.* Monograph 11. New York: International Universities Press, 1963.

White, R. W. Competence as an aspect of personal growth. In Albee, G. & Joffee, J. (Eds.), *Primary prevention of psychopathology: Social competence in children.* Vol. 3. Hanover, N.H.: University Press of New England, 1979.

3

A Psychoanalytic View of Burnout

Harvey J. Fischer

The primary aim of this chapter is to distinguish the phenomenon of burnout from other states that appear to be similar, especially one that I have labeled "worn-out." To this end, I have tried to formulate an operational definition of this distinction, keeping in mind the necessity to make observations concerning essential variables. For example, if we are attending to the phenomenon of a broken leg, essential variables will appear in the relevant history. The leg may have been broken during a collision at a hockey rink, while tripping on a sidewalk, or in the context of osteopetrosis. Although we may begin by observing a discrete symptom, we soon begin to appreciate more comprehensively the condition from which the person suffers. We may become additionally concerned with bruises and concussions associated with a collision, or self-injurious tendencies associated with accidents, or the presence of a systemic physical disorder, as well as the broken leg itself.

In reading the literature concerning burnout, I came to recognize that certain essential variables were unremarked, although I had already appreciated their significance in my clinical work. I therefore determined to bring these data forward together with some considerations that seem to have general theoretical importance. To these purposes I have selectively reviewed the literature and rearranged their order in order to highlight what I wish to emphasize.

The phenomenon known as "burnout" was originally described by Freudenberger (1975). He referred to people who were "overly committed and excessively dedicated," who "worked long hours for minimal financial compensation," who "ignored their own discomforts and preferences almost without respite," who "used the job as a substitute for social life . . . and who spent their free time on the job," and who "believe that they are indispensable and must do everything by themselves" (pp. 2–10). We can agree with Freudenberger that such people have idealized their work and that burnout seems to be a consequence of the loss of that ideal. After a time, as Freudenberger notes, they may change drastically—becoming sullen, irritable, and angry, denigrating both staff and clients. They work even harder, becoming cynical and exhausted, making errors and showing symptoms of stress, meanwhile denying any need for help. Freudenberger is distinguishing a group of people who, because of their work, have had an "opportunity to fall into the omniscient stance" (Freudenberger & Robbins, 1979, p. 294). They attribute an inordinate sense of importance to their work, which they then take to be a documentation of their own importance. They enjoy a heightened sense of self-esteem in their work, as long as their work appears exalted to them. They guarantee the perception that their work is of eminent consequence by dedicating themselves to it "body and soul." We are familiar with people who define themselves only in terms of their work: "I'm a doctor" or "I'm a teacher," they say with a sense of pride. They devote themselves to their work, which comes before all else. Indeed, should the work of such people become interrupted through illness or retirement, we should expect that they would experience a traumatic blow to their self-esteem. It is apparent, however, that these people lead shallow lives, and while we therefore might not want them as friends, we might well seek to hire such extraordinarily dedicated people to work for us.

But Freudenberger has indicated that only some of these people who idealize their work are subject to burnout. His choice of the term "burnout" reflects his view that these people are subject to extraordinarily demanding situations (Freudenberger, 1975; Freudenberger & Robbins, 1979). This impression is shared by Maslach (1978) who believes that the cause of burnout is to be found in specific social and situational factors involving unique stress—"bad situations where many good people function" (p. 114). Chance (1981) reviewed several recent publications and found agreement that both organizations and society in general "spawn" burnout (p. 89). Farber and his colleagues (Farber & Heifetz, 1982; Farber & Miller, 1981) have also emphasized the role of environmental factors, particularly a lack of organizational support, in precipitating burnout.

There is no doubt that certain situations are generally regarded as unpleasant, stressful, or even dangerous. In such cases, we find that most persons who are subject to those conditions suffer from the general effects. Burnout, however, is not noted to be found in this kind of epidemiological distribution. In fact, as Maslach (1978) has remarked, "what is most emotionally painful for one staff person may not pose any special problems for the next" (p. 115). Since burnout is not a general phenomenon specific to any particular setting, the sufficient cause must be sought among personal psychological factors. Of course, at the same time, the identification of unwholesome environmental factors should be pursued with a view toward their amelioration.

It is my impression upon viewing the literature that attention is now being given to the recognition of those environmental aspects that are capable of exerting debilitating effects on staff personnel, and to consideration of both preventive and recuperative measures. I suggest that the victims of such conditions might best be seen as having been "worn out," and they should be carefully differentiated from cases of burnout, since the causes and the indications for their management are quite different. In addition, as the burden of this chapter attempts to demonstrate, we should see that the part of these victims that has become "worn out" is their sense of self-esteem. Those who are burned out, rather than worn out, cling tenaciously to a *high* sense of self-esteem. In short, those who complain of burnout are, in fact, worn out—the true victims of burnout continue in their task in a martyrlike fashion. It seems likely then that the condition of "worn-out" is considerably more prevalent than that of burnout and may well constitute a major sociological problem. Even though burnout does not present such an epidemic threat to society, its victims also deserve some share of our efforts to help them.

Let us turn our attention to a typical case of burnout. As has been reported, such people have idealized their occupation and seem to have suffered disillusionment from a frustrating environment. Since they have "thrown themselves" into their work to such a major extent, we can understand that frustration might result in their suffering a major disappointment. Ordinarily, the marked discomfort of such a state of disappointment would motivate individuals to seek readjustments toward relieving their distress. They might reduce their involvement by withdrawing the idealization (taking the attitude that "it's just a job") or by leaving the situation. In any case, they would not suffer burnout. The type of individual identified by Freudenberger as burned out is the type who stays on, regardless of stress. He does not give up or reduce his ideal but works even harder, with all the ensuing consequences of tension and exhaustion. We therefore question what possesses this person to continue the pursuit of an ideal in the face of its manifest impossibility, and despite painful and increasing discomfort. For this person a basic law of human nature, the Pleasure Principle, seems to be inoperative; he does not seek to reduce his condition of unpleasure.

This author has had the opportunity to work with three of these individuals in psychoanalytic psychotherapy; this discipline, which concentrates upon understanding the subjective experience of the person (Schafer, 1976) has brought to light some new information. It became increasingly clear to me that these people, who were working beyond reasonableness, common sense, and even concern for their own well-being and health, were desperately engaged in trying to ward off something that appeared to them even more terrifying. My analytic inquiry was regularly met with a hostile attitude that had the same hallmarks as reported in the burnout literature: sullenness, irritability, cynicism, and denigration.

It is the experience of psychoanalysis to consider that a hostile attitude may arise as a reaction to what Kohut (1977) terms a "narcissistic trauma"—that is, a significant change in functioning attributable to a marked lowering of the individual's sense of self-esteem. And, in fact, an examination of the details of the changes in behavior in certain patients supports the conjecture that the burned out person is now behaving as though his sense of self-esteem were notably reduced.

Analytic investigation has identified two different forms of this alteration in attitude involving lowered self-esteem. In the first, a previously high sense of self-esteem appears to be replaced by a contrary position of low self-esteem, which the person maintains with considerable insistence. My studies have led me to consider this phenomenon as a manifestation of "negative grandiosity," or a devaluation of the self. In the second form of functioning with low self-esteem, the previous high self-esteem is now attributed to some external situation or individual. The person has come to regard that object as the source of his "necessary narcissistic supplies." It is this second form that is characteristic of those who suffer from burnout. Therefore, I came to understand that these patients resisted my well-intentioned effort to be sympathetic to what I had assumed was their fearful state because they did not, in fact, experience their state as fearful. They regarded my effort as irrelevant and mistaken. I corrected my approach by focusing on the sense of pride they had about their job, clarifying the importance of doing such work. Their hostility gave way and was replaced by a congenial attitude that, in several varieties, followed the pattern of a "mirroring transference" (Kohut, 1971). They basked in the light of being "admired," and expressed pleasure at being understood. They also reported feeling better at work. Eventually each came to appreciate the central role of their motivation to feel "special" and "superior." They reported that an intense and pervasive sense of pleasure accompanied the notion of being special. This "high" became a preoccupation that they described as analogous to drug addiction.

Although the course of therapy has not yet revealed the antecedents of this particular state (of feeling "special"), I am inclined to identify it as a variety of "the illusion of grandiosity." In choosing this term, I am referring to the assumption first described by Ferenczi (1913), that a neonate's subjective view proceeds from an attitude of "unconditional omnipotence," which is also described in the literature as the period of "primary narcissism." The same concept is addressed by Freud (1914) as "normal megalomania," "ego-libido," "ego-instincts," and "egoism." More recently this idea has been used as a foundation for the theoretical position of Kohut (1971, 1977) in his characterization of the "archaic grandiose-exhibitionistic self." My experience leads me to support Freud's notion (1914) that in the course of normal development the direct manifestations of such megalomania become subdued and covert, ultimately reappearing in the formation of one's ideals. I describe this process as the "taming of grandiosity," implying that this belief continues covertly as the individual adapts to society. Furthermore, I have designated this belief as an "illusion" to take into account the fact that it is "unrealistic" and objectively false. However, I also mean to suggest that, the illusion does, in fact, exist in the realm of "psychic reality" and serves to sustain one's basic sense of self-esteem. It is a constant anodyne to Hamlet's "slings and arrows of outrageous fortune." We are able now to understand why the victims of burnout, although suffering distress, ignore their discomfort and attend only to their reported "high." Their attention is centered upon the confirmation of their "illusion of grandiosity" which is afforded by their activity. As I have mentioned, there is as yet no available psychoanalytic data on the question of how this state came to be, i.e., on what influences on their sense of self-esteem motivated this change.

At this time, a different aspect of the clinical picture of burnout has become accessible to investigation. Observers have alluded to the depression suffered by these people, noting their sullenness, irritability, and cynicism. As Boesky (1980) reminds us, however, the view of the observer need not coincide with the view of the subject. Conclusions based upon manifest data alone are neither valid nor reliable concerning the person's subjective condition (Slap & Levine, 1978). Psychoanalysis regards depression, as well as all other affective states, as a motivated position that is accessible to investigation (Kernberg, 1975). My exploration has shown that these people, contrary to past assumptions, do not experience sadness when they are acting in the manner described. Although they express their mood in the classic terms of "helpless and hopeless" (Dorpat, 1977), a detailed analysis has brought to light their fear that they would be revealed as a "sham," as "incompetent," as being "only a child who is dressed up as a man." It seems that they have been harboring a "skeleton in the closet" of their self-esteem which has gone undetected for many years. This feeling was stirred up by the opportunity they perceived to grasp at a compensatory illusion of grandiosity through their work. This confirms Dorpat's finding that helplessness may serve as a screen for fantasies of omnipotence.

Returning to the consideration of the reported symptom of depression in burnout, we are now able to state, at least in these cases which have been studied psychoanalytically, that the behavior referred to has been mistakenly labeled depression. Instead, this behavior arises in a context of efforts toward maintaining an illusion of grandiosity. It is not that these people feel that they have lost their ideal but, rather, that they are desperately trying to maintain it. It is not that they have been "turned out," but that they are "burning up."

This chapter relates to those persons who both idealize their work (as shown by overcommitment and excessive dedication together with a sense of special importance), and who also take a militant attitude of determination to work even harder. This definition differs from the colloquial use of the term "burnout" as an excuse for poor performance and as a justification for both easier working conditions and higher pay. Such people do not meet adversity with obdurate perseverance (as does the true case of burnout) but, instead, are grudging, complaining, and seeking to reduce or avoid responsibility. This definition also differs from the view of burnout as a variety of depression—

depressed people would reduce their efforts instead of redoubling them. True cases of burnout organize the major portion of their lives to center about their work and, when adverse conditions are encountered, they marshal their resources and exert themselves to the utmost. This study has revealed the motive for such desperation: the pursuit of the "illusion of grandiosity." These pursuers have gone beyond reasonableness, common sense, and concern for health and well-being. It is suggested that this drive takes precedence over the Pleasure Principle as well as the principle of life preservation. It seems that when a choice must be made, people often value their self-esteem above their physical existence.

REFERENCES

Boesky, D. Introduction: Symposium on object relations theory and love. *Psychoanalytic Quarterly,* 1980, **49**, 48–55.

Chance, P. That drained out, used-up feeling. *Psychology Today,* 1981, **15**, 88–92.

Dorpat, T. Depressive affect. *The Psychoanalytic Study of the Child,* 1977, **32**, 3–27.

Farber, B. A. & Heifetz, L. J. The process and dimensions of burnout in psychotherapists. *Professional Psychology,* 1982, **13** (2), 293–301.

Farber, B. A. & Miller, J. Teacher burnout: A psycho-educational perspective. *Teachers College Record,* 1981, **83** (2), 235–243.

Ferenczi, S. Stages in the development of the sense of reality. (1913) In *Sex in psychoanalysis.* New York: Basic Books, 1950.

Freud, S. On narcissism: An introduction. *Standard edition.* Volume 13. London: Hogarth Press, 1958. (Originally published 1914.)

Freudenberger, H. J. *The staff burnout syndrome.* Washington, D.C.: Drug Abuse Council, 1975.

Freudenberger, H. J. & Robbins, A. The hazards of being a psychoanalyst. *The Psychoanalytic Review,* 1979, **66**, 275–296.

Kernberg, O. *Object relations theory and clinical psychoanalysis.* New York: Jason Aronson, 1975.

Kohut, H. *The analysis of the self.* New York: International Universities Press, 1971.

Kohut, H. *The restoration of the self.* New York: International Universities Press, 1977.

Maslach, C. The client role in staff burnout. *Journal of Social Issues,* 1978, **34**, 111–124.

Schafer, R. *A new language for psychoanalysis.* New Haven: Yale University Press, 1976.

Slap, J. & Levine, F. On hybrid concepts in psychoanalysis. *Psychoanalytic Quarterly,* 1978, **47**, 499–523.

4

Disrupting the Cybernetics of Personal Growth: Toward a Unified Theory of Burnout in the Human Services

Louis J. Heifetz
Henry A. Bersani, Jr.

When children first use words meaningfully—that is, when they begin to associate the names of objects with the objects themselves (Brown, 1958)—they do not immediately grasp the precise meaning of words. Instead, they make two sorts of errors that reflect their incomplete understanding. For example, they may use the word "dog" to refer only to their household pet. This is an instance of *underinclusion,* using the term too narrowly. On the other hand, they may use "dog" to refer to all furry animals, to women with very long hair, and to Princeton alumni in raccoon coats. These are instances of *overinclusion,* using the term too broadly.

There is reason to believe that we have not yet grasped the concept of "burnout," that we are groping toward understanding along paths strewn with errors of overinclusion and underinclusion. Articles in the popular press tend toward overinclusion while the theoretical and empirical literature tends toward underinclusion.

There is an unquestionable and understandable attractiveness to the idea of burnout. The label "burned out" often seems to serve as a partial remedy for the condition it describes. That is, in the absence of other evidence of professional accomplishment, burnout provides some consolation as a badge of martyred dedication. This is why even transitory states of fatigue and frustration may lead to the self-diagnosis of burnout. On the other hand, there does seem to be a growing awareness in the popular press that the concept of burnout, in its casual use, has become bloated and ambiguous. For example, a recent *Time* magazine essay was entitled "The Burnout of Almost Everyone"

(Morrow, 1981). Here "burnout" was criticized as a diagnostic black hole that encompasses almost any aspect of work that has some modest quotient of querulousness. Under such casual diagnostic criteria, the prevalence of "burnout" will soon be epidemic and its incidence should theoretically approach 100 percent.

The technical literature on burnout presents a very different view or, rather, a variety of very different views. How much agreement exists among these concepts—and what empirical evidence would address the points of disagreement—is not at all clear. One problem is that discussions of burnout offer widely differing levels of analysis. Some emphasize *taxonomy* and the importance of unequivocal, operational definitions of "burned out." Others highlight the clinical importance of burnout by emphasizing its negative *consequences* for consumer-provider relationships. Others focus on *prediction* by identifying personal traits or organizational characteristics that seem to be correlated with higher rates of burnout. Still others emphasize the underlying *mechanisms* of burnout.

What comes to mind after reading this literature is the fable of the seven blind men and the elephant. In the fable, each man grasped a different part of the elephant and described the elephant accordingly. The elephant was alternately "a great serpent" (the trunk), "a bedsheet hung out to dry" (the ear), "a tree trunk" (the leg), and so forth. Each man, because of his narrow focus of attention, overlooked the elephant's other features. In addition, each observer missed the underlying commonalities that tied the separate features together. In other words, what got lost was a unifying core—a sort of "pachydermal essence"—that was greater than the sum of its parts and that provided an organizing framework for understanding the separate parts.

OVERVIEW

We believe that the process of burnout has a unifying core that is only partially reflected by current models of burnout. The goal of this chapter is to propose a new model of burnout that more thoroughly and explicitly embodies this core. Rather than focus immediately on the various sources of stress that have been implicated in burnout, we will first consider what is required for satisfaction and fulfillment in human service work. After analyzing the motivational needs of committed human service providers, we will identify a small set of core requirements for meeting those needs. Taken together, the core elements constitute a "cybernetic process," a system for organizing the goal-oriented activities of human service work. Next, we will demonstrate how the apparently diverse sources of burnout that have been proposed by current models can all be understood as disruptions of this cybernetic process. Although there are several points of close agreement with other models of burnout, the cybernetic model argues for substantial reinterpretation of some of the widely alleged causes of burnout. We will use the cybernetic model to reexamine the dynamics of consumer-provider relationships and suggest strategies for enhancing them. Finally, we will explore some implications of the cybernetic model for personnel preparation.

CONCEPTUALIZING BURNOUT: ROOTS OR BRANCHES? ONE TREE OR MANY?

As previously noted, some theories of burnout concentrate on its various overt signs (the "symptoms" and "sequelae"), while other theories emphasize burnout's underlying causes and predisposers. Within a given theory, there may be connections drawn between overt symptoms and underlying processes. And, by synthesizing across theories, it is possible to infer some other intuitively compelling links between effects and causes of burnout. The resulting composite contains several manifestations of burnout (branches), each with one or more causes (roots). Certain roots seem common to several of the branches, but the relationships among the various roots are less clearly specified and less easily synthesized.

We would like to propose a model of burnout that more systematically outlines the connections among the roots and branches. The various branches can be assembled simply by drawing upon current descriptions of burnout. For the roots, however, current theories will not suffice, even in combination. *Our sense is that there is a single, integrated process that is engaged in by all human service providers who do not burn out. Each of the alleged causes of burnout— as well as others not yet specified—can be understood as a disruption of one or more parts of this single, integrated process.* Regardless of the specific source or site of the disruption, as long as the overall process is significantly impeded, burnout will occur. The particular form that the burnout takes does not depend on the nature of the disruption, but varies as a function of personality characteristics, coping styles, and other factors.

As Tolstoy observed in the opening sentence of *Anna Karenina:* "All happy families resemble one another; every unhappy family is unhappy in its own fashion" (Tolstoy, 1918, p. 1). What we are suggesting is that current approaches to burnout only deal with certain subsets or clusters of the fundamental forms of dissatisfaction and unhappiness among human service providers. We believe that all forms of burnout are produced by one or more disruptions of a single, organized system that, when intact, typically leads to satisfaction and fulfillment. Hence, a unified and more parsimonious framework for understanding burnout will require an initial emphasis on the process of professional fulfillment that is, in so many possible ways, disrupted. As a first step, we will consider the motivational energy that drives the process.

Basic Assumptions about Motivation

One common theme in discussions of burnout is some sort of motivational erosion: dedication becomes apathy; altruism becomes contempt; insomnia replaces the impossible dream; and crusaders become *kvetches*. The implicit assumption is that *burnout must be preceded by commitment*. For human service workers the focus of this commitment is fostering positive change—growth—in their clients. Any satisfactory theory of burnout must be limited to those workers whose clinical endeavors are substantially motivated by the desire to promote growth in their clients. Burnout may produce and perpetuate low levels of this motivation, but the process of burnout cannot begin unless the level of this motivation is high. Metaphorically, one must be "fired up" before one can burn out.

A second basic assumption about the motivation of human service providers is drawn from general theories of personality. Human beings strive toward mastery and are reinforced by the sense of self-efficacy that accompanies evidence of mastery (e.g., Erikson, 1950; Janis et al., 1969). This pursuit of mastery—driven by what Robert White (1959) called "effectance motivation"—varies across individuals and within individuals over time. It may slow drastically or even halt temporarily, but it rarely ends altogether. This species-wide effectance motivation takes a particular form for committed human service workers. Because of their investment in promoting growth in their clients, any evidence of their effectively doing so will rank high in their hierarchy of reinforcers. Similarly reinforcing will be anything that serves to enhance their ability to promote client growth. That is, the provider's growth as a growth promoter is valued along with client growth per se.

Thus, our model assumes two basic needs on the part of human service providers who are potential candidates for burnout: (1) *a need to promote growth in others,* and (2) *a need to grow personally on the job.* How does one determine whether or not satisfactory growth has taken place in one's clients or in one's self? As another assumption of our model, we believe that *professionals' subjective experience of growth—in their clients and in themselves—is strongest when it consists of the perception of milestones being approached, attained, and passed.* Consequently, the commitment and fulfillment of human service workers are rooted in the pursuit of milestones of growth, in their clients and in their professional selves. The effective, satisfying pursuit of these milestones is the antithesis of burnout. When burnout occurs, it is because one or more basic elements are missing from an organized system for pursuing the milestones.

Basic Elements for Satisfying Human Service Work

The core requirements for fulfillment as a human service provider can be outlined in a short list. With all elements present, burnout is highly unlikely. It should be remembered that, as we are conceptualizing burnout, only committed providers are at risk. In order to fulfill their commitment, they need the following:

1. Goals that are *clearly defined* and *consistent with their values and priorities.* These goals will involve growth in their clients and increases in their own levels of mastery as service providers.
2. Objective and reliable milestones that will accurately reflect the attainment of both sorts of growth goals.
3. A set of short-term indicators of progress that reflects sequential steps en route to the long-term growth goals. Like the longer-term milestones, these short-term indicators should be objective and reliable.
4. Procedures for gathering and interpreting data related to the short-term indicators.
5. Strategies for adjusting the pursuit of their goals on the basis of the data related to short-term progress.

To the extent that these five basic elements are present in service providers' *modus operandi,* they will thrive. To the extent that one or more of these elements is absent, service providers will burn out. These elements make up what we will call a *cybernetic process* for achieving client growth and personal growth.

Cybernetics (derived from the Greek word for "helmsman" or "navigator") is a field named and founded by Norbert Wiener (1954). Cybernetics is concerned with patterns in the flow of information and ways in which biological, chemical, and physical systems are controlled by information that they generate ("feedback information" or "feedback" for short). In general terms, a cybernetic process provides a means for organizing goal-directed activity. In particular, the feedback in a cybernetic process makes it possible to monitor progress toward the goal on a continual basis and to change course whenever necessary.

An everyday example of a cybernetic process can be seen in the behavior of automobile drivers. For a driver to reach a distant destination in satisfying fashion, several things are required. He must know what the final destination is and he must want to get there. He must have devices like maps and road signs that will let him know when he has arrived and will periodically inform him en route whether or not he is headed in the proper direction. These devices provide a gross level of feedback that guides the decisions made at intersections and other major choice points. There is also a finer level of feedback that influences the driver's moment-to-moment behavior. A driver constantly processes incoming perceptions—a flow of sensory feedback (primarily visual, then kinesthetic and auditory) that is generated by his driving actions—and makes rapid, fine-grained adjustments in response to the data. He changes lanes, alters speed, shifts gears, applies brakes, corrects the steering, and so on.

What distinguishes good drivers from mediocre from bad is the effectiveness of their cybernetic process: how clearly they have identified the final goal; how frequently they gather data to monitor their progress; how relevant those data are to the final goal; and how adroitly they change their behavior on the basis of the feedback. With a finely tuned cybernetic process, drivers—and human service professionals—reach their objectives with a maximum of efficiency and satisfaction. With a less sophisticated cybernetic process, both time and energy are wasted and some potentially reachable goals become unattainable. And with extreme deficiencies in the cybernetic process, the pursuit of goals degenerates into a tedious journey—disorganized, disoriented, and inevitably disappointed.

An Example of a Cybernetic Process

Figure 4.1 presents in "flow-chart" form a general cybernetic process that might correspond to the effective pursuit of client-growth goals in a wide range of human service settings. Pieces of the chart represent various actions taken in selecting goals, pursuing them, gathering feedback related to the goals, and altering service-delivery procedures in response to the feedback. The numbers are not meant to indicate any sequence in the actions; they are merely used to simplify references to the chart in the discussions that follow. For example, the sequence of steps 1-2-3-4-6-9-12 would indicate the simplest course of events for a human service provider: a single goal of intervention that is quickly achieved by means of the first intervention strategy used. The only feedback in this sequence occurs when the goal has been reached. A variation on this simple sequence would involve feedback at one or more interim points during intervention. This would be depicted by:

$$1\text{-}2\text{-}3\text{-}[5\text{-}7\text{-}10\text{-}16\text{-}3]\text{-}4\text{-}6\text{-}9\text{-}12.$$

The subsequence in brackets would be repeated each time that feedback confirmed satisfactory progress toward the goal.

A slightly more complex situation would involve a single goal that was partially achieved by means of one intervention procedure, but that then required a change in procedure in order to be completely attained. The decision to change procedures would be based on interim feedback, as would the decision to maintain the second procedure until the final goal was reached. The entire sequence of events could be described by:

$$1\text{-}2\text{-}3\text{-}5\text{-}7\text{-}[10\text{-}16\text{-}3\text{-}5\text{-}7]\text{-}11\text{-}13\text{-}15\text{-}17\text{-}3\text{-}[5\text{-}7\text{-}10\text{-}16\text{-}3]\text{-}4\text{-}6\text{-}9\text{-}12.$$

Here there are two subsequences in brackets. The first subsequence would occur each time that interim feedback showed that the first intervention procedure was effective. Feedback would eventually suggest changing to another procedure. The second bracketed subsequence would occur each time that interim feedback showed that the second procedure was making satisfac-

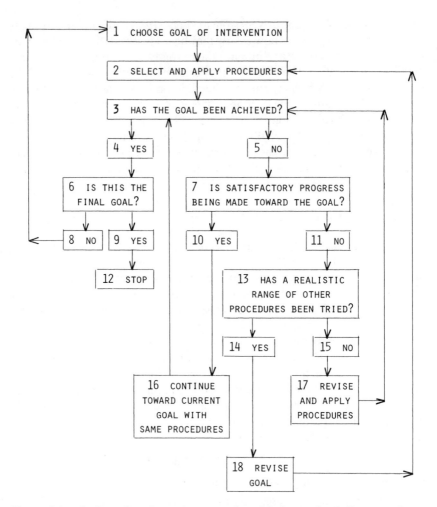

Figure 4.1.   Outline of a cybernetic process for achieving goals of client growth.

tory progress toward the final goal. This would enable the human service worker to confidently maintain the second intervention procedure until the goal was achieved.

In actual practice, of course, the sequence of events may be a great deal more complicated. There may be multiple goals of intervention for a given client. There may be many more than one or two potentially applicable intervention procedures. Translating these events into the structure of Figure 4.1 will produce strings of numbers that may appear quite cumbersome at first. However, by undertaking such a step-by-step analysis of the cybernetics of service-delivery, it will be possible to identify various deficits and breakdowns in the process. These cybernetic inadequacies are, we believe, the root causes of burnout.

Some Antecedents to the Cybernetic Model

Earlier we discussed the somewhat fragmented nature of current conceptualizations of burnout. The cybernetic model of burnout that we are proposing does not necessarily contradict these conceptualizations. In fact, many important features of current theories are quite compatible with the cybernetic model, which is intended to provide a more comprehensive and integrative framework for addressing burnout. Therefore, while considering the common kinds of disruption in the cybernetics of human service, we will attempt to show where elements of other models of burnout fit in the cybernetic model. Special emphasis will be given to five sources that have figured prominently in the brief history of the burnout construct:

1. Herbert Freudenberger, who coined the term in 1974, has provided several anecdotal accounts of burnout (especially in alternative institutions such as free clinics), has speculated about the underlying mechanisms of burnout, and has offered a variety of suggestions for preventing and remediating burnout (Freudenberger, 1974, 1975, 1977).

2. Christina Maslach, Ayala Pines, and their colleagues have been the leaders in developing an empirical foundation for the study of burnout. Their work—including the first well-validated burnout inventory—has emphasized the symptoms of burnout and the deleterious consequences for consumer-provider relationships (Maslach, 1976, 1978; Maslach & Jackson, 1978; Maslach & Pines, 1977; Pines & Aronson, 1981; Pines & Kafry, 1981; Pines & Maslach, 1978).

3. Cary Cherniss and his associates have stressed the organizational and cultural contexts within which individuals burn out. Their research has identified various correlates of job satisfaction in community mental health settings and has found specific sources of frustration in service delivery that are associated with burnout (Cherniss, 1980; Cherniss & Egnatios, 1978; Cherniss, Egnatios, & Wacker, 1976).

4. Richard Hackman and Greg Oldham have not focused specifically on burnout in the human services, but have addressed a larger and related topic: the motivational properties of jobs of many kinds. Their Job Diagnostic Survey, used to relate "job design" variables to worker motivation and productivity, has been valuable in the studies of burnout specialists (e.g., Pines & Kafry, 1981). The theoretical underpinnings of the Job Diagnostic Survey have clear relevance for a cybernetic model of burnout (Hackman & Oldham, 1975).

5. William Emener and Stanford Rubin have been mainly concerned with one type of human service worker, the vocational rehabilitation counselor. By examining the "roles and functions" of counselors—and by making comparisons among original expectations, current status, and desired changes—they have developed an unusual operational definition of burnout and have implicated "role strain" as a causal factor (Emener & Rubin, 1980; Rubin & Emener, 1979).

DISRUPTING THE PURSUIT OF CLIENT GROWTH

Ambiguity: The First Threat to the Cybernetic Process

Several theorists have addressed the importance of clear objectives of intervention. For example, Hackman and Oldham (1975) include "task identity" (working on start-to-finish jobs with clear closure) as one of the core dimensions of satisfying work. Cherniss and Egnatios (1978) cite poorly defined objectives as one of the major sources of frustration. The cybernetic process can be undermined at the outset by failing to express the goals of intervention (Step 1 in Figure 4.1) in clear, objective terms. Without such "operational definitions" of client growth, the entire process of goal pursuit, feedback generation, and course correction becomes open to uncertainty. Some useful guidelines for formulating clear goals have been provided by Bateman (1971) in education and by Mager and others in a variety of human service areas (Mager, 1972; Mager & Beach, 1967).

Functional Differences between Short-Term and Long-Term Goals for Clients

In our earlier discussion of milestones of client growth, we emphasized the motivational aspect of goal achievement for the committed professional. Clearly, the largest amounts of reinforcement come with the attainment of substantial goals over the relatively long haul. For example, completely desensitizing a phobia would be such an achievement. Bringing the reading scores of a learning-disabled child up to grade level would be another. Of course, there are also smaller amounts of reinforcement that come with the attainment of smaller goals. Such goals are often reached en route to larger milestones of client growth. For example, the phobic client reaches the third step on a 20-step desensitization hierarchy. Or the learning-disabled child masters the skill of decoding phonetically regular consonant-vowel-consonant trigrams. Hence, both short-term and long-term goals are important to the motivational needs of the human-service worker.

There is another, equally important function of goals, but this function is played mainly by the short-term goals. This is an *informational* function that is related to the feedback component of a cybernetic system. As long as the short-term goals have a logical, developmental connection to the long-term goal, then the short-term goals can act as a sort of "radar." This radar shows not only the current distance to the long-term goal, but also whether or not one is still "on course." Feedback on short-term goals is timely and sensitive enough to small changes that it can be used for course-correction activities. In contrast, feedback on long-term goals is too gross for efficient course correction.

An examination of Figure 4.1 shows the importance of short-term feedback (Step 7) in situations where the long-term feedback (Step 3) is currently negative (Step 5). A service provider in such a situation has three major choices: to continue pursuing the same long-term goal with the current procedures (Step 16); to continue pursuing the same goal with different procedures (Step 17); or to revise the long-term goal (Step 18). In order to choose wisely among these three alternatives, a service provider needs effective short-term feedback. Without such feedback there is no rational basis for choice among the three alternatives. Errors are bound to be made and may well set the stage for burnout.

Inadequate Cybernetics and Potential Burnout

Consider, for example, the situation in which the final goal of intervention is quite distant, but is in fact reachable. In other words, the service provider does have the skills necessary to help the client reach this particular developmental milestone. Yet, because of the absence of short-term feedback, a great deal of time must pass before there is clear evidence of progress. This might lead to the mistaken inference of a mismatch between the developmental goal and the service provider's capacities. Because of this erroneous conclusion, the goal would be abandoned prematurely, the effort already invested by the provider and the consumer would be wasted, and the provider's self-image would be unnecessarily undermined.

Now consider a different situation, one in which the provider is truly incapable of meeting the demands of the intervention goal. Very often such mismatches are not obvious in the early stages of intervention. If the goal is acknowledged to be substantial and long-term, and if there is no source of clear short-term feedback, the mismatch may go undetected for a painfully long period, wasting the time and efforts of provider and client alike. On the other hand, an effective feedback system would reveal the mismatch more quickly, perhaps enabling providers and consumers to be rematched. Another appropriate course of action—assuming that a small discrepancy existed between the demands of the intervention tasks and the capacities of the service provider— would be some relatively brief training that would raise the provider's skills to an adquate level.

Theories of burnout emphasize the causal role of excessive demands, unsatisfactory training, and inadequate skills of service providers. In other words, there is thought to be a significant mismatch between the demands of the intervention tasks and the capacities of the human service worker (Cherniss & Egnatios, 1978; Emener & Rubin, 1980; Freudenberger, 1975; Maslach & Jackson, 1978; Maslach & Pines, 1977). Our own position is that "poor fit" per se has been given too much credit as a source of burnout. Rather, we believe, it is the *misdiagnosis* of poor fit that is often to blame. As outlined in the preceding discussion, the misdiagnosis can take two forms: (1) incorrectly diagnosing poor fit (a "false positive"); or (2) waiting too long to diagnose poor fit (a "false negative"). We have suggested that both sorts of misdiagnosis can be caused by inadequate cybernetics.

Alternative Conceptualizations of the Goals of Intervention

Among theorists of abnormal behavior, one of the enduring debates concerns the relevance of a "medical model" in understanding the origins of maladaptive behavior, correcting such behavior when it occurs, and preventing its occurrence in the first place (Maher, 1966; Szasz, 1961; Ullmann & Krasner, 1969; Zilboorg & Henry, 1941). Under a medical model of intervention, the "final" goal is generally assumed to be restoration to a preexisting state of health, in other words, a "cure." Lesser accomplishments—no matter how much progress they might represent—constitute failure. Noncritical acceptance of this element of a medical model can place impossible burdens on human service providers.

This is especially true outside medicine, but can even apply within medicine. For instance, there are areas in which a medical model of etiology and/or a medical model of intervention are appropriate, but where medicine's traditional definition of "success" is not particularly useful. Incurable cancer and mental retardation of organic origin are two such areas. It is no coincidence that medicine has been slow to promote the growth of hospices for the terminally ill and has been all too ready to recommend institutionalization for newborn Down's Syndrome babies. Both situations confront physicians with a lifelong struggle in which there can never be a "complete victory," thus violating their thoroughly socialized conception of "success."

Outside of medicine, the majority of human service problems do not fit into clear-cut, either/or, disease-versus-health definitions of success and failure. Most human development—physical, cognitive, social, and emotional—proceeds along more or less continuous dimensions (Mussen, Conger, & Kagan, 1963; White, 1966). Most human service work involves facilitating the movement of clients along some developmental dimensions. This is a fundamentally different task from the typical, medical goal of restoring homeostasis to a physical system whose equilibrium has been temporarily disrupted. Therefore, the designation of "final goals" in most human service work involves somewhat arbitrary choices of points along various developmental continua. Accordingly, there should be little significance attached to falling just short of a "final goal." Moreover, each step in the preceding developmental sequence should be viewed as an accomplishment in its own right.

We believe that burnout can be caused by a human service worker's failure to maintain an appropriately developmental orientation. A common theme in the literature concerns the unrealistic goals set by human service workers who burn out (Boy & Pine, 1980; Maslach & Jackson, 1978; Mattingly, 1977). A corollary problem is the dogged perseveration on these goals, even as they remain distant and elusive. One frequent consequence is that more and more hours are spent on the job, with less and less being accomplished (Freudenberger, 1974, 1975). By concentrating so heavily on the final goal, human service workers may overlook the manner in which this goal depends upon a much earlier series of developmental steps. They tend to assign an overinflated value to the "final" goal, which obscures and implicitly devalues the immediate goals of intervention. This makes three things unnecessarily difficult for the service provider: (1) planning a step-by-step course of intervention; (2) generating regular, short-term feedback to monitor progress; and (3) deriving satisfaction from short-term increments of client growth. All three can undermine the cybernetics of service provision and thereby be precursors of burnout.

In contrast, by adopting a developmental perspective, human service providers can do much to ensure effectiveness and satisfaction in their work. By acknowledging the continuities of human growth—and the hierarchical order within different areas of development—they can undertake procedures for "task analysis" (Bateman, 1971) or "goal analysis" (Mager, 1972). The result is a series of small goals that begins with the client's current level and proceeds systematically to the long-term goal that has been chosen. Here, however, the long-term goal has been identified as merely a particular point on a continuum; it is thereby demystified and less likely to frustrate the provider whose client does not quite reach the goal.

A Closer Look at the Dynamics of Consumer-Provider Relationships

Human service providers are certainly not the only victims of disillusionment in the workplace. Yet the term "burnout" is usually reserved for human service work, while more general terms like "job alienation" or "tedium" (Pines & Aronson, 1981) are used to describe the depletion of workers in factories and other settings that are not directly involved with providing essential help to other human beings. It is widely believed that human service providers and consumers come together in a special relationship that exposes the provider to unusual and ominous risks (Cherniss, Egnatios, & Wacker, 1976; Freudenberger, 1977; Maslach, 1976, 1978; Pines & Kafry, 1981). In particular, the provider shares the developmental problems of the consumer and channels large amounts of cognitive and emotional energy into the consumer's struggles to cope. Typically there is little return flow of understanding and support from the consumer to the provider. This asymmetry—with the human service worker accumulating a huge deficit in the emotional "balance of trade"—has been implicated as a major cause of burnout (Kadushin, 1974). Indeed, some theorists believe that the client-centered qualities of human service interactions "make the process of burnout almost inevitable" (Pines & Aronson, 1981, p. 54). As protection against this emotional stress, providers are urged to cultivate an attitude of "detached concern" toward their clients (Lief & Fox, 1963; Maslach, 1976).

It is on this point that we distinctly part company with the major theories of burnout. We do not agree that prolonged, close contact with people's problems—and the accompanying emotional asymmetry between consumer and provider—are in and of themselves sufficient cause for burnout. We believe that another level of the consumer-provider relationship is much more important in understanding burnout. Moreover, this level of the relationship is symmetrical. Just as the consumer depends upon the provider's help to achieve and *recognize* personal growth, so too does the provider depend upon the client's milestones of growth for a much needed sense of professional efficacy. It is not the heavy emotional investment per se that drains the provider; rather, it is an investment that has insufficient dividends. And the most highly valued dividends are the developmental gains of the client, not the client's expressions of appreciation for those gains. A hypothetical question provides some insight into the comparative value for service providers of these two forms of reinforcement for their efforts: "What would be preferable—a client who has a developmental success, but not outwardly appreciative of the service provider's involvement, or a client who was a developmental failure, but treated the service provider as a valued comrade in a losing cause?"

It seems clear that the first client would be a much greater source of satisfaction than the second. Clients who do not progress deprive service providers of an essential psychological nutrient. Once it becomes obvious that efforts on behalf of these clients are ineffective, the withdrawal of the service providers is hardly surprising. Attempts to render service have been extinguished (a term that has a technically specific meaning in learning theory, but is strikingly similar in conventional language to "burnt out"). And retreat, which reduces painful reminders of one's ineffectiveness, is negatively reinforced. Beyond simple detachment from nonreinforcing clients (Maslach, 1976), it is only a few short steps to resentment and dehumanization (Maslach & Pines, 1977). "Blaming the victim" (Ryan, 1971) is one way of retaliating against a client who has, in effect, withheld the thing that service providers hold most dear—evidence of their own efficacy.

Cultivating "detached concern" may have some utility, but it should be secondary to enhancing the service provider's cybernetic process of setting goals and monitoring client growth. In light of the preceding discussion, it would be especially valuable to involve clients more actively as collaborators in the cybernetic process. For example, much of the "hard evidence" of a client's growth is not directly observable at the time of interactions with the service provider (student-teacher interactions provide the major exception). Hence, much of the needed feedback must take the form of the client's self-report.

And since, after all, the express purpose of consumer-provider contact is to *help the consumer,* there is an understandable tendency for clients to focus on negative information (Maslach, 1978). This may negatively distort, for consumer and provider alike, the amount of progress that has actually been made. Metaphorically, the glass may be seen as half-empty instead of half-full. And the message from consumer to provider, whether voiced or only implied, may be: " . . . so what have you done for me lately?"

An explicit part of service provision should be equipping clients to gather ongoing data on their progress as well as their problems. This could involve the provider and the client with choosing specific "homework" tasks to be accomplished between meetings and establishing objective criteria for successful completion of the tasks. The choice of goals should be realistic and developmental and, ideally, consensual. Meetings should begin with a discussion of the client's goal-related feedback and proceed to a consideration of upcoming tasks, objectives, and means for accomplishing them. In effect, consumer and provider become true partners in the sort of cybernetic process outlined in Figure 4.1. Among other benefits, this sort of collaboration removes the qualitative differences between "progress" and "problems." Progress can now be defined as "goals accomplished," while problems are recast as "goals to be accomplished next." And, although the data generated by the cybernetic process will not always be reinforcing, the collaborative and proactive nature of the process should provide a transcendent reinforcement to both partners.

PERSPECTIVES ON JOB DESIGN
AND THE GROWTH OF SERVICE PROVIDERS

Task Demand, Personal Capacity, and Stress

Although a great variety of burnout-related stresses have been discussed in the literature, they all have in common the notion that the demands of service provision have outstripped the capabilities of the service provider. It is probably rare to find an exact equilibrium between a provider's task demands and personal capacities. Discrepancies between demands and capacities involve either surpluses or deficits of capacity, and can be relatively minor or major in magnitude. The four possible combinations of direction and magnitude of the discrepancy produce four different psychological states for the service provider.

1. *Bored:* This involves a *major surplus* of capacity, where the needs of the client and the demands of the service tasks are adequately met by a provider operating in "low gear." This has been described by Freudenberger (1974) as "routinization" of the job.

2. *Relaxed:* This involves a *minor surplus* of capacity, where the task demands are still met comfortably, but require an extensive mobilization of the provider's capacities.
3. *Challenged:* This involves a *minor deficit* of capacity, where there's a gap between what needs to be done and what the provider can currently do, but a gap that is potentially bridgeable. In fact, such gaps can serve as catalysts to the growth of providers. As a consequence, this sort of "stress is not necessarily a bad thing" (Cherniss, Egnatios, & Wacker, 1976).
4. *Overwhelmed:* This involves a *major deficit* of capacity, where the provider is rapidly depleted by the demands of the task and even rendered helpless (Seligman, 1975) by the futility of the struggle.

Obviously, the greatest single cause of burnout is being in situations where one is overwhelmed. In addition, though, boredom can lead eventually to burnout (Maslach & Jackson, 1978). This represents an important divergence between the two major needs that we identified earlier in service providers: the need to promote growth in clients, and the need to grow personally on the job. In the bored region, feedback on client growth continues to be very positive, whereas professional growth is at a standstill. In the challenged region, the divergence also exists, except that conditions are reversed: client growth is sluggish, while professional growth is being stimulated.

As we mentioned earlier, the perception of client and provider growth is strongest when it consists of milestones being approached, attained, and passed. For professional growth, such milestones involve the progression from *challenged* to *relaxed* and, eventually, to *bored* for a particular task. What, then, is the "ideal" job description, the optimum blend of service tasks, the best mixture of circumstances for promoting client growth and professional growth and thereby responding to the service provider's two most important motivational drives? There would probably be no tasks whatsoever in the *overwhelmed* region; instead, the majority of tasks would be in the *relaxed* region, with about equal minorities of tasks in the *challenged* and *bored* regions.

Toward the Ideal Mix and Beyond Professional Preciousness

There has long been a great gap between the demand for human services and the supply of practitioners capable of rendering service. Greatly contributing to this gap is the phenomenon of "professional preciousness" (Sarason, 1972)—the tendency for various professional disciplines to conceptualize human service problems in ways that require the services of people trained and credentialed in that particular discipline.

Our analysis of professional growth suggests some possibilities for combatting "preciousness" while simultaneously enhancing the work life of professionals. The starting point is to stop regarding professional roles as indivisible and to acknowledge that any role is really just an aggregate of service functions that have coalesced for reasons that may be neither understood nor adaptive. Consider the problem of a function with which a professional has become *bored*. Rather than continue performing such a function, the professional could undertake the training of others in that function. For them (if they are properly selected), the function would begin in the *challenged* region and eventually progress to the *relaxed* region. For the practitioner-turned-trainer, training others would begin in the *challenged* region and eventually progress to the *relaxed* one. The entire process would have several salutary effects. The previously stagnating professional would experience milestones of personal growth. The trainees would have a similar experience. The pool of qualified practitioners would be enlarged, especially if paraprofessionals, nonprofessionals, and volunteers were eligible as trainees. A greater sense of synergy and community would be fostered among service providers. And there would be a greatly increased population of clients experiencing their own, more likely milestones of growth.

REFERENCES

Bateman, B. D. *The essentials of teaching.* Sioux Falls, S.D.: Dimensions Publishing, 1971.

Boy, A. V. & Pine, G. J. Avoiding counselor burnout through role renewal. *Personnel and Guidance Journal,* 1980, **59**, 161–163.

Brown, R. *Words and things.* Glencoe, Ill.: Free Press, 1958.

Cherniss, C. C. *Staff burnout: Job stress in the human services.* Beverly Hills, Calif.: Sage, 1980.

Cherniss, C. & Egnatios, E. Is there job satisfaction in community mental health? *Community Mental Health Journal,* 1978, **14**, 309–318.

Cherniss, C., Egnatios, E. S., & Wacker, S. Job stress and career development in new public professionals. *Professional Psychology,* 1976, 7, 428–436.

Emener, W. G. & Rubin, S. E. Rehabilitation counselor roles and functions and sources of role strain. *Journal of Applied Rehabilitation Counseling,* 1980, **11**, 57–69.

Erikson, E. H. *Childhood and society.* New York: Norton, 1950.

Freudenberger, H. J. Staff burn-out. *Journal of Social Issues,* 1974, **30**, 159–165.

Freudenberger, H. J. The staff burn-out syndrome in alternative institutions. *Psychotherapy: Theory, Research and Practice,* 1975, **12**, 73–82.

Freudenberger, H. J. Burn-out: Occupational hazard of the child-care worker. *Child Care Quarterly,* 1977, **6**, 90–99.

Hackman, J. R. & Oldham, G. R. *Motivation through the design of work: Test of a theory.* Tech. Rep. No. 6. New Haven, Conn.: Yale University, Department of Administrative Sciences, 1974.

Hackman, J. R. & Oldham, G. R. Development of the Job Diagnostic Survey. *Journal of Applied Psychology,* 1975, **60**, 159–170.

Janis, I. L.; Mahl, G. F.; Kagan, J.; & Holt, R. R. *Personality: Dynamics, development, and assessment.* New York: Harcourt, Brace, & World, 1969.

Kadushin, A. *Child welfare services.* New York: Macmillan, 1974.

Lief, H. I. & Fox, R. C. Training for "detached concern" in medical students. In H. I. Lief, V. F. Lief, & N. R. Lief (Eds.), *The psychological basis of medical practice.* New York: Harper & Row, 1963.

Mager, R. F. *Goal analysis.* Belmont, Calif.: Fearon, 1972.

Mager, R. F. & Beach, K. M. *Developing vocational instruction.* Belmont, Calif.: Fearon, 1967.

Maher, B. A. *Principles of psychopathology: An experimental approach.* New York: McGraw-Hill, 1966.

Maslach, C. Burned out. *Human Behavior,* 1976, **5**, 16–22.

Maslach, C. The client role in staff burn-out. *Journal of Social Issues,* 1978, **34**, 111–123.

Maslach, C. & Jackson, S. E. Lawyer burn out. *Barrister,* 1978, **5**, 52–54.

Maslach, C. & Pines, A. The burn-out syndrome in the day-care setting. *Child Care Quarterly,* 1977, **6**, 100–113.

Mattingly, M. A. Sources of stress and burn-out in professional child care work. *Child Care Quarterly,* 1977, **6**, 127–137.

Morrow, L. The burnout of almost everyone. *Time,* September 21, 1981.

Mussen, P. H., Conger, J. J., & Kagan, J. *Child development and personality.* 2nd ed. New York: Harper & Row, 1963.

Pines, A. M. & Aronson, E., with Kafry, D. *Burnout: From tedium to personal growth.* New York: Free Press, 1981.

Pines, A. & Kafry, D. Tedium in the life and work of professional women as compared to men. *Sex Roles,* 1981, **7**, 963–975.

Pines, A. & Maslach, C. Characteristics of staff burnout in mental health settings. *Hospital and Community Psychiatry,* 1978, **29**, 233–237.

Rubin, S. E. & Emener, W. G. Recent rehabilitation counselor role changes and role strain: A pilot investigation. *Journal of Applied Rehabilitation Counseling,* 1979, **10** (3), 142–147.

Ryan, W. *Blaming the victim.* New York: Pantheon, 1971.

Sarason, S. B. *The creation of settings and the future societies.* San Francisco: Jossey-Bass, 1972.

Seligman, M. E. P. *Helplessness.* San Francisco: Freeman, 1975.

Szasz, T. S. *The myth of mental illness.* New York: Hoeber-Harper, 1961.

Tolstoy, L. N. *Anna Karenina.* Oxford: Oxford University Press, 1918.

Ullmann, L. P. & Krasner, L. A. *A psychological approach to abnormal behavior.* Englewood Cliffs, N.J.: Prentice-Hall, 1969.

White, R. W. Motivation reconsidered: The concept of competence. *Psychological Review,* 1959, **66**, 297–333.

White, R. W. *Lives in progress.* 2nd ed. New York: Holt, Rinehart, & Winston, 1966.

Wiener, N. *The human use of human beings: Cybernetics and society.* Garden City, N.Y.: Doubleday, 1954.

Zilboorg, G. & Henry, G. W. *A history of medical psychology.* New York: Norton, 1941.

Part II:

The Nature and Dimensions of Burnout in the Human Service Professions

5

A Critical Study of Burnout in Teachers*

Mae Sakharov
and
Barry A. Farber

A worker's self-perception and perception of worth on the job are not "here and now" phenomena. As Sarason (1977) has noted, "Work is always experienced in relation to a perceived past, present and future" (p. 28). The primary aim of the present study was to investigate the phenomenology of the career development of teachers over time, toward the goal of isolating factors that contribute to the condition popularly known as burnout. An attempt was made to uncover those social-historical circumstances that affect an individual's work-related attitudes and behavior. In general, existing burnout studies have explored current, local working conditions instead of developing a historical, social analysis of the phenomenon.

Burnout has been defined as "a progressive loss of idealism, energy and purpose experienced by people in the helping professions as a result of the conditions of work" (Edelwich & Brodsky, 1980, p. 15). Early studies were of volunteers in free clinics that offered drug rehabilitation programs. These workers were described by Freudenberger (1974) as so emotionally drained that they began to identify with the clients whom they were serving. Maslach (1976), the first to compile empirical data on burnout, described it as a dehumanizing process, emphasizing the loss of concern and empathy in previously caring workers. According to Maslach, cynicism resulting from burnout often causes the worker to approach clients in derogatory ways, such as blaming them for their problems and labeling them with technical jargon.

Burnout has most often been discussed and written about in relation to teaching and teachers. Indeed, teacher burnout has been the theme of numer-

*We would like to thank Drs. Leslie Williams, Elizabeth Maloney, and Michael Lewis for their advice and helpful criticisms.

ous newspaper articles and television programs (Landsmann, 1978; McGuire, 1979; Reed, 1979; Serrin, 1979) as well as educational conferences (National Education Association, 1979). In January 1979, the New York State United Teachers union sent a questionnaire to a sample of its membership in order to determine sources of stress and burnout. The major causes reported were difficulties in managing disruptive children, incompetent administrators, and lack of administrative support in dealing with discipline problems ("Stress," 1980). Consistent with these results, a recent (1979) National Education Association (NEA) poll found that three-fourths of all teachers surveyed felt that discipline problems greatly inpaired their effectiveness in the classroom. Statistics compiled by the National Chapter of the NEA found that one in twenty teachers was physically attacked by students in the 1978–79 school year, and that more than 25 percent of the nation's 2.1 million elementary and secondary school teachers who reported attacks against them were dissatisfied with support from school administrators. Bloch (1976) has described the work environment of many teachers as resembling combat zones. He contends that those most susceptible to burnout are obsessional, passionate, idealistic, and dedicated persons who are unused to violence and hostility. They are unable to strike out or retaliate and instead internalize their rage and fear.

Other causes mentioned in the literature include poor salaries, lack of job mobility, involuntary transfers, public pressure, budget cuts, demanding parents, excessive paperwork, and excessive testing (Maslach, 1976; McGuire, 1979; Reed, 1979; Serrin, 1979). Burned out teachers, like other burned out professionals, complain of psychosomatic symptoms (e.g., exhaustion, insomnia, ulcers, headaches) as well as increased family conflicts (Cherniss, 1980; Freudenberger & Richelson, 1980; Maslach, 1976; McGuire, 1979).

This study advances the proposition that teacher burnout—as well as burnout in other professions—can be seen from a variety of perspectives, as there are many ways in which the problem is experienced and interpreted. For example, as noted above, the NEA attributes teacher stress to unruly students. Similarly, many teachers attribute job dissatisfaction to the jaded, antiintellectual attitudes of their students (Johnson, 1979). Hentoff (1979), on the other hand, takes a "teacher competency" approach and suggests that teachers rather than students have failed. He is particularly critical of teachers who become apathetic after they receive tenure. These examples indicate how one's stake in an issue can affect one's interpretation and response.

The hypothesis of this chapter is that burnout is not merely a psychological state or even a psychological reaction to a social situation, but the subjective experience of a predominantly social problem. This is not to imply, however, that social factors directly and exclusively determine individual behavior or that the individual is simply a reflection of social currents (Horkheimer, 1972). Rather, there is a dialectical interaction between the individual and society. It would be equally simplistic to attribute burnout to incompetent teachers or to broad social problems. This study regards burnout as a dynamic, interactive relationship between the individual teacher and the social world.

The methodology of the present study has been largely shaped by critical theory (Fromm, 1970; Horkheimer, 1972; Jay, 1973). This study does not attempt to test critical theory, but begins to examine whether the application of this political-social-historical approach to the problem of burnout will elucidate aspects of the phenomenon that are not currently explored in the literature.

INTRODUCTION TO CRITICAL THEORY

Critical theory is most closely associated with the Frankfurt Institute for Social Research (Arato & Gebhardt, 1978; Jay, 1973; Lasch, 1977). The Institute came into existence in the mid-1920s, bringing together political thinkers of the left who were disillusioned with the direction that the Russian Revolution had taken and disappointed that revolution not only had failed in the West but that Fascism had succeeded. It was felt that a rethinking of traditional Marxism was necessary. This required a critical reassessment of the traditional Marxist critique of exploitation and oppression. The Frankfurt Institute stressed subjectivity and insisted that constant self-criticism and self-reflection were necessary if past mistakes were to be avoided. The neo-Marxian emphasis on ideological criticism included the acknowledgment of biases in all research and theory, disclaiming the notion of neutrality.

Three topics of concern to the Frankfurt Institute are presented and briefly discussed below: alienation, individual psychology, and culture. Though the Frankfurt Institute dealt with many other issues, it is these three that are most relevant to professional burnout. From the perspective of critical theory, burnout can be interpreted as an instance of alienation, as a crisis of individual psychology, and as part of a larger cultural and social-political-economic problem.

Alienation

Marx first defined alienation in the *1844 Manuscripts* (Jay, 1973). It was not until 1924 that Lukacs, in his essay, "Reification and the Consciousness of the Proletariat" (Arato & Gebhardt, 1978), further developed the concept. Alienated labor was seen as a by-product of capitalism where human relationships were shaped largely by material interests. According to Lukacs (1971), "The problem of commodities must not be considered in isolation or even regarded as the central problem in economics, but as the central, structural problem of capitalist society in all its aspects" (p. 83). Both Marx and Lukacs recognized the effects of commodization not only within economics but also within the personal and interpersonal domains. According to them, relationships become increasingly "thinglike," or reified (Jacoby, 1975; Lukacs, 1971; Marcuse, 1964; Schneider, 1975). Reification causes people to become detached and thus alienated from the process and product of work, from other people, and ultimately from themselves.

Individual Psychology

The psychoanalyst, Erich Fromm, was a student of Freud and an early member of the Institute. Fromm brought Freud's perspective into critical Marxist theory. Later, Horkheimer, Adorno, and Marcuse would also attempt to synthesize Freud and Marx. Before the existence of the Frankfurt Institute, Marxism had relied on economic theories to explain domination, but a strictly materialist interpretation neglected the human and subjective aspects of social problems (Jay, 1973; O'Neil, 1976; Schneider, 1975), an oversight which the Frankfurt School criticized and sought to remedy.

According to Adorno, Freud "revealed the antagonistic character of social reality" (Jacoby, 1975, p. 28). Furthermore, noted Fromm (1970), "social psychology could discover in the child's psychological attitudes towards his parents, especially his father, the roots of the majority of the population's subservience to the ruling class" (p. 178). Horkheimer (1972) concluded that attitudes developed in the family are related to the manner in which people respond to state authority. According to the Frankfurt School, psychoanalysis could not develop a world philosophy in and of itself; it could only become meaningful in the context of a political-economic viewpoint. Thus, the combination of psychoanalysis and neo-Marxism provides a framework in which to study individual psychology in the context of prevailing economic, social, and political conditions (Baxandall, 1972; Fromm, 1970).

Culture

Traditional interpretations of Marx have either ignored or downplayed the role of culture, and that of ideology in particular (Arato & Gebhardt, 1978). For the Frankfurt School, the contradictions represented in the 20th-century phenomenon of mass culture (e.g., that it simultaneously meets and distorts real needs) were just as important to analyze as economic conditions, and, in fact, strongly related to them. Although members of the Frankfurt Institute differed on the effects of what Adorno called the "culture industry," there was general agreement that the culture industry exists and that, in its present form, its one-dimensionalizing effects are overridingly negative (Sacre, 1979). They also emphasized that, regardless of one's attitude to the culture industry, it can only thrive as it does because it addresses and exploits real needs (Sacre, 1979).

In short, within the paradigm of critical theory, burnout, though immediately experienced as an individual crisis, and though attributable to observable, seemingly irremediable problems, may also be seen as an instance of alienation that can be understood in much broader terms—as an almost inevitable characteristic of a worker's relationship to work and hence, to others and to himself in a capitalist society.

A CRITICAL APPROACH TO THE STUDY OF BURNOUT

Critical theory, as espoused by the Frankfurt School, assumes that specific social and political "givens" color any data with which they deal (Horkheimer, 1972). In contrast, the more established methodologies in social science research derive from traditional positivism and rationalism and assume that the process and products of data gathering can take place in a neutral or a natural context (Fay, 1975). A social scientist who works from the latter assumption focuses on the individual at the expense of the context in which the individual exists (Fay, 1975). The critical approach to research maintains that bias necessarily grows out of the interests of those who commissioned the research and from the prejudices of the researchers (Horkheimer, 1972).

The critical approach has a bias of its own, as proponents are eager to admit. As noted above, the critical approach would tend to interpret burnout as a specific example of alienation in a capitalist society. Teacher burnout would be seen as an inevitable outgrowth of a "repetition of ritualized tasks" (Freire, 1979). According to this point of view, many teachers, accustomed to a prescribed curriculum, have lost the desire to be spontaneous in their work with children. Despite, or even because of these biases, critical theory remains a method that seems potentially useful and perhaps unique in its ability to elucidate those aspects of individual, institutional, and social factors which, taken together, generate burnout.

METHOD

The critical method employed in the present study is characterized by the following features: (1) It has a *hermeneutic intention,* that is, it aims to establish an interpretive dialogue with helping professionals. The dialogue attempts to explore the meanings and themes of work that derive from professionals' personal and social histories; (2) It has a *critical social scientific* intention, that is, it focuses on the interplay between subjective experience and objective conditions (Jacoby, 1975; Fay, 1975). The interviews in this study therefore included questions dealing with personal history as well as questions that focused on an individual's current perceptions of work.

Helping professionals have historically not been vocal about the conditions of their work, and researchers have, for the most part, failed to investigate work experiences of professionals (see Sarason, 1977). The methodology of the present study sought to facilitate subjects' willingness to be self-critical as well as critical of the systems within which they work.

Subjects

Subjects were early childhood teachers, pediatric nurses, and pediatricians, all working in a large metropolitan community in the Northeast. Though this study is concerned primarily with early childhood educators, nurses and pediatricians were included in the sample to provide a means of determining whether burnout was indicative of a more general social condition. Subjects came from diverse ethnic and economic backgrounds. Since women have dominated the nurturing professions, it was decided to focus on a female population.

The choice of potential participants was established by a variety of means. In adherence to the stated hypothesis of this study—that burnout is the subjective experience of a predominantly social phenomenon—a concerted effort was made to find subjects working in a distinct variety of situations. The final sample included twenty early childhood teachers from different types of schools (day care, public, private, and special education facilities), five pediatric nurses, and five pediatricians. The subjects ranged in age from 23 to 65 with a mean age of 33. Seven subjects were minority group members.

Procedure

Preliminary interviews were undertaken with a small pilot sample of teachers, nurses, and pediatricians. These interview questions were extracted from the NEA nationwide teacher poll (1979) and *The Marienthal Study* (Lazarsfeld, 1971). Based on recurrent themes in the pilot data, a final open-ended, semi-structured interview was established.

Major topics covered in the final interview included: reasons for entering the helping profession; views regarding adequacy of professional training; attitudes of others regarding career choice; view of personal future in the profession; view of the future of the profession in general; attitude toward administration; and perceptions of sources and symptoms of job stress.

By following strategies developed by Glaser and Strauss (1967), the final typed transcripts were scrutinized to determine categories of responses. Categories and individual responses to them were charted according to the subjects' professions. The results were then reorganized into a time-frame that included: (a) reasons for career choice; (b) attitudes toward professional training; (c) assessment of current problems and issues in the field, and (d) personal commitment to one's profession.

RESULTS

In an interview study of this type, categorization of responses is mediated by the nature of the communication between researcher and subject. Assumptions must be made both about the validity of what the subjects express as well as the investigator's subsequent interpretations. It is with this caution that the results of this study are stated.

Reasons for Career Choice

The majority of subjects entered their profession because they wanted to care for children. Eighty percent expressed the specific desire to help and nurture children. Nurturant expectations were expressed in the comments of several teachers, such as the following:

> I love children and I feel that I should do something to bring out the better parts of them. . . . I like kids and I believe that I can provide for the children's educational and emotional needs. . . . It was my intimate experiences with children that drew me into teaching.

Most of the subjects saw nurturance as a way of bringing out the children's good personal qualities. In this way, they saw themselves contributing to society; they felt they could effect social change by working with children at a formative stage.

Almost half of the subjects felt that earlier volunteer work with children had a direct, positive influence on career choice. In contrast, a small percentage of subjects expressed the opinion that volunteer opportunities merely mirrored society's low expectations for women. Twenty-three percent of the subjects regarded their volunteer work as preparing them for stereotyped "women's work."

Attitudes toward Professional Training

How subjects experienced their professional training—the acquisition of skills, attitudes, and expectations—is related to how they fare in the world of work. In general, the subjects were fairly evenly divided in their assessment of their training. Thirty-seven percent of all subjects, including 45 percent of all teachers, described their academic training as putting them in good stead to meet the demands of their profession. Asked to evaluate the impact of professional training on her work, one public school teacher commented: "I feel that I probably was more fortunate than most teachers. My college specialized in Early Childhood Education. It was a small environment, with small classes, with 'real' professionals." Indeed many subjects attributed the excellence of their training to "high-quality" professors. Frequently cited attributes of high-quality professors included sensitivity, responsiveness, criticalness, and a holistic approach to education or health care. In addition, subjects who had a variety of field placements felt generally better equipped for work. Field work gave them exposure to different settings, job contacts, and knowledge of bureaucracy.

Thirty-three percent of the subjects (and 25 percent of all teachers) described themselves as having been "adequately" prepared. Representative of this point of view were the comments of a special education teacher working in a public school: "My training gave me a basic understanding of early childhood development and it also gave me an understanding of certain academic things but it only partially provided any preparation for what really happens in the classroom."

Thirty percent of all subjects, as well as 30 percent of teachers, felt poorly prepared; training was described as unrealistic and theoretical:

> I have been teaching for over twenty years. My original training didn't prepare me at all. It was too idealistic and painted a totally "rosy" picture of the profession. I've never found one working situation that matched what I was taught to expect in teacher training.

All subjects claimed a need to deal with "human" issues at work. All agreed therefore that a holistic approach to training—in which interpersonal as well as technical skills are emphasized—would have better prepared them for the realities of their profession.

Current Problems and Issues

Bureaucracy and Politics. Bureaucratic problems were seen as a major source of frustration on the job. Local education or health care administrators, under pressure from the central office, in turn put pressure on their staffs. In public schools, particularly, teachers are scapegoated. Two private school teachers had left the public system because it was too difficult to accomplish what they were hired to do. One of them stated that, primarily because of bureaucratic pressures, she would come home after a day of teaching in an inner-city school and need two hours of rest before she could do anything else. Most (83 percent) of those interviewed were impatient with bureaucratic indifference that treated children as the last, rather than the primary, concern.

Only 35 percent of all subjects interviewed regarded their administrations as being personally involved with them. Teachers in small programs such as day care, special education, and private schools had more contact with the administration. Several public school teachers reported that their administrations were either intimidated by the central office or personally ambitious to the extent that they harassed teachers to deter them from approaching administrative personnel with problems. One public school teacher described her administrator's techniques:

> Our principal is a very ambitious man. I think that he's concerned with getting himself up in the hierarchy as fast as he can go. If you are a good teacher he will leave you alone. But he will try to take advantage of you if you are a poor teacher or a teacher who is timid in any way. He will harass teachers into staying away from him. He posted a statement to this effect: "Any teacher who cannot control a child in the classroom is no teacher whatsoever."

Several subjects described the administration and individual workers as being under great pressure. In public schools, teachers must increase test scores for which the administration is accountable. Hospital administration must balance the budget, which results in low staffing patterns. Nurses feel this pressure especially when confronting life and death situations. Pediatricians in this study who were attached to hospitals complained of administrative pressure to publish.

Involuntary transfers are another aspect of bureaucracy. One public school teacher prepared for a particular class only to come in on the first day of school and find herself assigned to another classroom. In fact, 80 percent of the public school teachers interviewed had experienced involuntary transfers that they considered stressful. Conversely, all public school teachers agreed that the lack of "new blood" in schools had a demoralizing and deadening effect. With each layoff, the staff gets older and more inbred, with young workers usually the victims.

Health and Morale. Sixty-seven percent of the subjects felt that their physical health was adversely affected by their work. Though the causes of ill health were perceived differently by professional subgroups, work was generally described as stressful and exhausting. The most common complaint was that work was physically and emotionally depleting, resulting in overeating, over-smoking, depression, headaches, and stomachaches. One private school teacher complained that her blood pressure went up to a dangerous level while she was working in a public school. In the hospital, nurses described lowered resistance from working long hours without relief and from exposure to infections.

In addition, teachers, particularly public school teachers, described consistently bad publicity as affecting their morale on the job. For example, one public school teacher commented:

> We're under tremendous public criticism. Every time you pick up the paper, there is a lot of negative feedback about how the schools are failing. Public education is on the demise. Teachers seem to bear the brunt of all the blame.

Several interview questions dealt with how subjects were able to cope with such stresses. Generally, teachers tended to isolate themselves within the classroom while hospital workers tried to arrange time out from floor work. For example, teachers in most public schools found it necessary to close their classroom doors in order to gain "intimacy and a sense of distance from distractions." One public school teacher noted:

> I feel that what goes on in my room is no one's business. The classroom should be intimate and cozy and I use those words with the children. "Let's have a cozy day and turn off the lights and close the door." That's how I feel about it. It's my home and I wouldn't keep the door opened at my apartment. It's between me and my kids. I don't find any problem with that.

Similarly, a majority of nurses and pediatricians interviewed for this study described becoming overstressed and needing time to recuperate. For example, one pediatrician reported: "We need to get away. We need a hole to hide in."

Values and Attitudes. Working in low-income, high-risk schools has often been described as a cause of teacher burnout (see Reed, 1979). For this reason, several interview questions dealt with the effect of social class differences on attitudes toward work. Most (80 percent) of the teachers in this study felt that children should be taught middle-class values if they are to function in a world that is built on those values. In fact, according to one respondent, middle-class values do not conflict with the wishes of those parents who want to "come up in the world." For example, a public school teacher recalled working during the late 1960s:

> I used to be an idealist who believed in teaching according to the learning style of the culturally disadvantaged. Now though, I believe that middle class values are not in conflict with most of my students' families.

In this regard too, 75 percent of the teachers in this study, including 100 percent of those teaching in public schools, expressed the need for parents to become more involved with the education process.

Moreover, although disruptive children have been described as the major source of teacher burnout (McGuire, 1979; Reed, 1979; Serrin, 1979), most (90 percent) of the teachers agreed that, whatever problems they have on the job, children are not the cause. Several teachers admitted that they look to themselves rather than to the children as the source of their difficulties. One public school worker felt that "it is not the children themselves but the social conditions that make working with children impossible, i.e., overcrowding and bureaucratic paperwork."

Personal Commitment to Profession

Most of the teachers in this study (80 percent) were pessimistic regarding the future of the profession. The general decline of federal support for public education, coupled with the drop in the birth rate, has resulted in fewer opportunities in the field. Several teachers, in fact, described special education as the only area of potential growth.

Half of the teachers interviewed for this study were considering leaving the profession (although only a few were actively seeking other work). Many of the causes of their disenchantment have already been cited: bureaucratic indifference and pressure, parental apathy, involuntary transfers, increased paperwork, public hostility toward teachers. One other factor cited frequently by teachers was "lack of opportunity for professional advancement." Many teachers noted that either political or financial considerations took precedence over competence in hiring administrative personnel.

Those teachers who expressed a commitment to their profession cited two primary reasons for their position: rewarding relationships with students, and the availability of collegial support systems.

Rewarding relationships with students. Most teachers interviewed for this study worked in inner-city, depressed school districts where working conditions were perceived as oppressive and administration as neglectful or even hostile. Despite these conditions, many teachers expressed a dedication to "their" students. Many felt that at least within the confines of their classrooms, they enjoyed many positive, satisfying, and gratifying experiences with their students. Although admitting to occasional weariness, these teachers continued to want to understand, help, and teach their students.

Support systems. Good professional mentors—supportive, creative, and resourceful—seem to provide models of strength to deal with disappointments and pressures in daily work. Several public school teachers mentioned that the only way they could stay on the job was through the inspirational examples of colleagues. Dedicated teachers have a way of discovering each other. Even in a large school, they lunch together, discussing students and curriculum ideas, rather than feelings about defeat. A good example comes from two teachers working in a "bombed-out" school district where many children are exposed to a great deal of abuse and violence in their environment. These teachers, who were neither defeatist nor despairing, attributed their resilience to networks of colleagues and mentors. Other teachers mentioned the value of administrative support. One teacher, for example, cited a director of a day care program who involved the staff at all levels of decision making; another lauded a principal who valued her teachers and encouraged them to try out new ideas.

DISCUSSION

This study was concerned with uncovering professional, personal, and social conditions that characterize susceptibility to burnout. By applying methodologies derived from the Frankfurt School for Social Research and more contemporary critical theorists, this study attempted to "discover society within the psyche of the individual" (Jacoby, 1975, p. 96). The research method employed here, following Maslach (1976), was directed away from identifying "bad people" and toward uncovering characteristics of "bad situations" where many "good people" function (or dysfunction).

This study began with the hypothesis that burnout was an instance of alienation, a crisis of individual psychology that can be viewed as part of a larger cultural and social-political-economic problem. The results confirm this hypothesis. Eighty percent of the subjects in this study described a sense of professional futurelessness, combined with a cynical and disenchanted attitude toward present professional commitments. The results further indicated that burnout does not start with the isolated teacher in the classroom but is part of a configuration of factors that affect and are affected by personal histories. For example, one private school worker interviewed for this study described herself as being burned out in one professional situation but well-functioning in another.

Burnout as a Feminist Issue

"Women have never been free to develop their potential, femaleness has been defined by men to suit male needs" (Fromm, 1970, p. 73). Early writings of the Frankfurt School described women as an underclass with limited opportunities to change their status. Those professions included in the present study were either typically female (teachers and nurses) or medical specialties considered most appropriate for women (pediatrics). In this regard, half of all working women in the United States hold jobs in areas that are at least 70 percent female dominated, and one-quarter are in jobs that are 95 percent female dominated. In addition, women who have graduated from college have lower starting salaries than men who have completed the eighth grade (Bennetts, 1979). Many subjects expressed anger when they looked back at the limited opportunities available to them when they began work.

When asked why they remained on the job in light of their anger, the overwhelming majority of subjects indicated their love for and desire to help children. Nurturance as a way of life was a consistent theme throughout the study. Although female children are typically socialized to be nurturant and loving and male children trained to be achievement-oriented and competitive (Hammer, 1975), it does not necessarily follow that girls are devoid of ambition and that boys are uncaring. It is the society that has associated low status, low income, and female identification with professions that require nurturance.

The susceptibility to burnout on the job, then, may have personal-historical roots in conceptions of what a woman can and should do.

Unrealistic Expectations as a Source of Burnout in the Nurturing Professions

The present study attempted to investigate the complex interrelationship between theory and practice during training and how it affects later attitudes toward work. According to the critical approach, a synthesis of theory and practice is pivotal in overcoming worker alienation. Freire (1979), a contemporary critical theorist, commented on how this method would be applied to education: "The integration of theory and practice creates a situation in which one no longer studies in order to work, nor does one work in order to study; one studies in the process of working" (p. 6).

The majority of subjects found that their training had been too idealistic to be of use once they had left the university. The major complaint was not of poor academic preparation but that academic preparation was not related to the extensive "social work" required of them on the job. Teachers in public schools, for example, described having to spend much time keeping track of children's personal and health histories. Although hospitals have social workers, they are often short-staffed and nurses are expected to take care of Medicare and malpractice-form filling, as well as counseling an increasing number of teenage mothers and child abusers. Municipal hospital pediatricians find themselves in similar situations. Much effort goes into making themselves understood to parents of culturally different backgrounds.

Participants in this study also described feeling unprepared to deal with other social issues on the job, such as coping with bureaucracies (and organizational structure), understanding professional politics and funding procedures, and dealing with ethnic and social class differences. A repeated suggestion was that university programs include courses on the cause and treatment of staff burnout. In general, subjects did not want to become social workers, but described this function as a reality of their profession for which they should be prepared. According to the findings of this study, it is impossible to ignore the intrusion of the social world into the lives of the workers. Perhaps university training programs should reexamine what professionals actually do once they leave the classroom.

Assessment of Burnout Literature's Application to Early Childhood Situations

The teacher burnout literature has for the most part standardized its discussion of the phenomenon (McGuire, 1979; Reed, 1979; Serrin, 1979). The causes and solutions offered have generally not considered the age group that the teacher is working with or the teacher's specific circumstances. In this context, what distinguished the responses of the majority of early childhood professional workers in the present study from the results generally reported in the previous teacher burnout literature was the general agreement of respondents in the present study that whatever problems they may have on the job, their "child-clients" are not the causes. This response is in total opposition to the most frequently reported cause of teacher burnout—disruptive children (McGuire, 1979; Reed, 1979; Serrin, 1979).

Several conditions inherent in the early childhood profession can account for this finding. The most obvious consideration is the age of the children being serviced (0–7). Young children are for the most part easier to control and less apt to be disruptive. In addition, early childhood programs are often mandated to have a smaller staff-child ratio which makes management easier. It is significant that only one subject described problems working with children. The subject, a pediatric nurse, was on a floor with chronically ill children.

Another difference between the results of the present study and the results of previous burnout studies was that early childhood workers generally did not describe demanding parents as a source of job-related frustration. These results are consistent with the findings of Bronfenbrenner (1974), Gordon (1976), and Kruger (1975), who described the ideal working conditions with young children as a collaboration between parent, child, and teacher. Both teachers and health care workers saw the need for more well-planned parent participation, though each profession had different reasons for these views. Health care workers agreed that families often had difficulty understanding and implementing suggested treatments. On the other hand, teachers felt that many parents simply did not participate enough in their children's schooling. It can therefore be suggested that burnout does not result from parents who are too demanding, but rather from a lack of parental understanding of appropriate roles.

The results of the present study did, however, concur with many other commonly stated causes of teacher burnout (NEA Poll, 1979; "Stress," 1980; Reed, 1979) such as excessive paperwork, overcrowded conditions, involuntary transfers, inadequate income, unresponsive administrators, and public pressure. The school and hospital are part of a larger community; as such, difficulties within these institutions are reflections of the social world surrounding them.

Anxiety was manifested in a variety of physical complaints as well as a perceived loss of control at work. One defense mechanism for coping with such stress was self-imposed isolation. Teachers in public schools tended to protect themselves from the outside by "locking" themselves and their children in a protected classroom. Though effective as a temporary solution to stress, personal retreat obviously lessens the possibility for solidarity, network, and a sense of common cause among colleagues.

In summary, from the perspective of the early childhood workers interviewed for this study, burnout is characterized by (1) the experience of difficulties within the institution, as a microcosm of the social world; (2) isolation as a coping mechanism; (3) the development of a split between the warmth of isolation and the intensity of the world; (4) a recognition that children are victims rather than causes of problems; (5) a sense of futurelessness, and a cynical and detached attitude toward the present.

CONCLUSIONS AND RECOMMENDATIONS

The future in the nurturing professions, particularly in general education, looks bleak. This is perhaps reflective of the general economic, social, and psychological conditions of the 1970s. The reforms of the 1960s have been forsaken. Participants in this study were pessimistic about future possibilities and unable to imagine any solutions. They dream about simpler structures but are hopeless about achieving them.

Applying a critical approach to the study of burnout removes the onus of the problem from the individual and emphasizes instead the connection between the individual and society. If we assume that the structure of this society is not apt to change radically in the near future, the focus must therefore be on finding the most effective methods of remediation. A first step in overcoming the despair of burnout is to acknowledge its social context. When individuals realize that they are not alone, but part of a larger social experience, they can reach outward for solutions as well as solidarity.

A second step in overcoming burnout may be the establishment of strong institutional support systems (see Farber & Miller, 1981). Support systems can take several forms; for example, teachers' unions often provide a strong source of political support. During the course of this study it was found that schools with an active union chapter chairperson on the premises were less likely to have pessimistic staffs. Sarason (1977) suggests that "it is possible to improve the experience of work by engendering a sense of community" (p. 284). A psychological sense of community would not eliminate frustration and conflict but would provide an environment where it would be possible to "confront, clarify, and harmonize action with human values" (p. 287). Unfortunately, institutions do not often provide an atmosphere that facilitates worker solidarity. Moreover, bureaucracies have become larger and employees often have little power over their individual fates (Lasch, 1979). Nevertheless, attempts to establish a sense of community can only prove helpful in minimizing stress and preventing burnout.

Another area of potential change is within graduate training programs. These institutions appear generally to be out of tune with the realities of the work world. Preprofessionals are assigned appropriate course work but are not prepared for the disappointments that they will inevitably encounter on the job (Farber & Heifetz, 1982). Unrealistic expectations can be an impetus to disillusionment and burnout (Cherniss, 1980). Graduate education will have to deal more effectively with the totality of professional experience.

One means of more adequately preparing students might involve more extensive and well-supervised field work. Field work prepares students not only for the realities of work but also affords opportunities to interact with professionals who are already established in the field. Field work thus facilitates dialogue with experienced workers regarding the rewards and hazards of the profession. In addition, these experiences may foster mentor relationships that are a potential source of future professional support. Taken together, these suggestions point to the need to restructure graduate education, first to include more discussion of working conditions, second, to have more extensive and well-supervised field work components, and third, actively to encourage the student-mentor relationship.

Finally, the adoption of a feminist approach to the issue—which would involve recognizing the role of gender in the low status of the profession—could lead to the establishment of support systems, discussion forums, and political strategy sessions for women. The importance and predominance of women within the nurturing professions could thus be used to advantage, e.g., by publicizing the results of such meetings and by seeking actively to redefine nurturance as a privileged role all people, rather than women alone, can play. Sarason (1977) predicts that the changing role of women will have enormous consequences for society. It therefore becomes incumbent upon society to recognize the burnout phenomenon and to take steps to reduce its impact. The future of this country's teachers, as well as its children, may well be at stake.

REFERENCES

Arato, A. & Gebhardt, E. (Eds.). *The essential Frankfurt School reader.* New York: Urizen, 1978.

Baxandall, L. (Ed.). *Sex pol essays, 1929-1934 by Wilheim Reich.* New York: Vintage, 1972.

Bennetts, L. The equal pay issue: Focusing on "comparable worth." *New York Times,* October 29, 1979, p. A26.

Bloch, A. M. The battered teacher. *Today's Education,* 1977, **66**, 58-62.

Bronfenbrenner, U. *Is early intervention effective?* Washington, D.C.: Office of Child Development, U.S. Department of Health, Education, and Welfare, 1974.

Cherniss, C. *Professional burnout in human service organizations.* New York: Praeger, 1980.

Edelwich, J., with Brodsky, A. *Burnout: Stages of disillusionment in the helping professions.* New York: Basic Books, 1980.

Farber, B. A. & Heifetz, L. J. The process and dimensions of burnout in psychotherapists. *Professional Psychology,* 1982, **13** (2), 293-301.

Farber, B. A. & Miller, J. Teacher burnout: A psychoeducational perspective. *Teachers College Press,* 1981. **83** (2), 235-243.

Fay, B. *Social theory and political practice.* London: Allen & Unwin, 1975.

Freire, P. *Pedagogy in process.* New York: Seabury, 1979.

Fromm, E. *Crisis of psychoanalysis.* New York: Holt, Rinehart, & Winston, 1970.

Freudenberger, H. J. Staff burnout. *Journal of Social Issues,* 1974, **1**, 159–164.

Freudenberger, H. S. & Richelson, G. *Burnout: The high cost of high achievement.* Garden City, N.Y.: Anchor Press, Doubleday, 1980.

Glaser, B. G. & Strauss, A. L. *The discovery of grounded theory strategies for qualitative research.* Chicago: Aldine Press, 1967.

Gordon, D. Parenting, teaching and child development. *Young Children,* March 1976, 173–183.

Hammer, Signe (Ed.). *Women, body, and culture.* New York: Harper & Row, 1975.

Hentoff, N. The next school war—Flunking teachers. *Village Voice,* May 14, 1979, pp. 91–92.

Horkheimer, M. *Critical theory, Selected essays.* New York: Herder & Herder, 1972.

Jacoby, R. *Social amnesia.* Boston: Beacon, 1975.

Jay, M. *Dialectical imagination.* Boston: Little, Brown & Co., 1973.

Johnson T. A parting shot from teacher. *New York Times,* June 23, 1979, p. 21.

Kruger, S. Education for parenthood and school age parents. *Journal of Social Health,* 1975, **14** (5), 292–295.

Landsmann, L. Is teaching hazardous to your health? *Instructor,* April–May 1978, 49–50.

Lasch, C. *Haven in a heartless world: The family besieged.* New York: Basic, 1977.

Lazarsfeld, P. *Marienthal: The sociography of an unemployed community.* New York: Atheneum, 1971.

Lukacs, G. *History and class consciousness,* R. Livingston (trans.). Cambridge, Mass.: MIT, 1971.

Marcuse, H. *One dimensional man.* Boston: Beacon, 1964.

Maslach, C. Burned out. *Human Behavior,* September 1976, 16–22.

McGuire, W. *Teacher burnout statement.* National Education Association's 117th Annual Meeting, Detroit, Michigan, 1979.

National Education Association. Nationwide teacher opinion poll. Washington, D.C.: 1979.

O'Neil, J. *On critical theory.* New York: Seabury, 1976.

Reed, S. Teacher burnout a growing hazard. *New York Times,* February 6, 1979, p. A2.

Sacre, E. A. *A critical assessment of literature in the classroom: Curriculum implications.* Ed.D. dissertation, Teachers College, Columbia University, 1979.

Sarason, S. *Work, aging and social change.* New York: Free Press, 1977.

Schneider, M. *Neurosis and civilization.* New York: Seabury, 1975.

Serrin, W. NEA says teacher burnout causes thousands to leave jobs. *New York Times,* July 6, 1979, p. A8.

Stress. *New York Teacher,* January 1980, 1B–8B.

6

"Take This Job and Shove It!"
A Comparison of Organizational Stress
and Burnout among Teachers and Police*

Francis A. J. Ianni
and
Elizabeth Reuss-Ianni

Despite widespread professional concern with the syndrome popularly called "burnout," a consensus regarding its definition has yet to be reached. Most theorists, however, would agree that burnout is a distinct entity, characterized by several key features. First, it is a malady with specific contemporary roots in Western society. This does not preclude the possibility that it has always existed and has only recently been recognized or labeled, but rather suggests that it seems related somehow to modern living. Second, it is peculiarly related to the workplace. When it is discovered and recognized its first symptoms are almost always responses to the job and work satisfaction. Burnout seems to occur in those situations where the stresses of the job or work role become internalized, leading to either somatization of symptoms and loss of self-esteem, or both. Burnout is the disease of the human service worker, as much a function of the context of the professional's work environment as black lung disease is a function of the coal miner's work environment.

*The research reported in this chapter had a number of sources of financial support. The material concerning teacher stress is from the "Safe School Study," supported by the National Institute of Education and from our Social Organization of Schools Program which has been supported by the Ford Foundation and the National Institute of Education. The material on police stress is from our study, "The Social Organization of Police Precincts," supported by the National Institute of Justice. The adolescent study reported here is "A Study of Adolescents in Community Contexts," which was conducted under a grant from the Spencer Foundation.

The research literature on stress and its effects on individual and group performance is extensive (Bellak, 1975; Campbell, Converse, & Rodgers, 1976; Glass & Singer, 1972; Spielberger & Sarason, 1977). A review of this literature indicates that stresses and stressors can be viewed as developing from three distinctive sources. One source of potential stressors is within the individual. The subjectivity of burnout is reflective of the frequent observation that some individuals show greater or lesser tolerance for stress. Studies of stress-coping factors among police, for example, seem to indicate that such differentiating factors as anxiety levels and aggressiveness can distinguish between those officers who are likely to show dysfunctional rather than purposeful responses to stress (Baehr, Furcon, & Froemal, 1968; Diskin, Goldstein, & Grencik, 1977). These same studies, however, inevitably conclude that future research must focus on the special characteristics of police work and how it is organized if we are to understand how these individual characteristics are utilized or exacerbated by environments.

A second source of stressors is the sociocultural environment. Social and cultural change produces stresses for individuals and for organizations as they attempt to adapt. Sometimes even positive social change, such as increased educational opportunities for police or unionization among teachers, can produce stress as individuals and organizations try to adjust to new relationships (Dawson, 1974). All of the social problems we experience, such as marital instability, suicide, alcohol and drug abuse, changes in the quality of life and economic uncertainty, affect human service workers not only as individuals but in their professional relationships as well. Such sociocultural stressors, however, like the individual stresses described earlier, while obviously contributory, do not seem to produce the particular syndrome described as burnout unless they are mediated, aggravated, or complemented by some particular (usually bureaucratic) organizational structure. Police work, for example, is a high-stress occupation with factors such as danger, violence, and considerable discretionary authority causing obvious problems for health, safety, and effectiveness. But there are also role pressures—resulting from how police work is organized—that aggravate the stress (Denyer, Callender, & Thompson, 1975; Diskin et al., 1977). In addition, any number of sociocultural and environmental factors create stress in police work, quite apart from the dangers inherent in the job; for example, political pressure from community groups, media disdain for the role of policing, and the vagaries of the judicial system (Kroes, Margolis, & Hurrell, 1974; Hillgren, Bond, & Jones, 1976). The impact of these environmental variables, however, is heavily dependent on how the particular police organization or department structures the officer's relationship to that environment.

A third, less frequently cited area of stress is the relationship between the individual and the organization in which he or she structures the work role.

Recent research on effective organizational response to environmental uncertainty clearly indicates that the organization's ability to achieve the appropriate match between structure and environment is a key factor in reducing the stress effects of such uncertainty on employees (Lawrence & Lorsch, 1967). Administrative policies and procedures, power-dependency relationships, centralization or decentralization of decision making, task organization and performance measures, and a number of other organizational structure-specific factors have all been shown to produce stressors in the workplace that are equally as dysfunctional as the more dramatic and widely perceived environmental factors (Hilgren et al., 1976; Kroes et al., 1974; Reisner, 1974). Thus, while the inherent danger in the job of the policeman adds drama to the stress-provoking imagery of his environment, the structural features of police work are directly related to perceived stress as well as to job satisfaction. Similar analyses have been made of other human service occupations (Freudenberger, 1975; Kyriacou & Sutcliffe, 1977; Maslach, 1976).

In conducting a number of research studies that looked at psychosocial aspects of stress in person-organization relationships, we have found that the burnout syndrome is much more a phenomenon of stress in the person-organization relationship than it is a result of problems in the professional-client relationship. For example, disruptive students create the stress that leads to teacher burnout only if the ideology or sense of community provided by the organization is insufficient to withstand the threat, or the reality, of insult or injury from the environment.

TEACHERS, STRESS, AND THE SOCIAL ORDER OF THE SCHOOL

Whether as the result of coincidence or congruence, three major issues for the teaching profession seem to have developed at about the same time. The first of these is the process of unionization. The establishment of a "management-employee" relationship between the teacher and the administrator made many professional issues, such as class size and how to deal with disruptive students, subject to the same collective-bargaining procedures as such traditionally negotiable topics as salary and performance, and promotion criteria. Certainly, the concern with disruptive students was related to the second major issue: the growing evidence of school crime and violence associated with the loss of disciplinary control, and the subsequent concern for the psychological and physical safety of teachers expressed both within the profession and in the media. Finally, it was during this same era that "stress," and more particularly, "burnout" became recognized as problems for teachers as well as for other human service professionals.

The relationship between teacher stress and student behavior is well established and highly publicized. A special issue of the American Federation of Teachers Chicago newsletter (*Chicago Union Teacher,* 1978), for example, reported that "priority concerns" of teachers included dealing with "disruptive" children (ranked number two), being threatened with personal injury (number four), learning that a colleague was assaulted at school (number seven), and being the target of verbal abuse in school (number eleven). In an article entitled "The Battered Teacher," psychiatrist Alfred Bloch (1977) reported that many of the psychological stress symptoms of the 250 teachers he has treated are similar to those of survivors of war disasters, and that many teachers referred to their schools as "battle zones." What comes across in many of the portrayals of school disorders and their effects on teacher stress is just such a portrait of teachers under constant attack from students. We are not suggesting that school crime and violence and other problems in discipline are not significant stimuli in producing stress, but rather, that considered alone, they do not and cannot adequately explain burnout.

In the first place, it is questionable if America's schools really are as dangerous as they are sometimes made out to be. Media attention to school crime has created an impression of a school system where disorder and violence create significant dangers for teachers as well as for students. In 1975, the National Institute of Education, under a joint Congressional-Senate mandate in the "Safe School Study Act" (1974), undertook a comprehensive study to gather data on a range of offenses committed in schools, including those that are not reported to the police, and to obtain information on in-school conditions that might explain the offense data. The study, which got under way in 1976 and was reported in 1978, was set up in three interdependent phases. In Phase I, a mail survey was sent to a representative sample of over 4,000 public (elementary and secondary) schools throughout the country. Phase II was an on-site survey of a nationally representative cluster sample of 642 elementary and secondary schools. In Phase III, we, along with a small group of other ethnographers, developed case studies of a sample of ten schools deliberately selected for more intensive, qualitative study. Most of the schools chosen for Phase III had at some point experienced serious problems with crime and violence, but had changed for the better at some point in that history, while a few continued to have serious difficulties. The results of the Safe School Study raise some interesting questions as to how widespread disorder is in schools, and present some even more interesting evidence as to how that disorder affects teachers and how school organization can mediate such potential for stress. While public and media concern with crime and misbehavior in the schools has increased since the 1960s, the evidence from this study and others indicates quite clearly that, while acts of property destruction and violence increased from the early 1960s to the 1970s, both leveled off after the early 1970s. It appears that the great majority of schools—from 95 percent in rural areas to 84 percent in large cities—do not have a serious problem with school violence or vandalism.

More specifically for teachers, the studies indicate an increase in assaults on teachers from 1956 to 1974 but a leveling off thereafter. Overall, 12 percent of the teachers surveyed reported having something worth more than one dollar stolen from them in a typical month. Urban areas showed the highest percentages of such thefts. On the other hand, only an estimated one-half of 1 percent (some 5,200) of the one million secondary teachers in the country were physically attacked at school in a month's time. Most of the attacks reported by teachers were not serious: about one-fifth (19 percent) required medical treatment.

A little more than one-half of 1 percent (about 6,000) of all secondary school teachers are estimated to have had something taken from them by force, with weapons, or by threats at school in any given month. Once again, large cities show the highest percentages and rural areas the lowest. The differences between school levels are significant only in large cities, where junior high school teachers are more vulnerable than teachers in senior high schools. The estimate of the proportion of teachers raped in a month is very low (.04 or actually .08 percent since rape victims were female), and is presumed to be unreliable.

From these data we can provide some estimate of the risks faced by a typical teacher in the nation's secondary schools. A typical teacher has one chance in eight of having something stolen at school in a given month, one chance in 167 of being robbed, and one chance in 200 of being attacked in a month. A teacher's chances of being raped at school are very small. If these data accurately portray the social facts about violence and vandalism in the schools—and we are convinced that they do—then the question of why teachers should place such priority on student disruption and violence as a factor in stress becomes pertinent. Looking behind those social facts provides some answers.

Throughout the Safe School Study, and particularly in Phase III, we heard repeated mention of a "climate of fear" in the schools as a barrier to learning. If a climate of fear and apprehension can have an effect on learning, it can also be detrimental to effective teaching. Here, the reports are quite convincing. Almost half (49 percent) of all secondary school teachers report being *insulted* by students in a month, with the insulting behavior ranging from swearing to obscene gestures. This means that one out of every two teachers reports such behavior. The chances of this happening seem greatest in junior high schools in larger cities, where three-fourths (74.6 percent) of the teachers report it, and lowest in rural senior high schools, where four out of ten (39.6 percent) report it. Throughout these data there is a consistent tendency to find more of such insults in the junior, rather than the senior high school, and for a decline in such behavior to be apparent from urban, through suburban, to rural schools. There is also a consistency with what was found to be true of students, that teachers who report being sworn at are more likely than others to be victimized.

About 11 percent of secondary school teachers, or one out of nine, report that they have been threatened with injury by students, with junior high schools in large cities showing the highest proportions. Here again, the stress-related effects of such insults and threats on teachers become apparent: 12 percent, or one out of eight secondary school teachers report that they hesitate out of fear to confront students. Here, there is no difference by school level. This fear or hesitation is very pronounced in large cities, particularly among secondary school teachers; however, only 7 percent of rural teachers report such feelings. While we have no data on teachers swearing at or threatening students, there seems to be sufficient evidence to suggest that, particularly in urban secondary schools, many teachers operate within a climate of fear and apprehension. It is also apparent from all phases of the study that organizational size also defines the school climate. Large schools, particularly crowded schools, exhibit more violence. The higher the average number of students in the classes they teach, the greater the chance of victimization for the teacher.

In all three phases of the research program, and among all groups of respondents—students, teachers, and administrators—"improving discipline" was always rated as the most important factor in making schools safe and reducing fear. It was in Phase III, however, that we were able to look more closely at what "improving discipline" meant to the respondents. Within schools, as in any organization, there is a process of organizing behavior which regularizes as well as regulates person-to-person and person-to-organization relationships. Collectively, these "governance processes" mold and channel behavior and, in the case of teachers, provide a barometer for effectiveness as well as job satisfaction. Such regularizing of behavior, which is an organizational variable under the control of the school organization, can effectively mediate between the teacher and the stress potential of school disruption. There is abundant evidence in the Safe Schools Study that such organizational controls are a major factor in determining the level of crime and disruption in schools. Where school governance is seen as providing a rational organizational structure for maintaining order, and when teachers have a positive perception of their ability to maintain order in class, there is less dollar property loss. Where there is good coordination and mutual support evidenced between administration and faculty, there is also less property loss. Conversely, where teacher behavior indicates a lack of respect for students and where there is strong competition among students within a school, property loss measured in dollars tends to increase. Also, school crime and disruption are reduced in schools where students express an ability to identify with the teacher and where students report having access to teachers. Where ethnic and racial harmony are high, there is also less violence.

A number of organizational characteristics were found to be important determinants of reduced apprehension and attendant stress among teachers. The importance of the principal's style of leadership and his or her initiation of a structure of order seemed to differentiate safe schools from those that have trouble. The leadership role of the principal appears to be a critical factor in itself. Visibility and availability to teachers were characteristic of the principals in schools that seem to have made a dramatic turn-around from periods of violence. Conversely, in those schools that remained in difficulty or seemed to be headed toward increasing difficulty, we found that the principal was most frequently cited as the major problem. It is important to point out that strong leadership in this sense means a commitment to educational (professional) leadership, as well as control over the school. In each case where principals were described as providing a sense of direction, their educational leadership was emphasized. Teachers often described this as an important element of feeling "professionally in contact" with the principal's educational philosophy.

While the principal's style of personal leadership is important, we found that his ability to initiate a structure of order in the school was organizationally most important. Teachers frequently explained that they not only felt safer and more secure but could "work better" and felt "more freedom to teach" in a well-ordered school. In every successful Phase III school, we found that the structure of order that represents the enactment of the governance system was described as "fair, firm, and, most of all, consistent." It is interesting that this finding complements a number of recent research findings that indicate that achievement in a number of areas of school learning is also enhanced by a consistent structure of order.*

The data from the three phases of the Safe School Study, and from the Phase III case studies in particular, show quite clearly that organizational factors are important sources of other environmental stresses as well. In that report we concluded that "if a school is large and impersonal, discipline lax and inconsistent, the rules ambiguous and arbitrarily or unfairly enforced, the courses irrelevant and the reward system unfair, the school lacks a rational structure of order and the basic elements necessary to maintain social bonds" (Ianni, 1978, p. 9). While there has been considerable public and professional concern with the disruptive and dysfunctional results of the loss or straining of these social bonds among students, and between students and teachers, it was obvious throughout the study that social bonds among teachers, and between teachers and administrators, have also suffered. We found that high self-esteem and job satisfaction among teachers, the most commonly cited bulwarks against burn-

---

*See, for example, the U.S. Office of Education of Planning, Budgeting, and Evaluation Executive Summary, *Impact of Educational Innovation on Student Performance* (November 1976), which reports findings of Project Longstep conducted by the American Institute for Research, and *A Study of Compensatory Reading Programs* (October 1976), which reports the results of a large-scale study of Title I Compensatory Reading Programs. This study was conducted by the Educational Testing Service and RMC Research Corporation.

out, were important results of an organizational system in which teachers expressed general agreement with the administration's educational and procedural style. Cohesiveness and a feeling of "community" among teachers were frequently mentioned as associated with a strong sense of identification with the organizational mission, which would be called a "school spirit" variable among students. While there were labor-management differentiations between teachers and administrators that resulted from unionization in a number of the schools we studied, in those schools that were successful and where we found burnout to be almost nonexistent, teachers and administrators ran educational and behavioral development programs under the common professional rubric of "educators." Teachers in such schools also reported that they were there because they wanted to stay in those particular schools.

ORGANIZATIONAL STRESS, BURNOUT, AND THE TWO CULTURES OF URBAN POLICING

The uneasy organizational accommodation between the "labor" and "management" sectors in the new model of professional relationships we found in education is even more dramatically apparent in urban police work. While the public image of the policeman and the teacher are quite dissimilar in terms of role configurations, there is a considerable similarity in the organizational characteristics of the two professions. Like school systems, police departments, at least in urban areas, are structured by a central headquarters and a dispersed number of subunits called precincts, which, like schools, are associated with specific geographical areas or neighborhoods. Police managers, like educational administrators, start at the bottom; moreover, police officers, like teachers, advance (or fail to advance) in a system where there is no lateral entry or introduction of new personnel at the middle-management level. Finally, relationships between the police and their clients are, like those between teacher and student, characterized by the need to establish authority, the responsibility for social control, and considerable discretion in an arbitrary environment.

Early in September of 1976 we began a long-term study of the psychosocial organization of policing in New York City. What we learned through the two-year study, after hundreds of hours working with, observing, and interviewing officers in two precincts, is that the current psychosocial organization of policing is best described and understood in terms of the interactions of two distinct cultures: a "street cop culture" and a "management cop culture." These two cultures are increasingly characterized by competing, and often, conflicting perspectives on procedure and practice in policing. This situation is significant since much of the research and literature on policing describes the working of a monolithic, single "cop culture" that pervades all levels of the organization. The emergence of two cultures has implications for understanding what we believe to be the major source of stress and burnout in policing.

A pervasive conception of the "good old days" of policing is the organizing ethos of the street cop culture, orienting individual officers and precinct social networks and defining the day-to-day job of policing. In the good old days, we were told by street-level cops, the public valued and respected the cop, fellow officers could be counted on, and the "bosses" or higher-ranking officers were an integral part of the police family. Cops not only had public respect and the sense of security that came from belonging to a cohesive, interdependent organization, but were treated as professionals who knew their job and how best to get it done. A grateful public and an understanding City Hall seldom asked how. Everybody, say the cops, knew who the good guys were and who the bad guys were, and the political system and the community they represented agreed with their definitions. Being a policeman was something special; a cop put his life on the line and people appreciated and respected his willingness to do so. As a result, policemen were allowed to do their jobs without too many questions or too much interference from outside the department. Not only the street cops but everyone in the department was socialized to this ethos. Since there is no lateral entry into the department, everyone began his career as a cop and, they believed, everyone from the chief on down accepted the values of loyalty, privilege, and the importance of keeping department business inside the department. One monolithic culture permeated the department.

The police career path began with being a "good cop" who would then move to higher command positions or, in many cases, would choose to remain within the same precinct in the same assignment throughout his career. Success was based upon some combination of ability, luck, political, ethnic, or family connections, or having some "sponsorship" in the departmental hierarchy. Even for those who made it to the top, retirement frequently meant a job (such as director of security for a hotel) where one could use experience as a policeman to recognize the bad guys, and use connections in the department to "take care" of a situation or get information on someone or something.

It is important to emphasize that this notion of what the good old days were like in the department may or may not be realistic. In fact, many of the officers who spoke most longingly for those days were not even in the department then. The universality and persistence of this ethos is reminiscent of the Cargo Cult movements that sprang up in Oceania, and particularly in New Guinea, in reaction to the sudden impact of modern civilization on their Stone Age peoples. Faced with an awesome new technology, the tribal groups developed a new mythology about the "good old days" of their ancestors, when things were even better than when the colonizers arrived. The fact that the stories about the good old days of policing were in many cases learned from "old timers" or in growing up in a police family, gave them the authenticity, as well as the tenacity, that goes with tradition and legend. Again, we don't know if the department was ever really like what the legend describes, but we do know that most of the officers believed both that it was and that life and work were better for cops then than they are now. The good old days ethos also represents what they believe the job should be today.

Because this ethos was universal throughout the department, we were told, there was one culture that everyone, whether in the street or in headquarters, shared. But a number of social and political forces have weakened that culture and so the organic structure of the department is disintegrating. The changing political structure of the city introduced an escalating competition for scarce resources which has had the effect of pitting agency against agency in securing jobs and fiscal allocations. Political leadership has become increasingly management-oriented as the financial excesses of the old clubhouse days very nearly bankrupted the city. For the Police Department, as well as for other city agencies, this has meant greater emphasis on accountability and productivity, on management process, and products that could be quantified and measured in a cost-effective equation. The new politics also included those minority groups who were disenfranchised in the old days. Ever since the Civil Rights Movement, there has been growing political sensitivity about relationships with minority groups which holds the department accountable not only for providing adequate police service to those groups, but for affirmative action in seeking minority recruitment.

All of these forces have contributed to the development of a new headquarters management cop culture which is bureaucratically juxtaposed to the precinct street cop culture. This new management cop culture, say the cops, is positively oriented toward public administration and looks to scientific management and its associated technologies for guidance in running the department. Despite their new training and orientation, however, they must continue to justify their positions within the department, not by their new expertise or specialization, but because at one time they were also street cops. Regulations require that they continue to display the two most important symbols of the old culture: the shield and gun. Unlike other bureaucratic systems in which the upper echelon of the hierarchy is recruited from different socioeconomic and educational levels than the lower ranks, managers at all levels in police work come from the same socioeconomic and work experience groups as the "workers" or cops. But, the cops maintain, their bosses have forgotten about being cops and are now professional managers. "They would give us up in a moment if necessary in order to save their own careers, and they think we'll put up with anything because of our pension." Career paths for management cops begin when they are first assigned to headquarters; ultimately, they aspire to administrative careers in the department or, following retirement, in business or industry.

While there is some uneasy accommodation between these two cultures, they are increasingly in conflict, and this conflict isolates the local precinct functionally, if not structurally, from downtown headquarters. The isolation produces disaffection, strong stress reactions, increasing attrition, and growing problems of integrity. Most of the officers with whom we worked see the destruction of the street cop culture as an inevitable outcome of the changing organizational character and, with obvious resignation, say that this is what the bosses want anyway, because they can control cops more easily as individuals than as unified groups.

The existence of these two cultures of policing is, we believe, the major factor in burnout among urban police. Certainly, as we saw among teachers, increased danger, public devaluation, and resource-allocation problems resulting from budget cuts contribute heavily to their loss of self-esteem and job satisfaction. But the individual officer was shielded against these stressors when he was part of the professional police family. The incongruent value systems of the two cultures, differing in their expectations, are major factors in the growing alienation of the street cop. This displacement of quasifamilial relationships, in which loyalties and commitments took precedence over the rule book, by the more impersonal ideology of modern management is visible in any human service sector where professionals see their administrators as management, rather than as fellow professionals. Wherever this shift occurs, it produces intraorganizational conflict which, sooner or later, takes its toll in stress and eventually in burnout.

ORGANIZATIONS AND THE MANAGEMENT OF STRESS

Organizations are behavioral and emotional settings for the people who work in them. They shape self-concepts, aspirations, and other factors that affect the self-esteem of the individual. In short, organizations have important effects on how individuals perceive all types of stress. When an individual is in a role that requires him or her to define or interpret or in some way represent an organizational set of behavioral or attitudinal expectations to others, then he or she is, in effect, a "marginal" person—negotiating between the organization and the client- or student-generated stress and organizational or management tension stress. In this model, the human service worker is threatened or in some way buffeted by the client, and undergoes stress which leads to the "take this job and shove it" reaction. The frequent assertions that disruptive students, school crime or violence, and even student apathy are the principal causes of burnout among teachers is an example of this approach. The same model posits such management practices as reorganizations, involuntary transfers, bureaucratic red tape, lack of adequate compensation, and management insensitivity as examples of "the organizational side."

Organizations themselves can experience stress from their environments or they can suffer from internal conflicts such as contradictory goals and purposes. Either or both of these organization-specific problems can, and often do, produce organizational stress which is quickly communicated to personnel at all levels, but usually more immediately to the organization's service-delivery personnel. Sometimes this is because they feel they are being asked to behave in ways that violate their own professional or personal standards as, for example, being asked to implement policies or institute practices that they feel are either "too much" or "too little," too lenient or too harsh. At other times, self-image and, consequently, self-esteem are damaged when individuals feel manipulated by forces beyond their control, or when they think of their work role or status as demeaning or demeaned by others. Similar feelings of loss of self-esteem or lack of organizational purpose occur when what was once a comprehensive professional family of educators or police is divided into management and workers. What was once a family is now a factory. Workers and bosses are pitted against each other in labor-management disputes; in promotional and assignment decisions; as a result of external pressures from the media, the community, or the political system; when they feel that they have been manipulated or exploited by the organization; or when they feel they are manipulating their own clients or students as a result of imposed organizational policy.

The increasing use of arbitrary managerial decision-making devices—such as management-by-objectives systems—also produces lowered self-esteem and a sense of depersonalization and isolation for the professional who must translate all of this into contacts with real people. Even promotional systems— in which for each person promoted a number must be left behind—are stress-producing in all organizations; they are particularly a source of lowered self-esteem and job satisfaction in professionally structured organizations. Among police, for example, the selection and training process precludes lateral entry, thus making self-evaluation and self-judgment more immediate and personal. A similar situation exists among teachers. As with the police, promotion into the managerial or administrative ranks requires skills and training that are often not part of the shared professional experience. Promotion may therefore engender feelings of alienation from the group, depression, and lowered self-esteem. Finally, there is the problem of the management of aggression. People who are in any line of work that requires them to maintain face-to-face contact with irate customers or clients frequently have difficulty managing their own hostile reactions. What seems particularly important in understanding burnout, at least in the two human service areas of teaching and policing, is the compelling evidence that where the individual professional feels unsupported by the organization or agency, the aggression turns from the organization into a self-destructive feeling of "take this job and shove it."

A NOTE ON ADOLESCENCE
AND THE INTERNALIZATION OF STRUCTURE

Accepting the notion that organizations both create their own stressors and mediate—for better or worse—between individuals and extraorganizational sources of stress leads to the question of how "organizations" are "internalized" by individuals. While our interviews and observations in both the teacher and police studies gave us some indication of what is internalized and how this protects against or aggravates burnout, the methodology of the studies really did not permit asking or answering the question of "how." We do, however, have some tentative answers to this question from a long-term, multisite study of adolescence in which we focused on how community structure, or what we called the psychosocial organization of social institutions, is internalized by youth. We are not proposing to extend the concept of burnout to adolescent development, but rather suggesting that the internalization process may be similar in terms of its process and outcome.

The analytic distinction between internal and external influences on adolescents has had a corollary development in the study of organizations. Miller and Rice (1967), for example, went beyond the usual conceptualization of "informal" versus "formal" organization by incorporating an intrapsychic aspect. Some mechanism, they argued, must mediate between the formal organization (task organization) and the informal, more affective "sentient structure." It is this latter structure that relates the individual to the outside, external affiliations that breach the boundaries of the group. Miller and Rice are here proceeding with conceptualizations based on psychoanalytic ego psychology and object relations theory in which there is mediation by the ego between the environment and the inner world of the individual. "The mature ego is one that can define the boundary between what is inside and what is outside, and can control the transactions between the one and the other" (Miller & Rice, 1967, p. 16). In this regard, what seemed most important to us in our studies was to account for the reciprocally interacting effects of internal (intrapsychic) as well as external environments on the self-regulatory behavior of adolescents individually and in groups. Self-regulation occurs for adolescents as they develop conceptions about themselves and their environments and as they use these conceptions, beliefs, and self-perceptions to modify their behavior *and* the environment in which the behavior operates. What emerges, then, is considerable evidence that the development of ego identity during adolescence is not simply a function of peer relationships or "press toward autonomy." Rather, we find that the adolescent search for a psychic structure that will facilitate social competence is an interactional process in which the adolescent him or herself helps to *shape* the effective environment within which this transformation of the self will take place.

In the literature, two theoretical models of the social organization of adolescence have dominated both research and practice. In one model, which has historically been associated with epigenetic stage theories, the basic social competencies are developed out of familial interaction in childhood. The second model, which characterizes much of the social context literature, assumes that specific sets of skills or competencies are more or less independently developed in each of the variety of institutional contexts as a response to the demands of that system. However, in our analyses of the observational and psychodynamic data, we see a very different theoretical model beginning to emerge—one that indicates a synergistic rather than a sequential or independent pattern of relationships among institutional contexts in the lives of adolescents. The way in which the various institutional complexes are integrated by adolescents, rather than the individual impact of any single institution, emerges in our analyses as the most important determinant of the psychocultural environment that defines the transition to adulthood. For example, in the lower East Side of New York, the various social institutions are in open conflict with each other. Each institutional context loudly proclaims the incompetence of the other. Youth employment specialists decry the failure of the school, which in turn claims that the family has failed to prepare youngsters adequately for schooling. The consequences for adolescents are shown clearly in psychodynamic interviews that indicate considerable anxiety on the part of youth over the lack of continuity and congruence they feel in the integration (or, more accurately, lack of integration) in the psychosocial organization of adolescence characteristic of this particular social system.

Again, we are not proposing that this model of internalization of organizationally derived psychic structure with its attendant emotional consequences is as salient in the teacher and police stress studies we described earlier. Nor are we suggesting that adolescents who "drop out" are suffering from the same syndrome of lack of self-esteem and job satisfaction that leads to burnout in human service organizations. We do, however, believe that there is an obvious, but often ignored, organizational-structural factor in which external environments are internalized by individuals and in turn affect their behavior, attitudes, and beliefs. Indeed, individuals within organizations use their own conceptions of the environment—as well as their own beliefs, self-perceptions, and interpersonal networks—to modify both their own behavior and that of their immediate environment. As Bandura (1978) has noted, "Personal and environmental factors do not function as independent determinants; rather they determine each other (p. 345)." A comprehensive model of burnout, therefore, requires an understanding not only of personal and environmental factors, but of their interactional effects as well.

REFERENCES

Baehr, M. E., Furcon, J. E., & Froemal, E. C. *Psychological assessment qualifications in relation to field performance.* (Law Enforcement Assistance Administration Project 046). Washington, D.C.: U.S. Government Printing Office, 1968.

Bandura, A. The self system in reciprocal determinism. *American Psychologist,* 1978, **33**, 344–358.

Bellak, L. *Overload: The new human condition.* New York: Human Sciences Press, 1975.

Bloch, A. M. The battered teacher. *Today's Education,* 1977, **66**, 58–62.

Campbell, A., Converse, P., & Rogers, W. *The quality of American life.* New York: Russell Sage Foundation, 1976.

Chicago Union Teacher, March 1978.

Dawson, P. Social mobility and stress affecting police officers. *Police Review,* 1974, **82** (4273), 1574.

Denyer, T., Callender, R., & Thompson, D. L. The policeman as alienated laborer. *Journal of Police Science and Administration.* Northwestern University School of Law, 1975, **3** (3), 251–258.

Diskin, S. D., Goldstein, M. J., & Grencik, J. M. Coping patterns of law enforcement officers in simulated and naturalistic stress. *American Journal of Community Psychology,* 1977, **5**, 59–73.

Freudenberger, H. J. The staff burnout syndrome in alternative institutions. *Psychotherapy: Theory, Research, and Practice,* 1975, **121**, 73–82.

Glass, D. & Singer J. *Urban stress: Experiments on noise and social stressors.* New York: Academic Press, 1972.

Hillgren, J., Bond, R., & Jones, S. Primary stressors in police administration and law enforcement. *Journal of Police Science and Administration,* 1976, **4** (4), 445–449.

Ianni, F. A. Social organization of the high school and school violence. In *School crime and disruption: Preventive models.* Washington, D.C.: U.S. Department of Health, Education, and Welfare, June 1978.

Kroes, W., Margolis, B., & Hurrell, J. J. Job stress in policemen. *Journal of Police Science and Administration,* 1974, **2** (2), 145–155.

Kyriacou, C. & Sutcliffe, J. Teacher stress: A review. *Educational Review,* 1977, **29** (4), 299–306.

Lawrence, P. R. & Lorsch, J. W. *Organization and environment.* Cambridge, Mass.: Harvard University Press, 1967.

Maslach, C. Burned-out. *Human Behavior,* 1976, **5**, 16–22.

Miller, E. J. & Rice, A. K. *Systems of organization.* London: Tavistock, 1967.

Reisner, M. Some organizational stresses on policemen. *Journal of Police Science and Administration,* 1974, **2** (2), 156–159.

Reuss-Ianni, E. *Street cops vs. management cops: The two cultures of policing.* New Brunswick, N.J.: Transaction Press, in press.

Spielberger, C. & Sarason, I. (Eds.). *Stress and anxiety.* Vol. I and IV. New York: J. Wiley & Sons, 1967.

The National Institute of Education, *Violent schools—Safe schools.* Washington, D.C.: U.S. Department of Health, Education, and Welfare, 1976.

7

Dysfunctional Aspects of the
Psychotherapeutic Role*

Barry A. Farber

> Do not believe that he who seeks to comfort you
> lives untroubled among the simple and quiet words
> that sometimes do you good. His life has much
> difficulty and sorrow. Were it otherwise, he
> would never have been able to find those words.
>   —Rainer Marie Rilke

The primary purpose of this chapter is to examine the variety of dysfunctional consequences that may occur as a result of the stresses that psychotherapists face in their work. Psychotherapeutic work is often seen as unique, meaningful, and fulfilling, and admission to clinical training programs, particularly in psychology, has become increasingly competitive. In addition, psychotherapists themselves have reported that their work engenders much personal satisfaction, that it increases their knowledge and sensitivity, and that it heightens personal feelings of self-assurance, assertiveness, and self-reliance (Farber, in press). Yet there is a growing body of literature that suggests that the role of the psychotherapist is far more problematic than has usually been publicly acknowledged. Autobiographical accounts have questioned the personally fulfilling aspects of therapeutic work; medical journals have regularly noted the serious difficulties that psychiatry residents encounter in their training; epidemiological reports have noted disproportionately high suicide rates among psychiatrists; and recent research on the nature of professional work has indicated that disillusionment among human service professionals—a

*The author wishes to thank Jeannie Russell for her help in researching this topic and Louis J. Heifetz for his constructive comments on earlier drafts on this manuscript.

group that, of course, includes psychotherapists—is not an uncommon phenomenon. Psychotherapists may also be vulnerable to burnout (Farber & Heifetz, 1982; Freudenberger & Robbins, 1979; Pines & Maslach, 1978), though it should be kept in mind that many professionals, despite the stresses of their work, are not burned out. In short, while the difficulties and personally stressful aspects of psychotherapeutic work constitute but one part of the therapist's work experience, their potentially deleterious effects on both therapists and their patients compel our most serious attention.

Traditionally, professionals such as psychotherapists have been neglected in studies of work-related problems and attitudes. Sarason (1977) has attributed this historical neglect to three major factors: society's positive judgment about such work; the individual professional's uncritical acceptance of society's view upon entering the profession; and the resistance of professional organizations to self-scrutiny. As Sarason has pointed out, "to express dissatisfaction or boredom with, or a waning interest in, one's work—particularly if one's work is judged by society as fascinating and important as is the case of many professionals—is no easy matter" (p. 57). Moreover, admission of personal difficulties as a direct consequence of work may be particularly difficult for psychotherapists. The almost universal tendency to experience one's sense of self-esteem and self-definition in the measure of one's professional accomplishments is, in some ways, significantly heightened for therapists. Their professional work is often an extension of their normal interpersonal and intrapsychic lives. Stress, disillusionment, and dissatisfaction in their working lives might well be experienced as not just an alienation from their "means of production," but rather as reflections of a deeper split, an alienation from therapists' own selves, or the capacity to express themselves meaningfully. These factors then might explain why, until recently, there has been such a notable lack of research on the stresses and dysfunctional effects of the psychotherapeutic role—a lack that, on the face of it, is incongruous with the conspicuous role that psychotherapists play in American society.

If, however, therapists have been generally disinclined to confront their difficulties, other sources have shown no such reluctance. The popular media have for the last two decades portrayed the psychotherapist as a person with a great many problems. Much as Henry, Sims, and Spray (1971) have characterized the typical therapist as having certain political, ethnic, and demographic attributes (liberal, second-generation, urban Jewish), novels, plays, movies, and even cartoons have ascribed to the typical therapist a set of physical and mental attributes—often depicting him as a balding, bearded, Eastern European male who is not only humorless, controlled, impersonal, and egotistical, but whose personal idiosyncracies usually far surpass those of his patients. Such a therapist may simply be depicted as being unable to cope with his own family or feeling disillusioned and depressed; frequently, though, he may be seen as sexually obsessed or even exhibiting clear signs of psychopathology (Davidson, 1964; Martin, 1981; Psychiatry on the Couch, 1979; Rogow, 1970).

It would be simple to dismiss the media's caricature of therapists, were it not for the fact that similar observations have been made by more "reputable sources." Paul (1973) allows that "at least within the confines of his office the therapist is a rather strangely-acting human being," and that patient impressions of the therapist as "impersonal, thoughtful, serious and controlled" are quite accurate (p. 223). Rieff (1959) notes that "such careful and detailed concentration of the self as Freud encourages may more often produce pedants of the inner life than virtuosi of the outer one" (p. 329). Lieberman (1966) has speculated that a therapist may "require the continual experience of marginality and specialness of his society" (p. 57). And Burton (1972), in examining the lives of therapists from Freud to the present, comes to the conclusion that "most therapists experience themselves as closer to the shoals of psychosis than do other people" (p. 20). Comments on therapists' sanity, personality, family relations, and work satisfaction vary enormously, of course, in terms of respectability of observer and adequacy of observation. Moreover, those observations that deal with therapists' professional deportment are of relevance to this chapter only inasmuch as such behavior has observable "extra-professional" implications. Still, there are a number of personal declarations, critical observations, and experimental and epidemiological data that must be considered seriously in examining the various dysfunctional aspects of the psychotherapeutic role.

Some of the problems identified with the psychotherapeutic role are inextricably bound up with the process of doing therapy per se and are potential problems regardless of the age or experience of the practicing clinician. Other problems, though, are predominantly determined by specific stages of professional experience and are therefore more profitably considered in developmental terms; certainly, the critical issues and difficulties that confront the psychology and social work intern or psychiatry resident are different from those of the mid-career psychotherapist.

TRAINING TO BE A PSYCHOTHERAPIST

The process of training to be a psychotherapist can effect several kinds of positive growth, some primarily in the service of professional development, others of a more generally salutary nature: professional commitment, greater self-insight, and more mature social relationships (Holt, 1959); large gains in substantive knowledge and therapeutic insight (Pasnau & Bayley, 1971); increased self-assurance and humility (Maurice, et al., 1975); reduced alienation and authoritarianism (Henry, 1966; Khajavi, Hekmat, & Mehryer, 1973) and greater self-ideal congruence, primarily as a result of changes in self-concept (Perlman, 1972). The stressful atmosphere of the training period, however, may produce other, more problematic changes. Halleck and Woods (1962), for example, have contended that "few [psychiatry] residents have gone through the residency period without having experienced somewhere along the line, moderate to severe anxiety or depression," and that "perhaps no psychiatrist goes through training without at one time or another worrying about the loss of his sanity" (p. 341). Pasnau and Bayley (1971) have reported a significant increase in depression among first-year psychiatric residents. And Merklin and Little (1967) have characterized the transitory neurotic symptoms, psychosomatic disturbances, and symptomatic behavior of residency as "Beginning Psychiatry Training Syndrome" (p. 194), a condition they recognize as "distressing" but nonetheless essential to the making of a psychotherapist.

Several factors contribute to the difficulties of psychotherapeutic training. One of the primary sources of stress is the development of psychological-mindedness in beginning psychotherapists. As part of learning psychotherapy, residents and interns are required to understand the inner dynamics of their patients, and as a result, necessarily become more psychological-minded themselves, more aware of their own unconscious processes, motivations, and difficulties. The positive result of this process is that, as they become more aware of their own conflicts and problems, they become more empathic and more generally capable of conducting effective psychotherapy. The unfortunate implication is that they may overidentify themselves with patients, believing that they are more like patients than is truly the case (Holt & Luborsky, 1958). Beginning therapists may compare their own early development with that of patients and question their own tolerance for stress, their own defense mechanisms, and even their own sanity (Halleck & Woods, 1962; Merklin & Little, 1967; Book, 1973). As Frank (1973) has pointed out, "by calling people's attention to symptoms they might otherwise ignore and by labeling those symptoms as signs of neurosis, mental health education can create unwarranted anxiety" (p. 8). This may well be as true for the psychotherapist as it is for the client or general public.

This overidentification with patients' problems is, of course, consistent with the tendency of medical students to become convinced that they are suffering from whatever disease they're currently studying. As Merklin and Little (1967) have pointed out, however, the medical student has the certainty of an x-ray or laboratory to disaffirm his "affliction," while no such precise instrumentation is available to the psychiatric resident. It should be noted, too, that the development of psychological-mindedness is a process that occurs much more gradually among psychology and social work students who have studied psychological process for a number of years; therefore, the tendency toward overidentification with patients' pathologies is probably a somewhat less severe problem for the psychology or social work intern than it is for the psychiatry resident.

A second aspect of psychotherapeutic training that contributes to stress and insecurity in students is the difficulty attached to the actual treatment process.

Although achieving an understanding or psychopathology is a necessarily slow and gradual process, the new therapist must immediately deal with the exigencies of treating patients. Holt (1959), in fact, attributes the general decline of enthusiasm in beginning psychiatry residents to their realization that the practice of psychiatry is much more difficult than they had anticipated when they entered training. Here again, though, what is characteristic of psychiatry residents—their sudden realization of the difficulties of psychotherapeutic work—may not be so characteristic of psychologists or social workers who have had more extensive psychotherapeutic training in graduate school. For all beginning psychotherapists, however, the everyday difficulties and responsibilities involved in working with patients are exacerbated by the common practice of training institutions of assigning the most disturbed patients to the least experienced staff (Chessick, 1971; Merklin & Little, 1967; Ungerleider, 1965). Consequently, whatever initial enthusiasm or expertise new residents or interns may bring to the job will frequently fade as they are confronted with the inevitable resistances and/or miniscule change patterns of chronic patients. In addition, all beginning psychotherapists must struggle to find a comfortable therapeutic stance, to attempt to balance neutrality and objectivity with involvement and concern. In this regard, Halleck and Woods (1962) have commented on the "double bind" that the psychiatry resident faces: "If he does not become involved, he sees himself, or is chided by others, as being cold, aloof, or detached. If he does become involved, he often tends to overact and frequently suffers along with his patients" (p. 341).

The third major source of tension for beginning therapists can be traced to the supervisory relationship. While supervision is the most useful tool for teaching psychotherapy, it is also an inherently conflictual relationship. If the relationship is unsuccessful (and certainly not all competent therapists are effective supervisors), the student's already high level of anxiety may be further intensified; if the relationship succeeds in allaying anxieties, an exaggerated identification may result. Sharaf and Levinson (1964), in particular, have noted how psychiatry residents excessively admire their mentors in a quest for the mentor's apparent power and knowledge. An admired teacher or supervisor becomes viewed "not simply as a person having great skill and understanding, but as an omnipotent, charismatic figure who may, if all goes well, bestow his treasures upon the resident" (p. 136). Consequently, residents often greatly underestimate their own capabilities, feeling they are basically devoid of any knowledge or resources. Moreover, the detrimental implications of this "quest for omnipotence" extend beyond supervisory sessions; social relationships may also be adversely influenced by residents' needs to appear totally knowledgeable and competent.

For psychiatry residents, a fourth factor contributing to the stresses of training is "role confusion" occasioned by the loss of a supporting medical model. As medical students, residents are exposed to a paradigm that stresses an immediate, tangible relationship between etiology, pathology, and treatment. But while a failing heart may respond promptly to the administration of drugs (Book, 1973), psychotherapeutic intervention rarely produces such dramatic results and the student or beginning practitioner rarely receives such immediate gratification. Furthermore, the medical model, with its implicit support for the theory of Cartesian dualism effectively separates the patient from his disease, thus depersonalizing the physician-patient relationship and leaving the psychiatry resident quite unprepared for the personal nature of the psychotherapeutic relationship. In a similar vein, Sharaf and Levinson (1964) have noted that the resident must change from the medical notion of curing by "doing things" to patients to the psychological model of curing by "talking things over" with patients. This transition is not necessary for psychology or social work interns, who have been trained according to a psychological model.

Thus, the beginning psychotherapist faces several types of stresses during training: an emerging awareness of his or her own personal problems through the development of introspective capacities; the difficulties of the actual treatment process; the ambiguity involved in supervisory relationships; and in the case of psychiatry residents, adaptation to new, nonmedical roles. Anxiety, depression, and "quests for omnipotence" are commonly products of these pressures. In addition, a wide variety of "secondary symptoms"—reactions to anxiety and depression—have been either documented or described. For example, as a result of anxiety, beginning therapists may experience insomnia, fatigue, indecision, an inability to concentrate, and general irritability (Merklin & Little, 1967). On a therapeutic level, the beginning therapist's frustration may impel him or her to act aggressively toward patients, which may often lead patients to discontinue therapy (Book, 1973). Or, as a consequence of anxiety, beginning therapists may limit their perspectives, that is, they make premature closure in their points of view in order to cope with anxiety better (Chessick, 1971; Sharaf & Levinson, 1964). Finally, the stresses of training will inevitably affect the resident's family life. As Seashore (1975) has observed, "learning how to better use oneself in the helping process is likely to change one's basis for self-esteem, and alter what it is one values in oneself or others. This produces a significant amount of conflict among those who liked you for what you were, not for what you are becoming" (p. 3). The stress of changing patterns of interaction may lead to accommodations on the part of both partners; however, such stress also has the potential to lead to the breakup of previously stable relationships.

For most beginning therapists, resolution of the difficulties of training is gradual but does eventually occur. For example, in reflecting on their transition from residency to "career," recently graduated psychiatrists acknowledge the continued presence of stress—primarily in the form of anxiety and depression—but also report high levels of overall feelings of personal growth, maturity, confidence, and support by loved ones (Looney et al., 1980). For other residents and interns, however, the stresses of training keep them from ever fulfilling their potential. As Halleck and Woods (1962) have noted, there are those beginning therapists for whom further development of skills would necessitate a degree of anxiety that they are unwilling to experience.

THE STRESSES AND COPING PATTERNS OF MID-CAREER THERAPISTS

The very nature of psychotherapeutic work subjects the psychotherapist, at whatever level, to continual emotional demands. Freud (1937/1964) referred to psychotherapy as one of those "impossible professions," noting the extreme demands the therapeutic situation places upon the psychotherapist. Empirical and clinical investigations have consistently corroborated Freud's observations, finding that face-to-face contact with patients is a basic source of stress that is inherent within the psychotherapeutic situation (Bermak, 1977; English, 1976; Farber & Heifetz, 1981, 1982; Freudenberger & Robbins, 1979). Therapists must continually deal with the widest range of human emotions and are often themselves the target of irrational expressions of love, hate, envy, or need. Therapists must also deal with criticism and failure, as well as with the necessity of offering painful interpretations to their patients (Basescu, 1977). Psychotherapists, in fact, are constantly called upon to be empathic, understanding, and giving, yet they must control their own emotional needs and responsiveness in dealing with their patients. As Freudenberger and Robbins (1979) have noted, a therapist is "full of feelings—feelings of hurt, anger, joy and sadness that he must share but is often unable to share with or communicate to anyone, especially not his patients" (p. 291). Therapeutic work is also frustrating; progress is necessarily slow and erratic, and validation of one's efforts is difficult, if not impossible. And finally, the therapeutic process may engender feelings of personal vulnerability in the therapist, particularly when he or she is working with severely disturbed patients. Searles (1965), for example, notes that the gratification involved in working with schizophrenic patients is invariably obliterated by feelings of anxiety, helplessness, and threats to the therapist's own personal integration and sense of identity. In a similar vein, Jung (1966) has commented on how patients, by stirring up unconscious material in their therapists, may effect "a transfer of pathology."

One could argue that, to a certain extent, years of experience working as a therapist mitigate the impact of these potential problems; on the other hand, one could also hypothesize that it is the very weight of these years that makes the mid-career therapist more prone to disillusionment and burnout and more vulnerable to the cumulative effects of thinking about and working with patient's problems.

In addition to experiencing some of the same therapeutic stresses as the beginning resident, the mid-career therapist faces a different set of challenges, challenges that are unique to his or her position and level of experience. For example, a full-time clinical practice will usually not offer the same opportunities for a diversified schedule of activities that are offered by a psychiatric residency or psychology internship. The sedentary and often secluded nature of full-time practice may severely restrict the occasions for peer interaction or even physical exercise, and thus limit opportunities for even minimal release of tensions. Greben (1975) notes that psychoanalysts suffer from a kind of environmental deprivation that results from their repeated performance of a complex but limited task. These physical and mental constraints may explain why psychiatrists as a group are the physicians with the highest rate of cigarette smoking and the least success in quitting (Tamerin & Eisinger, 1972), and why psychiatrists, of all medical specialists, may be especially prone to alcohol abuse (see Knutsen, 1977).

A second distinctive problem of the more experienced psychotherapist is that he or she works without the support and expertise of a supervisor. The lack of reliable feedback about one's work is a primary source of anxiety for most psychotherapists who, in several ways, may suffer from the absence of collaborative aid (Schlict, 1968). For example, experienced therapists do not get adequate feedback on their performance in either individual sessions or long-term cases and may have difficulty evaluating the course of therapy, modifying therapeutic procedures, or setting a termination date. In general, therapists may have unallayed doubts concerning their therapeutic competence, and in particularly difficult cases, they may acutely miss the solace, reassurance, and advice of a colleague.

Another issue of particular salience to the mid-career therapist concerns the effects of therapeutic practice on the therapist's spouse and children. Therapeutic work often leaves too little time for family and outside interests. In addition, therapeutic work is emotionally depleting and often, when the therapist gets home, he or she is no longer in a mood to be a sympathetic listener; indeed, family issues may seem banal compared to the problems of patients. It is the patient then who is most often afforded priority in terms of the therapists' time and emotion (Cray & Cray, 1977; Farber, in press; Freudenberger & Robbins, 1979). Therapists may also interact with members of their families in unexpected and unsettling ways, for example, by interpreting or analyzing behavior; conversely, therapists' family members may treat them with considerably less admiration and deference than their patients.

The mid-career therapist must also cope with the universal stresses of what Marmor (1968) has called "middle-life crisis"—physical signs of aging, existential doubts regarding one's mission in life, the death of close friends and relatives, and the consideration of one's own mortality. It is during this period, too, that therapists often have the greatest financial and emotional strains placed upon them by their families. Even then, at the height of a career, when the experienced therapist is most technically proficient, most esteemed by colleagues, and most professionally established, he or she is subject to both personal developmental crises and occupational stresses.

CAREER DISSATISFACTIONS

Studies that have investigated the career dissatisfactions of psychotherapists have reported consistently similar themes. One common theme, that of isolation, includes therapists' feelings of physical confinement, of separation from professional colleagues, and of social distance stemming from the difficulties of explaining psychotherapeutic work to friends (Daniels, 1974; London, 1976; Maciver & Redlich, 1959; Rogow, 1970). A second theme reported in the literature emphasizes concerns over the efficacy of psychotherapeutic treatment, in particular the lack of research-validated roles and techniques, and the difficulty in evaluating treatment results (Daniels, 1974; Farber & Heifetz, 1981; Maciver & Redlich, 1959; Rogow, 1970). A third theme, "image status," relates to the misconceptions of the therapeutic role by patients, other professionals, and the general public (Daniels; Mawardi, 1980; Rogow). In this regard, too, both Daniels and Rogow have noted the tendency of psychiatrists to view their psychiatric colleagues as aloof, arrogant, unimaginative, rigid, and even pathologically disturbed.

Another theme emphasizes the pressures inherent in the therapeutic relationship and the lack of sufficient rewards; therapists have reported that although therapeutic work is extremely frustrating, likely to exacerbate personal weaknesses, and entails great responsibility, they receive neither adequate financial remuneration nor adequate patient appreciation for their efforts (Daniels; Farber & Heifetz; London; Mawardi; Rogow). A fifth theme concerns the personally depleting aspects of therapeutic work: emotional depletion, physical exhaustion, and social difficulties after work (Farber & Heifetz). A final theme points to problematic working conditions of institutionally based therapists, in particular "excessive workload" and "organizational politics" (Farber & Heifetz). Daniels (1974) suggests that many of these themes are interdependent, that, for example, professional isolation fosters the development of professional arrogance, and therefore of an unsympathetic public; and that the realistic difficulties involved in evaluating therapeutic progress contribute to a public image of mental health professionals as either "omnipotent" or "impotent."

Coping with Stress: Adoption of a Psychodynamic Stance

It has been shown that experienced therapists face potential stress from many sources. In addition to stressful patient contact, they may experience family demands and conflicts, the existential crises of mid-life, and a variety of daily pressures, disappointments, and frustrations.

One common reaction to these pressures is for therapists to take refuge in their psychodynamic paradigm, to adopt a psychodynamic stance regardless of its appropriateness to a given situation (Farber, in press; Henry, Sims, & Spray, 1973; Rieff, 1966). According to this point of view, many clinicians tend to "live in a unidimensional world defined in terms of psychodynamic language" (Henry et al., 1973, p. 217). Therapists may maintain a therapeutic perspective in their relationships with others outside the office; they may bring their special skills and psychological understanding into their homes. In short, therapists who are exponents of psychodynamic theory use these theoretical and therapeutic constructs to structure their views of self and others. Over time, then, the tendency to adopt a psychotherapeutic perspective may become a reflexive, if defensive, reaction to professional and personal stresses—a familiar, predictable, and organized system of ordering the world. "The psychologically trained man (in or out of the therapeutic regimen) lives alert to the interpretative opportunity," according to Rieff (1966), "his whole life becomes a source of material for interpretation" (p. 102). Paul (1973) probably echoed the thoughts of many other psychotherapists when he stated that the therapeutic mode is generally inappropriate to personal and social relationships. Nevertheless, conceded Paul, "we've all known therapists who are always therapists" (p. 224).

As a result of immutably adopting the stance and attitude of psychodynamic psychology, the therapist may not only tend to act as a therapist indiscriminately (i.e., by interpreting the behavior of others), but may also tend to act as a hypertrophied version of a psychoanalyzed person (i.e., being in total control of his or her emotional life at all times). Meyer (1971) has noted that when analytic thought is overdeveloped, it can interfere with other functions, "especially those of feeling and intuition, and in general with the spontaneity essential to sexual, artistic and athletic achievement" (p. 335). And Rose (1974) has pointed out that an individual who becomes an "interminable analyst" may assume the analytic aversion to action and moral judgment and the analytic propensity toward thought and verbalization, detachment and emotional neutrality. These values, as Rose has indicated, should represent strategies of treatment and research; they are, however, sometimes introjected by therapists who, in place of developing their own personal style of relating to others, adopt the professional style of a psychoanalyst. In this regard, Rieff (1963) believes that "psychological man" practices a cultivated detachment that enables him to keep a safe distance from family and friends, and Henry et al. (1973) have noted that a "distancing aura" is characteristic even of therapists' interactions with spouse and children; these relationships tend to be "emotionally temperate, mutually satisfying, but clearly controlled" (p. 218) and are more likely to revolve around shared intellectual and recreational activities than on patterns of affective communication.

The psychotherapist who becomes a psychological man, an "interminable analyst," may indeed find salvation through the understanding and mastery of the unconscious. To some observers, the detachment and control of the psychotherapist is in fact an attractive, alluring facet of the therapist's "mystique"; to others, though, this "cultivated detachment" and "calculated sense of the therapeutic value of spontaneity" (Rieff, 1966) symbolizes the profound loss of an ineffable spirit. A dramatic example of this loss of spirit is found in *Equus* (Shaffer, 1974). In this play, the protagonist, a British psychiatrist, agonizes over whether to "cure" an adolescent who has blinded six horses, and thereby risk cauterizing the boy's capacity for passion—a capacity the psychiatrist himself has long since lost and now desperately envies.

Mid-Career Disillusionment

More than 20 years ago, Kelly (1961) found that 50 percent of clinical psychologists no longer believed in what they were doing and wished they had entered a different profession. Although more recently Garfield and Kurtz (1976) found that 90 percent of clinical psychologists were either "very satisfied" or "quite satisfied" with their careers, and Norcross and Prochaska (1982) found that 82 percent were either very satisfied or quite satisfied, other data have tended to support Kelly's original findings. Farber (1978), for example, found that among a heterogeneous group of psychotherapists, 50 percent have, at times, regretted their choice of profession; Norcross and Prochaska (1982) found that 42 percent of clinical psychologists would choose a different career if they were starting over again. In addition, personal testimony disparaging psychotherapy as a healing profession still appears regularly, lending further evidence that disillusionment with the field is still widespread. For example, Kernberg (1968) has written about "professional identity diffusion," attributing it primarily to therapists' lack of confidence in the psychodynamic model. Mandell (1977) has suggested that psychotherapy has become "degenerate." And Rogow (1970) has claimed that the entire field of psychiatry is undergoing an "identity crisis" manifested by practitioners' increasing skepticism about the goals, methods, and achievements of their profession. Intuitively, it might seem that psychotherapy (as well as other helping professions) should, of all careers, be most personally satisfying, and yet, as Sarason (1977) has shown, work *is* a problem for many highly educated, professional people.

Alan Wheelis, a psychoanalyst, and perhaps the most articulate of those to whom the practice of psychotherapy has become a professional dilemma, has written a succession of books and articles epitomizing the angst of the practicing clinician. For Wheelis, disillusionment with the psychotherapeutic role begins with the therapist's "awareness of the limited efficacy of insight" (1958, p. 230). Because the foundation of psychodynamically oriented therapies rests on the assumption of insight as the essential curative ingredient, it is difficult for therapists to accept that for many patients, "insight is more a subject of discussion than an instrument of change" (p. 230). The therapist then begins to question the honesty of his role, until presently other dissatisfactions become salient: the failure of the therapeutic role to provide an expected intimacy with people; the failure of the therapeutic role to provide vocational satisfactions; the failure of the therapeutic role even to alleviate the psychic distress of the therapist. To Wheelis though, it is the ultimate failure of the therapeutic role to create meaningful existence for the therapist that is most disillusioning—a failure that results in the therapist's feeling "a sense of futility, an intimation of unimportance attaching to creative effort" (1963, p. 147).

Wheelis' views, although attacked by some professional colleagues as a simplistic touting of "19th century romanticism" (Lowinger, 1966), are supported by many others who share his basic dissatisfactions. Burton (1972), for example, also tends to view dissatisfying aspects of the profession as reflecting intrinsically negative features of psychotherapeutic work. "Being a psychotherapist" says Burton, "requires working with the bedrock of existence and involves a perpetual philosophical questing. Irritability and dissatisfaction constantly wait at the door to be let in" (p. 318). Similarly, Reik admitted that in 35 years of analytic practice he had several times had the wish to change professions, feeling that being a psychoanalyst seemed to be "less a profession than a calamity" (Natterson, 1966, p. 249).

Feelings of Superiority

As a result of practicing psychotherapy, some therapists adopt a fixed psychodynamic stance that results in emotional detachment; others, perhaps incapable of affecting this imperturbality, are prone to feelings of disillusionment; still others may react to therapeutic work by developing what Marmor (1953) has called "the feeling of superiority." According to Marmor, "the constant exercise of authority" tends to create "unrealistic feelings of superiority in the authority figure" (p. 370). Although Marmor has discussed this occupational hazard as if it were equally true of all psychotherapists, it would appear the psychiatrists, imbued as they are with a great deal more authority than other mental health workers, might well be more prone toward adopting attitudes of superiority.

However, several factors other than the exercise of authority—factors common to the work of all psychotherapists—may also come to influence the development of these feelings. For example, because patients often seek the services of a professional clinician only after they have exhausted all other alternatives, the therapist may be thrust into the position of "savior," where he or she is considered not merely a realistic source of help but an idealized parent-figure as well. Patients, many of whom have themselves achieved considerable success, come to the therapist in need; they are depending and dependent upon help. A second aspect of psychotherapeutic work that may lead to grandiosity is the isolation that often plagues those in full-time private practice. As a consequence of limited communication with others, the psychotherapist may tend to "overestimate the virtue of his own particular approach and ability in contrast to those of his colleagues" (Marmor, 1953, p. 371). And a third factor that may exaggerate the therapist's self-esteem is the tendency for people, when meeting psychotherapists, to regard them with awe or to attribute to them magical powers of omniscience. Finally, a feeling of superiority may arise in the therapist as a defense against the anxieties inherent in the psychotherapeutic role—the enormous responsibilities of working with disturbed people, the need to adapt continually to shifting problems and to check continually on one's objectivity, the realistic difficulties in achieving and defining therapeutic success, and the disparity between patient and public expectations and therapeutic limitations. And according to Marmor, supervising therapists have an extra potential stress to contend with: they are not only subject to the idealization of their patients, but supervisory relationships often make it incumbent upon them to demonstrate their superior expertise to the resident or trainee.

The impact of these work stresses may cause psychotherapists to maximize their successes, minimize their failings, and regard themselves as eminently successful and powerful. Though "feeling superior" may be an unconscious by-product of many occupations, it is of particular importance to the psychotherapist inasmuch as it may directly interfere with the establishment of an effective psychotherapeutic relationship. A secondary manifestation of these feelings of grandiosity is the tendency for therapists to be "defensively arrogant," to be "less tolerant or more aggressive" than others, and to be "destructively critical of other colleagues" (Marmor, 1953, p. 374). In this regard too, Chertok (1966) has noted that the whole history of psychotherapy is marked by acrimony among psychotherapists.

Burnout

As has been noted throughout this chapter, certain difficulties are inherent in therapeutic work—difficulties relating primarily to the nature of the therapeutic role (e.g., attentiveness, responsibility, personal vulnerability) and to the nature of the therapeutic process (e.g., the slow, often erratic pace of therapeutic progress). As Farber and Heifetz (1982) have suggested, however, these stresses are for the most part accepted by therapists as inevitable and even necessary components of the job; they can, in normal circumstances, be dealt with moderately well with only minimal erosion of the therapist's faith in psychotherapy. Burnout, then, is not the inevitable result of psychotherapeutic stress. It is when psychotherapeutic work is particularly frustrating and only minimally *successful*—as is often the case when a therapist is overworked or dealing with particularly difficult patients—that disillusionment and burnout are likely to occur. And it is also when stresses at home lower the therapist's threshold for coping with daily therapeutic frustration and impair his or her ability to attend effectively to the patients' needs, that disillusionment and burnout in the winter (Farber & Heifetz, 1982). It is of note, too, that the longer staff members work in mental health settings, the less they like working with they begin to feel lonely, empty, inconsequential, and burned out (Farber & Heifetz, 1981, 1982; Freudenberger & Robbins, 1979).

It is interesting that many therapists feel that they are particularly prone to burnout in the winter (Farber & Heifetz, 1982). It is of note too that the longer staff members work in mental health settings, the less they like working with patients, the less successful they feel with them, and the more custodial rather than humanistic are their attitudes toward mental illness (Pines & Maslach, 1978).

Burnout, as explained by Pines and Maslach (1978), is a syndrome of "physical and emotional exhaustion, involving the development of negative self-concept, negative job attitudes, and loss of concern and feelings for clients" (p. 233). In addition, the emotional frustrations attendant to burnout may lead to increased family conflicts and/or refusal by the professional to discuss job experiences with either family or friends (Maslach, 1976). Psychotherapists who are burned out may lose concern for their patients, become disillusioned with the therapeutic process and doubt their own professional abilities, and become cynical, detached, and unfeeling. Again, though, it should be kept in mind that burnout is most often an extreme reaction to stress. Therapists may use a number of defensive techniques to try to ward off incipient feelings of burnout (Pines & Maslach, 1978): detached concern (balancing a sense of care with objectivity and distance); intellectualization (reacting to stressful situations in intellectual rather than emotional terms); compartmentalization (making sharp distinctions between personal and professional roles); withdrawal (spending less time with patients and interacting with them more impersonally); and reliance on others to diffuse personal responsibility.

Psychosis and Suicide

Given the nature and intensity of the stresses that psychotherapists undergo as a consequence of their work, it is not surprising that an image of the therapist as an embodiment of all the disturbing, "crazy" experience that therapeutic practice consists of is so very common. Insofar as this is merely a reaction of the lay public to a professional experience that seems dangerous, disconcerting, and incomprehensible in its contents and methods, its relevance to the "real life" of the psychotherapist can be discounted. However, this mantle of craziness or specialness is very often assumed by therapists themselves and interpreted as a valuable, or at the least, an inescapable concomitant of therapeutic work. "Craziness" can be understood as a consequence of clinical work inasmuch as "therapeutic practice itself provides continual reaction of personal inner states" (Henry, 1966, p. 54) and inasmuch as therapeutic practice interferes with the tendency toward repression, a defense mechanism that preserves the tranquility of psychic life (Stekel, 1964). "Craziness," though, can also be understood as a means for psychotherapeutic understanding of patient dynamics. "Craziness," or more precisely the ability to be in touch with and utilize regressive and primitive thoughts and feelings, is a state that can be used in the service of empathy and insight. In the shamanic traditions as well, it is knowledge of his own wounds that enables the shaman to heal the patient. Perhaps this is why psychotherapists, rather than vehemently denying the accusation of craziness, have in several instances actually promoted this view themselves. For example, Burton (1972), in reviewing the autobiographies of 12 prominent therapists, observed that they "accept the fact—even parade it, in a sense—that they are unlike other men. . . . To be 'crazy' is to be inventive and innovative" (p. 316).

Although no precise figures are available as to the incidence of psychosis or "breakdowns" among psychotherapists, their disproportionately high suicide rate is usually considered an indication of a similarly disproportionate prevalence of psychological disturbance. A high suicide rate among psychiatrists (58 to 65/100,000) as compared to that of the general population (11/100,000) has been reported by a number of different research teams (Blachly, Disher, & Roduner, 1968; DeSole, Singer & Aronson, 1969; Freeman, 1967; Pond, 1969). Each investigator reported a slightly different suicide rate by using somewhat different definitions of suicide and this has led to some dispute over the validity of these findings (Rosen, 1973). A past chairman of the American Psychiatric Association Task Force on Suicide Prevention has, however, concluded that physician suicide is not overreported and that psychiatry still has a noticeably higher suicide rate than other medical specialties (Ross, 1975). In response to the publication of these suicide rates, one psychiatrist suggested that medical students be warned that psychiatric practice may not fulfill either their conscious expectations or unconscious needs (Braun, 1973), and another (Ellerbroek, 1972) went so far as to contend "that professionals in the field should maintain a high index of suspicion as to the validity of psychiatric teachings until we have the lowest suicide rate of any professional group, not the highest" (p. 364).

The issue of suicides among psychiatrists has sometimes been considered simply in terms of whether working in the field of psychiatry predisposes an individual to suicide, or whether psychiatry attracts more suicide-prone individuals (Freeman, 1967). Recently, it has come to be recognized that the disproportionately high suicide rate among psychiatrists is a complex problem, not conducive to simple "either/or" explanations. The nature of psychiatric work and the nature of the psychiatrist have, of course, been implicated as causes of psychiatrist suicides, but many other factors have also been advanced: that psychiatrists think about suicide because they work with suicidal people; that psychiatrists are too proud to talk about their problems, and that family and friends are reluctant to intervene; that psychiatrists' preoccupation with their role leads them to neglect recreational and restorative activities; that psychiatrists' grandiose expectations are inevitably unattainable; and that for beginning psychiatrists in particular, the attainment of psychoanalytic insight may be too severe a burden (Freeman, 1967; Ross, 1973). Further research appears to be necessary in order to determine whether certain types of psychiatrists or psychotherapists (e.g., those who treat schizophrenics, those who are primarily analytically oriented, those who are in full-time practice) are more prone to suicide than others.

EXPLANATORY MODELS OF PSYCHOTHERAPEUTIC ROLE DYSFUNCTIONING

To this point, personality traits of psychotherapists such as grandiosity or emotional distancing, and personality breakdowns such as psychosis and suicide, have been attributed primarily to the stresses of the therapeutic role per se. One immediately apparent alternative hypothesis is that many who enter the field may already be very sensitive or neurotic individuals with unique backgrounds and specific needs. This view is supported by psychoanalytic theory, as well as by an examination of the early lives and graduate careers of mental health workers. For example, as far back as 1913, Ernest Jones wrote about the potential dangers of a "God complex" in those with strong interests in psychiatry and psychology. A prevailing current view is that a therapist's motivation for pursuing clinical work is based on a search for personal therapeutic help (Holt & Luborsky, 1958; Searles, 1965). For example, Menninger (1957) has noted that "psychiatrists, more than members of other specialties and more than the average man, have at some time suffered overmuch from a sense of loneliness, unlovableness and rejection" (p. 104). Eron's findings (1955) on fourth-year medical students indicated that students planning to specialize in psychiatry were significantly more anxious than those planning to enter pediatrics, internal medicine, or surgery. And Sharaf, Schneider, and Kantor (1968) showed that those who were certain of their choice of psychiatry as a specialty were more intraceptive (psychological-minded) than other groups of medical students.

It appears then that these two opposing points of view are somewhat analogous to the nature-nurture controversy, that is, whether certain disconcerting personality patterns of psychotherapists are a function of longstanding characterological dispositions or whether they are generated by the deleterious effects of psychotherapeutic training and practice. And as is true of most nature-nurture arguments, both positions in this case seem somewhat correct. One of the psychiatrists interviewed by Rogow (1970) illustrated this point: "I lean toward the view that analysts are fairly neurotic people, in general, very sensitive people. . . . What you start out with is, in a way increased. Maybe you get to be more objective as you go along, but I think there's a corresponding increase in personal vulnerability, too" (p. 100). Similarly, Wheelis (1958) has noted that those personal difficulties, which for some people have provided the impetus for pursuing a mental health career, may eventually become "aggravated by practice of that profession" (p. 206).

Henry's (1966) interactive model therefore is probably the most appropriate perspective from which to view therapists' problems. According to Henry, mental health professionals tend to have backgrounds that lead them to experience "a special sense of isolation" and a "heightened awareness of inner events" (p. 49). Often they report notable incidents in their childhoods that made them feel "different"—the death or remarriage of parents, a severe personal illness, family financial difficulties, infrequent peer contact. These stressful experiences produce a sense of "personal distinctness, social marginality and low intimacy" (p. 53). These feelings then are likely to motivate individuals to pursue mental health careers; in addition, the feelings themselves are perpetuated by therapeutic work so that even family life and social relations become minimally affective. Similarly, the evolution of introspective capacities during childhood facilitates entry into the field and is itself reinforced by performing psychodynamically oriented psychotherapy. As a result of their practice, therapists become increasingly self-reflective as well as increasingly psychological-minded in their relations with others (Farber, in press). The practice of psychotherapy serves to reactivate early experiences, memories, and emotions continually—feelings that may help sustain therapists' curiosity and involvement in their own problems as well as those of their patients.

In sum, therapists often are perceived as "different" by themselves and others. This difference, often rooted in childhood, is based on a sensitivity to inner states and feelings, a sensitivity that is sometimes personally painful and distressful to others, but which is also enlightening and fulfilling to therapists themselves. According to Henry (1966), "the career of a mental health professional . . . is a commitment to a lifestyle, as well as an investment in a line of work" (p. 54). As such, those difficulties and rewards that stem from sensitivity, introspection, and psychological-mindedness are not simply embedded in the therapeutic role, buy in the whole fabric of therapists' lives.

Prevention and Treatment

"It must be recognized that the psychotherapist uses his feelings, his self, to a degree that is unique. And that self has to be adequately cared for to function well" (McCarley, 1975, p. 224). Freud (1937/1964) recommended that therapists care for themselves by periodically returning to therapy. Similarly, it has been suggested that therapists renew themselves in either a supportive therapeutic group atmosphere or within the context of "refresher courses" with colleagues (McCarley, 1975). More commonly though, suggestions regarding the prevention and treatment of the stresses of therapeutic work have clustered around the need for therapists to pursue extratherapeutic activities: hobbies; social and recreational events; vacations and sabbaticals; interdisciplinary contacts; coursework outside one's area of expertise; and even psychological work such as consulting, teaching, and research that takes place outside the confines of one's professional office (Farber & Heifetz, 1981, 1982; Freudenberger & Robbins, 1979; Grinberg, 1963; Marmor, 1953; Rose, 1974). In addition, it has been recognized that therapists need to be able to express negative feeling toward their work freely without fear that such admissions will either go unacknowledged or be interpreted as incompetence. In this vein, it has been suggested that seminars and conferences in the field begin to focus on common problems as well as on appropriate technique, on the inevitability and cybernetic value of failures as well as of successes, and on the limitations rather than the infinite possibilities of the therapeutic process (Farber & Heifetz, 1982).

Taken together, these suggestions emphasize the need for therapists to alleviate personal and professional pressures while pursuing opportunities for growth and fulfillment outside the therapeutic context. While these suggestions make intuitive "sense," their efficacy, as either preventive or ameliorative measures, has never been assessed.

CONCLUSIONS

The emphasis throughout this chapter on the dysfunctional aspects of the psychotherapeutic role has, unfortunately, obscured the fact that many therapists view the experience and effects of psychotherapeutic practice in primarily positive terms. For example, many therapists are more impressed with the positive effects of psychological-mindedness (increased insight into self and others) than they are with its potential for impeding spontaneity or dampening emotionality; in addition, therapeutic work is still seen by a majority of therapists as offering the opportunity for personal affirmation and self-fulfillment (Farber & Heifetz, 1981). The data presented here thus lend support to previous research indicating that stress and disillusionment in human service professionals can coexist with high levels of job satisfaction (see Cherniss & Egnatios, 1978); nevertheless, as was noted earlier, there is still a need to address those aspects of therapeutic work that are personally and professionally debilitating. Disillusionment and burnout may, after all, affect not only therapists and their families but also the effective delivery of mental health services.

Burton (1972) has asserted that "psychotherapy is a peculiar mixture of play and reality, of studied rationality and fantastic idiosyncracy, of established maturity and puerile infancy, of sheer honesty and gross deception. All of this becomes critically focused in the one personality of the healer and the visible motif is often one of chaos" (p. 317). This is perhaps an exaggerated view but certainly the psychotherapist is affected by the nature of psychotherapeutic work. Given the growing popularity of psychotherapy—as both a career choice for students and an option for troubled individuals—further research into psychotherapeutic role difficulties seems crucial. At present, the literature is replete with random case studies and anecdotal evidence. In fact, it is ironic that of all related topics, the most complete and systematic data have been collected on suicide rates of psychiatric residents and psychiatrists. Only at the point of self-imposed death are the difficulties of psychotherapeutic work (and the potential for these difficulties to create unbearable personal stress) no longer ignored. Clearly, then, there is a need for further objective measurement of the effects of psychotherapeutic practice upon psychotherapists. With such studies may come increased knowledge regarding the prevention and remediation of the occupational stresses of performing psychotherapy.

REFERENCES

Basescu, S. Anxieties in the analyst: An autobiographical account. In Frank, K. (Ed.), *The human dimension in psychoanalytic practice*. New York: Grune & Stratton, 1977.

Bermak, G. E. Do psychiatrists have special emotional problems? *The American Journal of Psychoanalysis*, 1977, **37**, 141–146.

Blachly, P. H., Disher, W., & Roduner, G. Suicide by physicians. *Bulletin of Suicidology*, December 1968, 1–18.

Book, H. On maybe becoming a psychotherapist, perhaps. *Canadian Psychiatric Association Journal*, 1973, **18**, 487–493.

Braun, M. Suicide in psychiatrists. *Journal of the American Medical Association*, 1973, **223**, 81.

Burton, A. *Twelve therapists*. San Francisco: Jossey-Bass, 1972.

Cherniss, C. & Egnatios, E. Is there job satisfaction in community mental health? *Community Mental Health Journal*, 1978, **14**, 309–318.

Chertok, L. An introduction to the study of tensions among psychotherapists. *British Journal of Medical Psychiatry*, 1966, **39**, 237–243.

Chessick, R. D. How the resident and the supervisor disappoint each other. *American Journal of Psychotherapy*, 1971, **25**, 272–283.

Cray, C. & Cray, M. Stresses and rewards within the psychiatrist's family. *The American Journal of Psychoanalysis*, 1977, **37**, 337–341.

Daniels, A. K. What troubles the trouble shooters. In Roman, P. M. & Trice, H. M. (Eds.), *The sociology of psychotherapy.* New York: Jason Aronson, 1974.

Davidson, H. The image of the psychiatrist. *American Journal of Psychiatry,* 1964, **121,** 329–334.

DeSole, E. E., Singer, P., & Aronson, S. Suicide and role strain among physicians. *International Journal of Social Psychiatry,* 1969, **15,** 294–301.

Ellerbroek, W. C. Suicide in psychiatrists. *Journal of the American Medical Association,* 1972, **222,** 364.

English, O. S. The emotional stress of psychotherapeutic practice. *Journal of the American Academy of Psychoanalysis,* 1976, **4** (2), 191–201.

Eron, L. D. The effect of medical education on medical students' attitudes. *Journal of Medical Education,* 1955, **30,** 559–566.

Farber, B. A. The effects of psychotherapeutic practice upon the psychotherapist: A phenomenological investigation. (Doctoral dissertation, Yale University, 1978). *Dissertation Abstracts International,* 1979, **40-01B,** 447.

Farber, B. A. The effects of psychotherapeutic practice upon psychotherapists. *Psychotherapy: Theory, research and practice,* in press.

Farber, B. A. & Heifetz, L. J. The satisfactions and stresses of psychotherapeutic work: A factor analytic study. *Professional Psychology,* 1981, **12,** 621–630.

Farber, B. A. & Heifetz, L. J. The process and dimension of burnout in psychotherapists. *Professional Psychology,* 1982, **13** (2), 293–301.

Frank, J. D. *Persuasion and healing.* Baltimore: Johns Hopkins University Press, 1973.

Freeman, W. Psychiatrists who kill themselves: A study of suicide. *American Journal of Psychiatry,* 1967, **124,** 846–847.

Freud, S. Analysis terminable and interminable. *Standard Edition.* Vol. 23. London: Hogarth, 1964. (Originally published 1937.)

Freudenberger, H. J. & Robbins, A. The hazards of being a psychoanalyst. *The Psychoanalytic Review,* 1979, **66** (2), 275–296.

Garfield, S. L. & Kurtz, R. M. Clinical psychologists in the 1970s. *American Psychologist,* 1976, **31,** 1–9.

Greben, S. E. Some difficulties and satisfactions inherent in the practice of psychoanalysis. *International Journal of Psychoanalysis,* 1975, **56,** 427–434.

Grinberg, L. Relations between psychoanalysts. *International Journal of Psychoanalysis,* 1963, **44,** 362–367.

Halleck, S. C. & Woods, S. M. Emotional problems of psychiatric residents. *Psychiatry,* 1962, **25,** 339–346.

Henry, W. E. Some observations on the lives of healers. *Human Development,* 1966, **9,** 47–56.

Henry, W., Sims, J., & Spray, S. L. *The fifth profession.* San Francisco: Jossey-Bass, 1971.

Henry, W., Sims, J., & Spray, S. L. *Public and private lives of psychotherapists.* San Francisco: Jossey-Bass, 1973.

Holt, R. R. Personality growth in psychiatric residents. *AMA Archives of Neurology and Psychiatry,* 1959, **81,** 203–215.

Holt, R. & Luborsky, L. *Personality patterns of psychiatrists.* New York: Basic Books, 1958.

Jung, C. J. Psychology of the transference. *The practice of psychotherapy.* Vol. 16, Bollingen Series. Princeton: Princeton University Press, 1966.

Kelly, E. L. Clinical psychology—1960: Report of survey findings. *Newsletter: Division of Clinical Psychology, American Psychological Association,* 1961, **14,** 1–11.

Kernberg, O. Some effects of social pressures on the psychiatrist as a clinician. *Bulletin of Menninger Clinic,* 1968, **32,** 144–159.

Khajavi, F., Hekmat, H., & Mehryar, A. Patterns of alienation and authoritarianism among mental health professionals and trainees. *Journal of Community Psychology,* 1973, **1** (2), 164–167.

Knutsen, E. J. On the emotional well-being of psychiatrists: Overview and rationale. *The American*

Journal of Psychoanalysis, 1977, **37**, 123-129.

Lieberman, M. A. Comments on W. E. Henry's "Some observations on the lives of healers." *Human Development*, 1966, **9**, 57-60.

London, R. W. The lonely profession: A study of the psychological rewards and negative aspects of the practice of psychotherapy. (Doctoral dissertation, University of Southern California, 1976.) *Dissertation Abstracts International*, 1976, **37**, 1491B.

Looney, J. G.; Hardy, R. K.; Blotcky, M. J.; & Barnhart, F. D. Psychiatrists' transition from training to career: Stress and mastery. *American Journal of Psychiatry*, 1980, **137** (1), 32-36.

Lowinger, P. Psychiatrists against psychiatry. *American Journal of Psychiatry*, 1966, **123**, 490-493.

MaCiver, J. & Redlich, F. Patterns of psychiatric practice. *American Journal of Psychiatry*, 1959, **115**, 692-697.

Mandell, A. J. *Coming of [Middle] age: A journey.* New York: Summit Books, 1977.

Marmor, J. The feeling of superiority: An occupational hazard in the practice of psychiatry. *American Journal of Psychiatry*, 1953, **110**, 370-376.

Marmor, J. The crisis of middle age. *Psychiatry Digest*, 1968, **29**, 17-21.

Martin, L. B. The psychiatrist in today's movies: He's everywhere and in deep trouble. *The New York Times,* January 25, 1981, Section 2, pp. 1, 27.

Maslach, C. Burned-out. *Human Behavior,* 1976, **5**, 16-22.

Maurice, W. L.; Klonoff, H.; Miles, J. E.; & Krell, R. Medical student change during a psychiatry clerkship: Evaluation of a program. *Journal of Medical Education,* 1975, **50**, 181-189.

Mawardi, B. *Physician career satisfaction: Another look.* Paper presented at the annual conference of the Association of American Medical Colleges, Washington, D.C., October 1980.

McCarley, T. The psychotherapist's search for self-renewal. *The American Journal of Psychiatry,* 1975, **132**, 221-224.

Menninger, K. A. Psychological factors in the choice of medicine as a profession. *Bulletin of the Menninger Clinic,* 1957, **21**, 51-58, 99-106.

Merklin, L. & Little, R. B. Beginning psychiatry training syndrome. *American Journal of Psychiatry,* 1967, **124**, 193-197.

Meyer, R. The practice of awareness as a form of psychotherapy. *Journal of Religion and Health*, 1971, **10**, 333-345.

Natterson, J. M. Theodor Reik. In Alexander, F., Eisenstein, S., & Grotjahn, M. (Eds.), *Psychoanalytic pioneers.* New York: Basic Books, 1966.

Norcross, J. C. & Prochaska, J. O. A national survey of clinical psychologists: Views on training, career choice, and APA. *The Clinical Psychologist*, 1982, **35**, 1, 3-6.

Pasnau, R. O. & Bayley, S. Personality changes in the fist year of psychiatry residency training. *American Journal of Psychiatry*, 1971, **128**, 79-84.

Paul, I. H. *Letters to Simon.* New York: International Universities Press, 1973.

Perlman, G. Change in self and ideal self-concept congruence of beginning psychotherapists. *Journal of Clinical Psychology*, 1972, **28**, 40-48.

Pines, A. & Maslach, C. Characteristics of staff burnout in mental health settings. *Hospital and Community Psychiatry*, 1978, **29** (4), 233-237.

Pond, D. A. Doctor's mental health. *The New Zealand Medical Journal*, 1969, **69**, 131-135.

Psychiatry on the couch. *Time*, April 2, 1979, pp. 74-82.

Rieff, P. *Freud: The mind of the moralist.* New York: Viking, 1959.

Rieff, P. In S. Freud, *Therapy and technique.* New York: Collier Books, 1963.

Rieff, P. *The triumph of the therapeutic.* New York: Harper & Row, 1966.

Rogow, A. *The psychiatrists.* New York: G.P. Putnam's Sons, 1979.

Rose, G. Some misuses of analysis as a way of life. Analysis interminable and interminable 'analysts.' *International Review of Psycho-analysis*, 1974, **1**, 509-515.

Rosen, D. Suicide rates among psychiatrists. *Journal of American Medical Association*, 1973, **224**, 246-247.

Ross, M. Suicide and the psychiatrist. *American Journal of Psychiatry*, 1973, **130**, 937.

Sarason, S. B. *Work, aging, and social change.* New York: Free Press, 1977.

Schlicht, W. J. The anxieties of the psychotherapist. *Mental Hygiene,* 1968, **52,** 439–445.

Searles, H. F. *Collected papers on schizophrenia and related subjects.* New York: International Universities Press, 1965.

Seashore, C. *In grave danger of growing: Observations on the process of professional development.* Paper presented at the Washington School of Psychiatry Group Psychotherapy Training Program, June 1975.

Shaffer, P. *Equus,* New York: Avon, 1974.

Sharaf, M. R. & Levinson, D. J. The quest for omnipotence in professional training. *Psychiatry,* 1964, **27,** 135–149.

Sharaf, M. R., Schneider, P., & Kantor, D. Psychiatric interest and its correlates among medical students. *Psychiatry,* 1968, **21,** 150–160.

Stekel, W. *Sadism and masochism.* Vol. 2. New York: Grove Press, 1964.

Tamerin, J. S. & Eisinger, R. A. Cigarette smoking and the psychiatrist. *American Journal of Psychiatry,* 1972, **128,** 1224–1229.

Ungerleider, J. T. That most difficult year. *American Journal of Psychiatry,* 1965, **122,** 542–545.

Wheelis, A. *The quest for identity.* New York: Norton, 1958.

Wheelis, A. To be a God (1963). In *The Illusionless man.* New York: Norton, 1966.

8

Aspects of the Impaired Physician

Betty Hosmer Mawardi

This discussion of the impaired physician phenomenon is based on the results of investigations carried out at Case Western Reserve University School of Medicine during the last 20 years. The data, collected for two major career studies, are primarily in the form of personal interviews I conducted with 400 graduates of Case Western Reserve's School of Medicine.

The first study (Mawardi, 1979a) involved a large random sample of graduates from the classes of 1935 through 1945. They were physicians, well established in their respective careers and communities, who had received a traditional medical education. Their career patterns were investigated in depth. The study inquired about the types of patients and medical problems these physicians most preferred to work with and why; the patients and medical problems they most disliked having to work with and why; how they handled patients whom they disliked or felt inadequate to treat; what aspects of their practices they found stressful or boring; how they worked with other physicians and members of the health team; what methods they developed for improving their efficiency; and ways in which they kept current with progress in their field. Interviews have just been completed with 200 graduates from the revised program in medical education that went into effect in 1952. This revised program introduced changes in the curriculum, in the philosophy of the student-faculty relationships, and in the learning environment (Ham, 1962). The major curricular change meant that the basic sciences of medicine were taught by an integrated, interdepartmental, functional, organ systems approach (i.e., cardiovascular system or endocrine and reproductive system) rather than by separate courses given by the independent departments. Students were introduced to clinical medicine early in their careers by being assigned to a pregnant woman's case upon entry to medical school. The students followed the women through the remainder of their pregnancies, were present at the births, and eventually added other family members to their "patient load." Additional increments of responsibility for patient care were planned and added throughout the four years.

In order to graduate, each student was required to conduct a research project in the summers after the first and second years and to report the research results in thesis form in the senior year. Students were treated as maturing individuals, as graduate students, and as junior colleagues to the faculty members rather than in the authoritarian methods of previous years. Faculty worked unceasingly to produce special courses and clerkships that allowed the students to develop as individuals, assuming ever greater responsibility for their own learning as well as for the patient care. Self-education was emphasized. Free time was built into the program; this meant that the students were given 27 percent of the working week completely free from school commitments for the first two and one-half years in order to encourage them to make their own decisions as to when, where, or how much to study. The number of examinations was reduced to just one three-day comprehensive examination at the end of the first year (or Phase I) and a second at the end of Phase II, plus five to eight interim learning exams per year. Examinations were taken anonymously and students were "identified" only if their work was judged unsatisfactory. An attempt was made to encourage cooperative rather than competitive behaviors among the students by eliminating the use of grades and class standings. These were some of the major principles or precepts of that revised program. If they no longer sound revolutionary or "new," it is because they have been adopted by approximately one-third of the medical schools in the United States and by many schools in foreign countries.

A major objective of the present career study was to evaluate most of these educational principles many years after the medical students had graduated, when they were advanced in their careers. There was considerable interest in which features of that revised program were now viewed by the graduates, from their present perspective of years of practice, as being very helpful and cogent or merely ephemeral insofar as their careers in medicine are concerned.

This follow-up study consists of a stratified random sample of graduates from those classes of 1956 through 1965. It is a longitudinal investigation that employs a format similar to that of the earlier study. In addition to looking at the graduates' current reactions to their medical education, analyses are focused primarily on satisfactions, dissatisfactions, sources of stress, and alternative ways of coping. The complex analyses of results are now in progress, but some things are already becoming very clear. Accurate diagnosis with successful therapy is still the source of greatest satisfaction while service to humanity and good physician-patient relationships again come in a close second; time pressures continue as the strongest dissatisfaction. These major findings are the same as in the previous study; however, the current investigation has revealed some new sources of stress. Sources of stress that were not present in the previous work include the great increase in malpractice suits, having to give up certain aspects of medical work (for example, surgery) as a consequence of insurance restrictions or cost, fear of physical harm, and certain features of peer review (Mawardi, 1979b). A variety of outside interests and a reduced work week provide some alleviation and respite from the stress factors that could precipitate impairment.

WHAT CONSTITUTES PHYSICIAN IMPAIRMENT?

Impairment and burnout are not identical concepts, although they are closely related. Physical impairment occurs when medical, physical, or psychological conditions impinging upon the physician cause a deviation from the delivery of optimum medical care. The impairment may be temporary or chronic. Burnout is a more pervasive phenomenon that affects both personal and professional aspects of a physician's life; it results in a state of emotional, physical, and attitudinal depletion. Burned out physicians are less satisfied with their work. Ultimately, this may take a toll on the physician and can be a significant precursor to physician impairment.

The impaired physician as a *concept* has only become well known within the last decade. The *reality* of the impaired physician has, of course, been present much longer; in an effort, though, to deflect the attention of patients and society from the situation, very little has been voiced publicly by the medical establishment. Physicians themselves have often recognized impairments or disabilities in colleagues and have resolved not to refer their own patients to them. But they have also adhered to the tacit professional ethic of "live and let live." This "conspiracy of silence" is based on the fear that revelation of impairment would somehow lessen the esteem in which medicine and physicians have been held for so long. While lapses by colleagues are not condoned, their disclosure is seen as particularly jeopardizing the reputation and respect of the profession. Physicians are sworn to uphold the "Hippocratic oath," one of whose principle's is: "I will maintain the honor and noble tradition of the medical profession." It has been the *appearance* of this noble tradition that has long been presented to the public.

What is meant by an "impaired physician"? Physician impairment can range from slight distortions in acumen or judgment following a medical emergency to major impairments such as alcoholism, drug addiction, depression, and suicidal ideation. These latter disabilities are clearly serious and have provoked considerable discussion in the field (see Jones, 1977; Murray, 1976; Sargent et al., 1977). They may, however, have less deleterious effects on patient care since physicians who are impaired to this extent may no longer be involved in doctor-patient relationships. On the other hand, impaired, still-practicing physicians may work at lowered or reduced efficiency for months or years, posing potential hazards to each of their patients.

Many cases of physician impairment do not constitute gross and irreversible incompetence: for example, the physician who, because of a growing clinical practice, has not allowed sufficient time to keep abreast of material in medical journals or to take necessary courses in continuing education; or the physician who has just taken a couple of drinks at a Saturday night dinner party at a friend's home and receives an emergency call from one of his patients; or the conscientious physician who has been up two nights in a row with critically ill patients, yet, sleep deprived and exhausted, faces a full schedule of appointments at his office the next day; or the physician who is serving the medical community but who is found making fraudulent claims for Medicaid services; or the chronically disorganized physician, always running late, whose office is characteristically full of patient patients who may have to wait hours to see the doctor without so much as an explanation or an apology. The patients of these doctors are all victims of impaired physicians, regardless of whether the impairment stems from ignorance, ineptitude, deteriorating skills, greed, compulsion, other character or personality frailties, or mere mood fluctuations and fatigue. The above situations are just a few examples from the myriad of real instances that regularly occur and engender concern for physician competency and the quality of medical care being delivered daily. It is acknowledged, therefore, that some of these impairments are relatively minor and even nonculpable, though the results may nonetheless be potentially tragic.

Other impairments (e.g., drug addiction) take more dramatic form and affect physicians themselves more seriously. The most extreme case of physician "impairment" is, of course, suicide. The suicide rates of physicians have exceeded the rates of both the population at large and comparable professionals. Reports of these rates vary by investigator and by criteria of suicide. In general, suicides of physicians over the age of 60 (or 65) have not been included on the supposition that they may reflect concurrent instances of terminal illness. Furthermore, possible accidents, such as drowning or single-car or plane crashes, have not been taken into account. Despite these omissions, the estimated rates for male physicians are as high as 88 per 100,000 or eight times the rate of the general population (Ross, 1967). More frequently, the estimates are lower but vary widely among the medical specialties. Blachly, Disher, and Roduner (1968), whose figures still are most often cited, indicate a range of rates from 61 per 100,000 for psychiatrists to 10 per 100,000 (about the general population rate) for pediatricians. Some investigators have expressed doubts that the rates are actually that high (Rich & Pitts, 1979) although Rose and Rosow (1973) demonstrated how greatly physician suicide numbers are underestimated. It does seem certain that the suicides of physicians, when they happen, are most likely to occur in the 35–54 age group which is the most productive phase of the doctor's life (Hussey, 1974). Moreover, the suicide rate for female physicians is substantially higher (Pitts et al., 1979).

Explanations for these high suicide rates could not be found in the initial analyses of the career study data on physician satisfaction (Mawardi, 1979a). Indeed, the research showed that pediatricians, despite their low suicide rate, were the least satisfied with their careers, and psychiatrists, despite their high suicide rate, were among the most satisfied group of doctors. Since no significant correlations could be found between satisfaction and impairment, other explanations were sought. The most compelling of these alternative explanations was found in the work of Vaillant, Sobowale, and McArthur (1972). Also based on the data of a longitudinal study, they traced the roots of physician impairment to the somewhat unhappier-than-usual childhoods of physicians. Some might suggest therefore that the incidence of physician impairment could be reduced through more effective screening of medical applicants, but Vaillant et al. caution that society might then also be selecting out the very individuals whose empathy and capacity for helping patients renders them most vulnerable to burnout and impairment. At issue, then, is whether it is just to deprive physicians of their "calling" and their future patients of their services, because of their higher probability of developing dysfunctional behaviors.

PREVENTION AND TREATMENT

The more extreme forms of physician debilities—alcoholism, drug addiction, and suicide—have come to public and professional attention in recent years. Since 1973, the American Medical Association has sponsored several programs on the impairment of physicians. The first was a half-day symposium during the AMA's 1973 medical education meetings at which Casterline (1973) revealed that the medical profession in the United States each year loses the equivalent of the annual graduates of seven medical schools (700 physicians) due to suicide (100), drug addiction (200), and alcoholism (400). These figures include only those doctors who are no longer practicing; they do not include those who are victims of drug addiction and alcoholism but who continue to practice, albeit in a diminished capacity.

Clearly this is a distressing picture. The situation is grievous indeed when one considers what the loss of these health providers means to the health communities of the nation. When these physicians finally leave their practices, their expertise and experience are lost to the community at large and an additional financial burden is placed on state and national governments in educating their replacements. Serious though this loss of trained physicians may be to the profession and to the public, the greatest concern is for the potential danger to patients of impaired physicians. As the medical establishment has become more aware of the ramifications of physician impairment, countermeasures have been introduced. In 1969, the Florida legislature pioneered the development of a "sick doctor statute" which changed the state's rules for professional discipline in order to protect the public (AMA Council on Mental Health Report, 1973). Texas enacted a similar law in 1971, and other states have subsequently followed suit. It has often been necessary to coerce physicians into treatment programs, since they frequently deny illness, lack insight into the problem, avoid medical assistance, and minimize the problem outright (AMA Council, 1973, p. 687). Several states have initiated programs of physician rehabilitation. Licenses to practice have been revoked, not as a punitive measure but with the understanding that they will be restored when the physician is rehabilitated. Institutions, separate from those available to the general public, have been established exclusively for physicians who have drug or alcohol problems. It has been determined that physicians are more likely to seek help for these problems if their identities are protected and confidentiality is assured. Regrettably, it has been reported (Cranshaw et al., 1980) that the incidence of suicide by physicians on probation is disturbingly high.

The tremendous increase in malpractice suits during the last decade has done much to alter the practice of medicine itself. Two changes resulting from malpractice considerations have added greatly to the cost of medical care. One is the large-scale trend toward practicing "defensive medicine," wherein the physician orders expensive extra tests and procedures with the sole purpose of establishing a patient record that will stand up in court. The second is the added cost of expensive malpractice insurance that has been passed on directly to patients. But there has been a positive effect that is not often discussed beyond professional circles. That is, some of the worst offenders among the disabled physicians have not been granted insurance at all and are no longer able to practice an inferior quality of medicine.

Some peer review systems also give promise of serving to protect the public from impaired physicians by seeking to replace the conspiracy of silence with a "conspiracy of constructive compassion" (AMA Council, 1973, p. 687). Under some of these more recent programs, it appears possible that physicians who know of another physician's impairment and say nothing about it may themselves be held liable for any malpractice. This action may remove additional disabled physicians from practice; yet is poses ethical dilemmas to hold physicians responsible, and indeed liable, for their colleagues' behavior. Only recently has there been attention to this dilemma in the literature (Horsley, 1978). To relieve physicians of the burden of peer evaluation, the state could establish and enforce criteria for licensure that would insure minimum standards of good practice and would be designed to protect the public from the more flagrant cases of physician impairment. This would be more in concert with the insurance company model previously cited as opposed to the "brother's keeper" model proposed in the legislature.

In response to the need for physician review, hospitals, licensing boards, and medical societies have established their own mechanisms of review. They investigate serious instances of incompetence and disability, especially following complaints. Although some of the reforms may facilitate disciplinary action against problem physicians and thus protect the level of medical practice, there is evidence that other legislation could contribute to a possible lessening of the quality of clinical care. Rigid standards of practice, for example, may unacceptably limit the autonomy and judgment of individual physicians.

THE PHYSICIAN'S PERSPECTIVE

So far we have taken into consideration primarily the patient and society, the apparent victims of the impaired physician. What about the physicians themselves? Physicians in their professional roles enter into the doctor-patient relationship as providers of health care to their patients. The doctor-patient relationship can be defined as:

> a professional dyadic interaction usually developed around a health problem where the differential roles of the person involved include a sick or troubled seeker after health and a trained therapist. The sick person comes to the therapist seeking help in his illness and the knowledgeable therapist is expected to provide that help or to know where it is available. He gives assistance to the best of his training and ability, in exchange for which, he receives a fee. Responsibilities of each presuppose that the sick person wants to or is trying to get well [i.e., he does not enjoy and wish to maintain the sick role *per se* and that he will cooperate in putting forth some effort to recover] and that the therapist will honestly do the best he can to assist the sick person to regain his health and not "use" or mistreat the sick person. Expected emoluments or gains for each are improved health or alleviation of symptoms for the one and financial reward and professional enhancement for the other [Mawardi, 1979a, p. 200].

Moreover, the existence of such a relationship is a sanction toward moral action. For example, in order to facilitate the doctor-patient relationship, certain moral and legal conditions—such as confidentiality and the nonabandonment of patients—are imposed. In addition, the doctor-patient relationship may be looked upon as a contractual one in which there is an obligation on the part of the doctor to maintain his or her own health in order to provide competent health care service.

Eventually, the doctor-patient relationship develops an entity of its own and is recognized for its own importance and therapeutic qualities. The satisfaction derived from this relationship is the most positive motivation influencing physicians to maintain their competence and avoid impairment (Mawardi, 1979b). This satisfaction permits physicians to carry out, to the best of their abilities, their part of the obligations implied by the contractlike responsibilities of that doctor-patient relationship. Without career satisfaction of some kind, resulting from what the physician is doing or the circumstances in which he is practicing, impairment occurs. As a result of the lack of any career satisfaction, too much of the physician's time and energy may be diverted to the pursuit of other satisfactions. This subtracts from the time and energy that can be allotted to patient care and continuing education.

According to some physicians, the development of hobbies and strong interests outside of medicine helps prevent impairment and burnout. Although outside interests may become engrossing, and thus reduce the amount of time spent in the practice of medicine, they are certainly preferred alternatives to the physician's turning to alcohol or drugs. Some of the most popular interests of physicians include tennis, sailing, camping, traveling, flying, painting, writing, politics, and investments. Some of these leisure-time activities have spurred involvement in second careers (Mawardi, 1981).

An additional positive influence promoting physician competence is the movement in recent years toward group practice. Group practice provides the opportunity for high-quality health care, primarily by relying on a number of skilled colleagues for dependable, adequate medical coverage for physicians. The time thus released enables physicians to have more or less regular hours, limit the number of patients seen daily, be on call at night without having to treat patients the next day, enjoy vacations and leisure time without the possibility of being suddenly called away, and subscribe to continuing education courses. Groups also serve to relieve some impairment by insisting that their members meet certain qualifying criteria of the various American boards. In addition, groups require that their associates complete requisite numbers of postgraduate educational credits each year; they provide ready collegial consultation; and they also provide challenge, support, and advice in the service of keeping abreast of current developments in the field. Finally, groups often have built-in retirement plans that help alleviate the disability problems that may come with advancing age. Group practice can be a powerful influence on the quality of medical care and the manner in which it is delivered in the United States today. Why isn't all medicine then practiced in groups? To some, group membership implies limitations on individual autonomy. This is an overriding deterrent for a number of physicians.

Doctors in solo practice, however, are a paradox. They enjoy their autonomy and their image as individualists ("I like this way of working because I'm really the last of the rugged individualists"). They perceive that they can behave and practice medicine as they please. On the other hand, they are probably among the most encumbered persons in our society. They put in long hours at strenuous work and are always on call. They have little leisure time and don't take vacations. They have little time to spend with their families or friends. They may know another's children better than they know their own. In response to an interview question ("If time and money were satisfactorily arranged so that you could have a year completely free, what would you do?"), some solo practitioners found it impossible even to imagine getting away for a year. But, they believe, and they believe that their patients believe, that they are practicing the "best" kind of medicine. They are always available to their patients, day or night. Their patients know exactly whom they'll reach when they call and who will respond to their call. Particularly if the physician practicing solo is the only medically trained person in the area, he or she can scarcely be held culpable for occasional and minor instances of less than optimal performance that result from fatigue and overwork. The uneven geographical distribution of physicians and other medical services is in part responsible for what may appear to the casual observer to be only further examples of physician impairment.

Not all physicians in solo practice are like those described above. Some solo practitioners do manage to escape from professional pressures. They organize themselves and their practices in a manner that reduces stress. They are able to provide high-quality medical care characterized by the continuity in doctor-patient relationships which is regarded by many physicians and patients alike as the *sine qua non* of health care. Some graduates from the revised program in medical education now "confess" to inserting free-time periods in their schedules. Among these same graduates, whose medical education had emphasized an individual's responsibility for continuing training, several have taken an entire year or two to update their skills or to acquire new ones. Usually, this has meant that the practice was essentially abandoned for a period of time, but, in the physician's eyes, the overriding advantage to physician and patient alike was an increase in the physician's knowledge and skill. These same graduates, whose medical educations promoted an environment of cooperation instead of competition, have begun more frequently to call upon their colleagues for advice, thus adding to their knowledge as well as reducing their isolation. Building up cordial relationships with fellow physicians may also permit the solo practitioner to develop a means of obtaining occasional coverage for his or her practice.

This chapter has discussed various kinds and degrees of physician impairment in the practice of medicine and has considered some of the sanctions that impel the physician toward moral action in medical practice. It has also examined some of the results of sanction from peer review, insurance companies, and organizations granting relicensure and recertification; it has examined sources of satisfaction in the doctor-patient relationship and the implications of changes in styles of practice. The attention newly paid to physician impairment and burnout may well prove helpful in generating new solutions to these problems; it remains to be seen, though, whether these "solutions" generate new problems and impairments.

REFERENCES

American Medical Association Council on Mental Health Report. The sick physician: Impairment by psychiatric disorders, including alcoholism and drug dependence. *The Journal of the American Medical Association,* 1973, **223**, 684–687.

Blachly, P. H., Disher, W., & Roduner, G. Suicide by physicians. *The Bulletin of Suicidology.* Chevy Chase, Md.: National Clearinghouse for Mental Health Information, December 1968, pp. 1–18.

Casterline, R. L. *Deviant behavior in physicians.* Paper presented at the 69th Annual Congress on Medical Education at the American Medical Association, Chicago, February 1973.

Cranshaw, R.; Bruce, J. R.; Eraker, P. L.; Greenbaum, M.; Lindemann, J. E.; & Schmidt, D. E. An epidemic of suicide among physicians on probation. *Journal of the American Medical Association,* 1980, **243**(19), 1915–1917.

Ham, T. H. Medical education at Western Reserve University: A progress report for the sixteen years, 1946–1962. *New England Journal of Medicine,* 1962, **267**, 868–874 (October 25) and 916–923 (November 1).

Horsley, J. E. When to "tattle" on physician misconduct. *RN,* 1978, **4**(12), 17–20.

Hussey, H. H. Suicide among physicians (editorial). *Journal of the American Medical Association,* 1974, **228**(9), 1149–1150.

Jones, R. E. A study of 100 physician psychiatric inpatients. *American Journal of Psychiatry,* 1977, **134**(10), 1119–1123.

Mawardi, B. H. *Physicians and their careers,* Ann Arbor, Mich.: University Microfilms International, 1979. (a)

Mawardi, B. H. Satisfactions, dissatisfactions, and causes of stress in medical practice. *The Journal of the American Medical Association,* 1979, **241**, 1483–1486. (b)

Mawardi, B. H. *Reshaping a career: The count-down to retirement.* Paper presented at the Conference on Successful Retirement, The Cleveland Clinic Foundation, Cleveland, September 1981.

Murray, R. M. Characteristics and prognosis of alcoholic doctors. *British Medical Journal,* 1976, **2**, 1537–1539.

Pitts, F. N., Jr.; Schuller, A. B.; Rich, C. L.; & Pitts, A. F. Suicide among U.S. women physicians, 1967–1972. *American Journal of Psychiatry,* 1979, **136**(5), 694–696.

Rich C. L. & Pitts, F. N., Jr., Suicide by male physicians during a five-year period. *American Journal of Psychiatry,* 1979, **136**(8), 1089–1090.

Rose, K. D. & Rosow, I. Physicians who kill themselves. *Archives of General Psychiatry,* 1973, **29**, 800–805.

Ross, M. Suicide is preventable. *Medical Tribune,* April 5, 1967.

Sargent, D. A.; Jensen, V. W.; Petty, T. A.; & Raskin, H. Preventing physician suicide: The role of family, colleagues, and organized medicine. *Journal of the American Medical Association,* 1977, **237**(2), 143–145.

Vaillant, G. E., Sobowale, N. C., & McArthur, C. Some psychologic vulnerabilities of physicians. *The New England Journal of Medicine,* 1972, **287**, 372–375.

9

Job Satisfaction and Burnout in Social Work

Srinika Jayaratne
and
Wayne A. Chess

A vast array of research and literature is available on job satisfaction in the American work force but little of this information addresses human service professionals. The target groups in these research efforts have been blue-collar and white-collar workers, and in some instances, farm workers and managerial personnel (see, for example, Caplan et al., 1975; Quinn & Sheppard, 1974; Quinn & Staines, 1978). In contrast, the literature on burnout is primarily concerned with human service professionals (see, for example, Cherniss, 1980; Maslach, 1976; Maslach & Jackson, 1981; Pines & Kafry, 1978).

A review of these two "sets" of literature reveals some notable similarities and dissimilarities. The job satisfaction literature discusses the notions of stress and strain and their physical and emotional impact extensively but they never use the term or discuss the notion of burnout. This is primarily because the term "burnout" appeared in the literature only recently. The burnout literature tries to draw a distinction between burnout and job satisfaction, but then proceeds to discuss stresses and strains similar to those identified in the job satisfaction literature, relating them to emotional and physical well-being. One distinct difference between these two sets of literature is that the job satisfaction research tends to be empirical while the burnout literature (with a few exceptions) tends to be comprised primarily of case studies and studies that are qualitative in nature. It is also perhaps fair to state that, as a function of its longer history, job satisfaction has been conceptualized somewhat better both theoretically and methodologically than has the phenomenon of burnout (see, for example, Dunnette, Campbell, & Hakel, 1967; Locke, 1969, 1976; Nord, 1977).

Within the profession of social work, literature on job satisfaction is relatively scarce, with the most recent information being in unpublished dissertations (Gann, 1979; Glicken, 1979). The majority of the published social work literature tends to be on burnout rather than on job satisfaction (Barrett & McKelvey, 1980; Daley, 1979; Mattingly, 1977), on child care workers rather than a broad spectrum of social workers (Barrett & McKelvey, 1980; Daley, 1979; Harrison, 1980; Wasserman, 1970), and primarily qualitative, with essays on personal experience or descriptions of specific programs (Karger, 1981; Mattingly, 1977; Pines & Kafry, 1978). The result, therefore, is a body of literature which is severely constrained in terms of its generalizability to social workers at large.

The present study was conceptualized within the framework of job satisfaction and its relationship to work stress and health. This formulation is in keeping with most analyses dealing with work stress, job satisfaction, and mental and physical health (see, for example, House, 1981; LaRocco, House, & French, 1980; Kahn, 1970; McGrath, 1970). Figure 9.1 presents our conceptualization of the perceived relationships and is based primarily on the work of the above-mentioned authors. As evidenced in this figure, however, our model includes some factors that have been commonly investigated by both job satisfaction and burnout researchers (for example, role ambiguity, role conflict, and workload), some factors that seem to have been investigated only by job satisfaction researchers (for example, comfort and promotions), and some factors that fall strictly within the domain of burnout (depersonalization and emotional exhaustion). While the conceptual model used here was developed within the context of job satisfaction, we believe that it is directly applicable to the study of burnout as well, and is therefore employed to investigate aspects of both phenomena.

STUDY VARIABLES

Job satisfaction has been viewed in a number of different ways, but all definitions construe it as a multidimensional concept (see, for example, Dunnette et al., 1967; Locke, 1969; Nord, 1977). The approach used in the present study was developed at the Institute for Social Research at the University of Michigan, by researchers studying quality of employment and worker health (Caplan et al., 1975; Quinn & Sheppard, 1974; Quinn & Staines, 1978). The measurement strategy relies on the person's perceptions of the work situation rather than on the absolute nature of the work context. It is deemed similar to what Kurt Lewin (1951) called the "psychological environment," and it is basically a report of an individual's subjective assessment of a situation.

Quinn and his colleagues concluded that job satisfaction is best measured by using both a general affective measure of satisfaction and a series of measures of satisfaction with various facets of the job. In the present study, the global

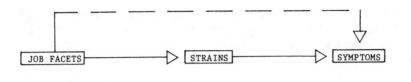

Comfort   Job Satisfaction   Anxiety

Challenge   Burnout   Depression

Financial Rewards   depersonaliztion   Irritability

Promotions   emotional exhaustion Somatics

                    Nonstress   Mental/Physical

Role Ambiguity

Role Conflict

Workload

                    Stress

Fig. 9.1.   Conceptual model and study variables.

facet-free measure of job satisfaction is the single item: "All in all, how satisfied would you say you are with your job?" The response options are on a four-item Likert scale ranging from "very satisfied" to "not at all satisfied." In attempting to measure various facets of the job, we had to decide which aspects of the job would be most important. Our selection of job facets was guided by prior research, our conceptual model, and our interest in bridging the notions of job satisfaction and burnout. All of the facet indices used in this study were based on a Likert-scale response format. Data on scale construction, validity, and reliability are available in Caplan et al. (1975), Quinn and Sheppard (1974), and Quinn and Staines (1978).

The seven job facets measured are:

1. *Comfort:* this index consists of seven items and has a score range from 7 to 28. The lower the score, the greater the perceived comfort. This is a measure of the creature comforts offered by the workplace. An item example: "The physical surroundings are pleasant."
2. *Challenge:* this index consists of six items and has a score range from 6 to 24. The lower the score, the greater the perceived challenge. This is a measure of how stimulating the job is perceived to be by the worker. An item example: "The problems I am expected to solve are hard enough."

3. *Financial Rewards:* this index consists of three items and has a score range from 3 to 12. The lower the score, the better the perceived rewards. This is a measure of pay, security, and fringe benefits. An item example: "The pay is good."
4. *Promotions:* this index consists of three items and has a score range from 3 to 12. The lower the score, the better the perceived promotional opportunities. This is a measure of the worker's perceptions of promotional changes, as well as the fairness of the process. An item example: "Promotions are handled fairly."
5. *Role Ambiguity:* this index consists of four items and has a score range from 4 to 20. The lower the score, the less the perceived role ambiguity. This is a measure of the perceptions a worker has about the clarity of the work situation. An item example: "Work objectives are well defined."
6. *Role Conflict:* this index consists of four items and has a score range from 4 to 16. The higher the score, the less the perceived conflict. This is a measure of the conflicting demands that a worker reports as being present in the job. An item example: "On my job, I can't satisfy everybody at the same time."
7. *Workload:* this index consists of four items and has a score range from 4 to 20. The higher the score, the lower the perceived workload. This is a measure of the worker's perceptions of the amount of work that needs to be done. An item example: "How often does your job require you to work very hard?"

In measuring burnout, we relied on the operational definition and scales developed by Christina Maslach and her colleagues (Maslach, 1976; Maslach & Jackson, 1981). We employed the dimensions of "depersonalization" and "emotional exhaustion" in order to measure the extent of reported burnout, but we did not use the scales in their original form. While the depersonalization scale was used in its entirety, only the intensity dimension was measured. In addition, we did not allow a "never" category in our response alternatives, as Maslach does, and we simply presented a seven-point response option. To measure emotional exhaustion, we use the single item, "I feel burned out from my work," rather than the full scale. This decision was predicated by the observation that since this item alone had such a high factor loading (.81) with the total scale (Maslach & Jackson, 1981), we could use this single item and get a reasonable reading on the extent of emotional exhaustion. As before, we employed only the seven-point intensity measure and did not use the "never" category. Our decisions were dictated by a pragmatic need to shorten the questionnaire. In view of these changes, our data are not directly comparable to scores obtained by using the Maslach scales in their original form.

Since both job satisfaction and burnout are undoubtedly related to job turnover, we decided to include a measure of "intent to turnover." Here we employed a single item from the quality of employment surveys: "Taking everything into consideration, how likely is it that you will make a *genuine effort* to find a new job with another employer within the next year?" The responses ranged from "very likely" to "not at all likely."

The final series of scales included in the study are indices of mental and physical health. The measures of anxiety, depression, irritability, and somatic complaints used here were employed by Quinn and his colleagues as well as by Caplan et al. (1975) in their national surveys. Again, information on scale construction, reliability, and validity are available in Quinn and Sheppard (1974) and Quinn and Staines (1978).

In summary, this study incorporates a series of measures dealing with job satisfaction and burnout, and a series of indices tapping dimensions of mental and physical health. All of the measures have been theoretically and conceptually tied to the model presented in Figure 9.1. In addition, the measures used in this research have been employed previously in studies of job satisfaction and burnout, and have reasonably high validity and reliability, with the possible exception of the burnout scales which are being used in a modified form.

STUDY DESIGN AND SAMPLE

Since we were interested in obtaining a diverse sample of social workers, we decided to randomly sample the membership of the National Association of Social Workers. NASW is the primary professional association for social workers in the United States, with a membership of around 85,000. A ten-page questionnaire, a cover letter, and a commitment-to-cooperate postcard were mailed to each of 1,173 randomly selected potential respondents. If the commitment postcard was not received from a potential respondent within three weeks, then that person was sent a second questionnaire and cover letter. This procedure resulted in the return of 853 questionnaires, a response rate (72.7 percent) considerably higher than that obtained from previous studies with this population, and certainly a very good response rate by any criterion (Kirk & Fischer, 1976; Taber & Vattano, 1970).

We have restricted the current analysis to those respondents who are working full-time (40 hours/week or more), on the assumption that part-time workers may have somewhat different perceptions of the work context. This resulted in an analytic sample of 553 respondents. The respondents are mostly female (57.7 percent) and predominantly white (87.0 percent). Slightly less than two-thirds are married, and the majority (60.5 percent) have an annual income of over $20,000 from their social work jobs. In terms of work characteristics, a little more than half the sample received their MSW degrees after 1971, are employed in public agencies, and have been in their current positions for more than three years. There appears to be a tendency toward turnover, with over 50 percent having held four or more positions.

RESULTS

Perhaps the most gratifying finding in this study is the extent of satisfaction with the job reported by the respondents. Of the social workers in our sample, 35.4 percent indicate that they are very satisfied with their work, and an additional 46.3 percent report that they are somewhat satisfied. On the other hand, our respondents also tell us they are job hunting, with 43.1 percent of the sample indicating that they are very likely or somewhat likely to "make a *genuine effort* to find a new job with another employer within the next year." Of the workers reporting satisfaction with their jobs, over a third (34.0 percent) hope to find new employment, a perplexing, although not surprising, finding (Armstrong, 1978; Kermish & Kushin, 1969).

In theory, we would expect a very high inverse relationship between job satisfaction and intent to turnover. In the present sample, the zero-order correlation is − .58 between these two variables. This is, of course, a significant correlation coefficient but it is somewhat lower than was anticipated. This raises the possibility that workers may be using somewhat different frames of reference in assessing job satisfaction and intentions to turnover. That is, they may use one set of criteria to evaluate the job and another set to decide whether or not to remain on the job. In order to understand the situation better, we conducted multiple regression analyses on job satisfaction and intent to turnover, using the different job facet indices as predictors.

Two features clearly stand out from these analyses. First, whereas 45 percent of the total variance is explained by the job facets in the determination of job satisfaction, only 26 percent of the variance is accounted for in intent to turnover. On face value alone, it appears that the model employed here fits the notion of job satisfaction better than it fits the notion of turnover intent. By implication then, some significant variables related to job discontinuance appear to have been omitted from the model. What these may be is, of course, an empirical question.

The second feature of these analyses is that the same set of variables emerge as significant predictors in both job satisfaction and turnover intent. Challenge, financial rewards, and promotions are common predictors in both dimensions, while role ambiguity appears to have a marginal role in the assessment of job satisfaction. Some specific aspects of the regression analyses are also worthy of note here. Of the 45 percent variance accounted for in job satisfaction, challenge alone is responsible for 36 percent, which clearly illustrates the importance of this job facet to these respondents in the evaluation of job satisfaction. A similar finding was reported by Weinberger (1970) in a study of job satisfaction and retention of social workers. On the other hand, financial rewards account for 16 percent of the total 26 percent variance explained in turnover intent. Thus, the facet of financial rewards appears to be a prime determinant in the decision to turnover. Challenge added an additional 7 percent to the explained variance in this instance.

Thus, while the factors associated with job satisfaction and turnover are virtually the same, different weights are attached to the facets, depending on which dimension is being considered. But, since the same grouping of job facets are involved, from an interventional perspective, one could argue that agency action that addresses the dimensions of challenge, promotions, and financial rewards may result in higher levels of job satisfaction and decreased turnover. It is of particular interest here that these characteristics of the job are directly under the control of (and can be manipulated by) organizational structure, procedure, and policy.

One other comment needs to be made with regard to these analyses. Those variables identified as "stressors" in the literature (role ambiguity, role conflict, and workload) contribute very little toward explaining job satisfaction or turnover intent. This raises some interesting questions. The burnout literature has consistently argued that role ambiguity, role conflict, and workload (among others) are important contributors to the "burnout syndrome" (Barrett & McKelvey, 1980; Harrison, 1980; Pines & Kafry, 1978). As noted earlier, the literature has made a conscious effort to distinguish between burnout and job satisfaction, arguing that these are interrelated but not identical dimensions (Harrison, 1980; Maslach & Jackson, 1981). The current data lead to two observations in this regard. First, while the stressors may predict burnout, they do not help explain job satisfaction. Therefore, without directly testing the notion, it could be speculated that job satisfaction and burnout are of a different order. Second, it is perhaps fair to say that the dimensions of challenge, promotions, and financial rewards have not been investigated systematically by researchers studying burnout. If these facets were included, would they emerge as stronger correlates of burnout—that is, stronger than role ambiguity, role conflict, and workload? Both these issues will be addressed later in this chapter.

While the analyses have thus far considered the relative weights attached to the different job facets in assessing job satisfaction, they did not indicate whether or not there are absolute differences in felt satisfaction with the facets. That is, would those individuals who report higher levels of job satisfaction report lower levels of role ambiguity and role conflict, and conversely, higher levels of challenge and comfort, etc.? In theory, one would expect this to be the case. In all instances (with perhaps the exception of workload), this is indeed true, as indicated in Table 9.1. We performed analyses of variance on the different variables and, with the exception of the role conflict and workload dimensions, aposteriori Scheffé comparisons indicated that the mean differences are significant between all three levels of satisfaction. In other words, the "very satisfied" group is not only different from the "not satisfied" group, but it is also different from the "somewhat satisfied" group, and the "somewhat satisfied" group is significantly different from the "not satisfied" group. In role conflict, there is no significant difference between the somewhat and not satisfied groups, and in workload, the only significant difference is between the

Table 9.1. Analyses of Variance on Predictor Variables by Levels of Reported Job Satisfaction.

Satisfaction		Comfort	Challenge	Financial Rewards	Promotions	Role Ambiguity	Role Conflict	Workload
Very Satisfied	Mean:	14.07	8.31	4.95	7.00	6.59	9.63	7.89
Somewhat Satisfied	Mean:	16.67	10.45	6.38	8.70	8.06	8.56	7.50
Not at all Satisfied	Mean:	17.75	13.93	7.20	10.33	9.90	8.23	8.32
		$F = 41.155$	$F = 148.23$	$F = 45.293$	$F = 74.763$	$F = 48.294$	$F = 10.360$	$F = 2.609$
		$p \leq .001$	$p \leq .0001$	$p \leq .0001$	$p \leq .0001$	$p \leq .0001$	$p \leq .0001$	$p \leq .07$

somewhat and not satisfied (an anomalous finding in this instance). These data clearly indicate that overall job satisfaction is directly related to and varies with perceptions of satisfaction with the different job facets.

These analyses have led us to some tentative conclusions. First, the job facets of challenge, promotional opportunities, and financial rewards seem to be the most important predictors of job satisfaction and turnover intent. Second, the stress variables of role ambiguity, role conflict, and workload contribute very little toward the explanation of job satisfaction or turnover intent. And third, expressions of overall satisfaction with the job do indeed covary with perceptions of satisfaction with the various job facets.

It was pointed out earlier that the stressors of role ambiguity, role conflict, and workload have been correlated with burnout in the literature. On the other hand, the analyses that are up-to-date with the present sample indicate that these variables seem to have little to do with job satisfaction. The zero-order correlation coefficients in the present study between job satisfaction and depersonalization is $-.25$, and between job satisfaction and emotional exhaustion, $-.40$. The strength of these relationships suggests that job satisfaction and burnout are overlapping dimensions and that they are certainly not identical. Given the reported relationship between stress and burnout noted above, one would predict that these variables would emerge as significant correlates of burnout. In order to examine this question, we proceeded to conduct multiple regression analyses on the burnout dimensions using the same set of job facets as predictors.

The results of these analyses are presented in Table 9.2. They are not what we anticipated. Challenge emerges as the only significant predictor of depersonalization, and promotional opportunities as the only significant predictor of emotional exhaustion. Role ambiguity, role conflict, and workload do not emerge as significant predictors in these analyses. Furthermore, the total variance explained is very low in both instances (12 percent of depersonalization and 8 percent of emotional exhaustion), suggesting that the model used in these analyses may be relatively incomplete. In contrast, note that these same predictors account for 45 percent of the variance in job satisfaction.

In summary, it does indeed appear that job satisfaction and burnout are of a different order, at least as measured by the indices used in this study. Not only are the correlation coefficients between the two dimensions low, but the same set of predictor variables also relate somewhat differently to each dimension. One of the most pervasive findings in the present study is that the stress variables do not play a significant role in either the assessment of job satisfaction or in the reporting of burnout. Rather, the job facets of challenge, promotions, and financial rewards, either together or individually, emerge as significant predictors in both instances. These findings are clearly at odds with previous studies on burnout where stress factors were found to be highly related to burnout.

Table 9.2.   Job Facets as Predictors: Multiple Regression Analyses On
Depersonalization, Emotional Exhaustion, and Job Satisfaction.

Depersonalization	Beta Weight	t-stat	Significance
Comfort	.09	1.175	ns
Challenge	.29	4.639	.0001
Financial			
Rewards	.01	0.048	ns
Promotions	.05	0.815	ns
Role Ambiguity	.03	0.506	ns
Role Conflict	.06	0.879	ns
Workload	.04	0.524	ns
	R = .35		R^2 = .12
Emotional Exhaustion			
Comfort	.05	0.769	ns
Challenge	.04	0.691	ns
Financial			
Rewards	.08	1.541	ns
Promotions	.19	3.659	.0005
Role Ambiguity	.04	0.676	ns
Role Conflict	.04	0.716	ns
Workload	.01	0.828	ns
	R = .28		R^2 = .08
Job Satisfaction			
Comfort	.09	1.720	ns
Challenge	.41	9.761	.0001
Financial			
Rewards	.12	3.074	.01
Promotions	.19	4.755	.0001
Role Ambiguity	.08	2.033	.05
Role Conflict	.03	0.540	ns
Workload	.05	0.994	ns
	R = .67		R^2 = .45

In our final analyses, we looked at the consequences of dissatisfaction and burnout. In order to conduct these analyses, we simply divided the respondents by their reported levels of satisfaction (very satisfied, somewhat satisfied, not at all satisfied) and burnout (high, medium, and low scores on the emotional exhaustion scale). We then compared the scores obtained on the various mental and physical health measures across the three groups. It was anticipated that greater symptomatology would be reported by those who indicated higher levels of burnout or greater job dissatisfaction.

The data were as expected, with lack of satisfaction with the job and/or feelings of burnout being directly related to the various mental and physical symptoms. We performed analyses of variance on the different symptom scales using the three levels of satisfaction and burnout as stratification categories. All of the main effects analyses were significant, with the exception of the anxiety dimension, where no differences appeared between the satisfied and the dissatisfied, and the burned out and the not burned out. When aposteriori Scheffé comparisons were performed, as before, all of the levels showed significant differences in both the satisfaction and burnout dimensions. The one exception was the depression index in both instances; the difference between the very satisfied and the somewhat satisfied, and the low and medium levels of burnout were nonsignificant. In all other instances, all comparisons were significant. In effect, those individuals who are dissatisfied with their jobs, as well as those individuals who are burned out, report significantly higher levels of depression, irritability, and somatic complaints. That is, the consequences of burnout and job dissatisfaction appear to be the same with respect to the reporting of these particular mental and physical symptoms.

CONCLUSION

For the present sample, it appears that job satisfaction, burnout, and intention to turnover are all related in terms of causal attributes. The challenge of the job, promotional opportunities, and financial rewards emerge as the best predictors of job satisfaction and turnover. On a somewhat similar vein, challenge emerged as the only significant predictor of depersonalization, and promotions as the only significant predictor of emotional exhaustion. What is most important is that the stress factors of role ambiguity, role conflict, and workload, which have been tied to burnout in the literature, did not appear to be important predictors of burnout, job satisfaction, or intent to turnover. On the whole, however, the predictor variables employed in the present study seem to better explain job satisfaction in terms of the total variance accounted for while they explain relatively little of the burnout dimensions. It appears, then, that the model used here is more applicable to the study of job satisfaction, and that other variables should be considered for use in studies of burnout.

While the above explanation is based on the observation that job satisfaction and burnout are of a different order, the same does not seem to hold true when one considers the consequences of job dissatisfaction and burnout. Both groups record high levels of depression, irritability, and somatic complaints. It is conceivable that the difference may be one of degree, with burned out individuals recording higher levels of the symptoms than dissatisfied workers. This would, however, imply that job satisfaction and burnout are on a unitary dimension, a position contrary to that noted above.

The present analyses have posed several questions about the nature of and relationship between job satisfaction and burnout, both in terms of their causal and consequential elements. Clearly, the present data do not "fit" what has been found to be the case in much of the previous research on burnout. The reasons for this can be numerous. On the basis of the present data, however, we would like to suggest some recommendations for future research in this area.

First, burnout research should systematically incorporate nonstress variables as predictors along with stress factors. Failure to do so may result in a skewed and incomplete perspective. Second, given the potentially high level of overlap between job satisfaction and burnout, further effort should be made to assess the extent of the differences between the dimensions critically, or to discover whether or not we are dealing with a unitary dimension. And third, the predictive model employed here appears to be viable but incomplete, particularly in assessing burnout. Other predictor variables derived from a theoretical and conceptual basis should be included in the model, such as professionals' perceived level of competence and autonomy.

From the perspective of the worker under stress, these data would suggest that the existence of stress does not necessarily lead to turnover or even to dissatisfaction with the job. That is, workers may report feelings of burnout and still remain on the job, be relatively happy with their work, and perhaps even perform well. But, since signs of depression, irritability, and somatic complaints are common to both lack of satisfaction with the job and burnout, efforts to help workers cope with these strains would undoubtedly be beneficial. Here, stress-management procedures, self-support groups, and other strategies recommended in the burnout literature may be of particular value in helping workers cope. While we have argued that the job dimensions most strongly related to strain are under the control of the organization, it is conceivable that they are difficult to alter. Under these circumstances, the availability of a mechanism within the agency to handle such issues would be of significant value.

REFERENCES

Armstrong, K. L. *How can we avoid burnout?* Berkeley, Ca.: Berkeley Planning Associates, 1978.

Barrett, M. C. & McKelvey, J. Stresses and strains of the child welfare workers: Typologies for assessment. *Child Welfare,* 1980, **59**, 277–285.

Caplan, R. D.; Cobb, S.; French, J. R. P.; Van Harrison, R.; & Pinneau, S. R. *Job Demands and Worker Health.* Washington, D.C.: U.S. Department of Health, Education, and Welfare, 1975.

Cherniss, C. *Professional burnout in human service organizations.* New York: Prager, 1980.

Daley, M. R. Burnout: Smoldering problem in the protective services. *Social Work,* 1979, **24**, 375–379.

Dunnette, S., Campbell, J. P., & Hakel, M. D. Factors contributing to job satisfaction and job dissatisfaction in six occupational groups. *Organizational Behavior and Human Performance,* 1967, **2**, 143–174.

Gann, M. L. The role of personality factors and job characteristics in burnout: A study of social service workers. Unpublished doctoral dissertation, University of California, Berkeley, 1979.

Glicken, M. D. A regional study of job satisfaction of social workers. Unpublished doctoral dissertation, University of Utah, 1977.

Harrison, W. D. Role strain and burnout in child protective service workers. *Social Service Review,* 1980, **54**, 31-44.

Haynes, K. S. Job satisfaction of mid-management social workers. *Administration In Social Work,* 1979, **3**, 207-217.

House, J. S. *Work stress and social support.* Reading, Mass.: Addison-Wesley, 1981.

Kahn, R. L. Some propositions toward a researchable conceptualization of stress. In J. E. McGrath (Ed.), *Social and psychological factors in stress.* New York: Holt, Rinehart, & Winston, 1970.

Karger, H. J. Burnout as alienation. *Social Service Review,* 1981, **55**, 270-283.

Kermish, I. & Kushin, F. Why high turnover? Social staff losses in county welfare agency. *Public Welfare,* 1969, **27**, 34-35.

Kirk, S. A. & Fischer, J. Do social workers understand research? *Journal of Education for Research,* 1976, **12**, 63-70.

Lewin, K. *Field theory in social science,* New York: Harper & Row, 1951.

LaRocco, J. M., House, J. S., & French, J. R. P. Social support, occupational stress, and health. *Journal of Health and Social Behavior,* 1980, **21**, 202-218.

Locke, E. A. What is job satisfaction? *Organizational Behavior and Human Performance,* 1969, **4**, 309-336.

Locke, E. A. The nature and causes of job satisfaction. In M. D. Dunnette (Ed.), *Handbook of industrial and organizational psychology.* Chicago, Ill.: Rand McNally, 1976.

Maslach, C. Burned-out. *Human Behavior,* 1976, **5**, 16-22.

Maslach, C. & Jackson, S. E. The measurement of experienced burnout. *Journal of Occupational Behavior,* 1981, **2**, 99-113.

Mattingly, M. A. Symposium: Stress and burnout in child care. *Child Care,* 1977, **6**, 85-89.

McGrath, J. E. *Social and psychological factors in stress.* New York: Holt, Rinehart, & Winston, 1970.

Nord, W. R. Job satisfaction reconsidered. *American Psychologist,* 1977, **32**, 1026-1035.

Pines, A. & Kafry, D. Occupational tedium in the social services. *Social Work,* 1978, **23**, 499-509.

Quinn, R. P. & Sheppard, L. J. *The 1972-73 quality of employment survey.* Ann Arbor, Mich.: ISR, 1974.

Quinn, R. P. & Staines, G. *The 1975-76 quality of employment survey.* Ann Arbor, Mich.: ISR, 1978.

Taber, M. A. & Vattano, A. J. Clinical and social orientations in social work: An empirical study. *Social Service Review,* 1970, **44**, 34-43.

Wasserman, H. Early careers of professional social workers in a public child welfare agency. *Social Work,* 1970, **15**, 96.

Weinberger, P. *Job satisfaction and staff retention in social work.* San Diego, Calif.: San Diego State College School of Social Work, 1970.

10

Organizational Mediators
of the Quality of Care:
Job Stressors and Motivators
in Human Service Settings*

Russell A. Eisenstat
and
Robert D. Felner

Human service institutions, such as hospitals, schools, and mental health agencies, have been subject to frequent and often harsh criticism for the quality of care they provide. One of the central themes underlying much of this dissatisfaction has been that these institutions are often seen as impersonal, cold, and dehumanizing both by those they are charged with caring for and by professionals (Barton, 1976; Goffman, 1961; Vail, 1966). In one scathing indictment of these settings, Goffman (1961) states that institutions such as mental hospitals provide "a series of abasements, degradations, humiliations, and profanations of self" (p. 14) for those they are supposed to be serving.

There are certainly a myriad of factors that contribute to the failure of a human service agency to provide humane, high-quality care. Chronic shortages of funds and other resources, complicated, unresponsive state and federal administrative bureaucracies, and poor service linkages and communication are but a few of the persistent problems that constitute the less than optimal larger systemic environment in which human service agencies function (Sarason, 1977; Sarason & Lorentz, 1979). As these are deficiencies over which the individual agency has little control, it may be asked whether much can be done

*The authors wish to express their appreciation to May G. Kennedy, and Michael Blank for their assistance in designing and conducting some of the research on which this chapter is based. Thanks are also due to Clayton P. Alderfer and J. Richard Hackman for their helpful discussion of some of the ideas in this work.

at the agency level to improve care. The answer is a clear yes. Agencies operating within the same systemic contexts can and do differ dramatically in the quality of care they provide. This makes it clear that while ultimately, larger delivery system factors may act to limit the quality of care provided by agencies in a given service system, within these constraints, structural and organizational aspects of the agencies themselves are primarily responsible for shaping the nature of client care. It is with these variables, which may be modified at the agency or setting level to impact on quality of care, that we concern ourselves in this chapter.

The basic foundation from which the quality of care offered by an agency ultimately derives is its direct service staff. While careful organizational planning, modern facilities, and sophisticated treatment procedures certainly enhance the quality of care when the staff are skilled and committed, they are of little value without such individuals. It may be argued that whether or not such individuals are present in an agency is, to a great extent, determined by the larger delivery system factors we have previously cited. Adequate funding and the perception of the agency as part of a responsive and well-functioning system may assuredly play an important role in both attracting and retaining competent individuals. Another factor, however, that may be of such overriding importance as to influence the quality of care offered by settings that have even the most highly qualified staff, is the nature and context of the human service work experience.

Recently, both administrators and social scientists have shown an increased awareness of the needs of the workers who provide direct care (Cherniss, 1980; Freudenberger, 1975; Maslach, 1976; Sarason, 1977). It has been proposed that because of the intense emotional demands of the human service worker's job, he or she may become "burned out." Pines and Maslach (1978) have described this phenomenon as "a syndrome of physical and emotional exhaustion, involving the development of [a] negative self concept, negative job attitudes, and a loss of concern and feelings for clients" by workers (p. 223). Similarly, Cherniss (1980) has pointed out that the dictionary defines burnout as: "to fail, wear out, or become exhausted by making excessive demands on energy strength or resources" (Websters Collegiate Directionary, p. 16). These definitions make it clear that a stress model is implicit in the notion of burnout. In this framework, workers' coping abilities and resources are ultimately overwhelmed by the demands of their jobs. Approached in this way, human service work appears almost analagous to a progressive disease: when they are faced with an overwhelming set of job demands, it seems inevitable that workers will ultimately succumb to "burnout."

Evidence currently available does to some extent substantiate this bleak view of human service work. Indeed, a recent study (Eisenstat & Felner, 1981a) supports the view that the excessive quantities of work, insufficient opportunities for training, and inadequate performance feedback from other staff that characterize many human service jobs may lead workers both to become emotionally exhausted and to develop more negative attitudes and behaviors toward their clients.

Many of the recommendations researchers have made for combatting burn-out stem directly from this stress model. These recommendations generally involve devising ways of strengthening workers' levels of emotional defense against the potentially overwhelming onslaught of job demands. For example, workers have been advised to form mutual support groups to aid in coping with job stress (Maslach, 1979), to take "time outs" from direct client contact (Pines & Maslach, 1978), and to moderate unrealistically high goals for client progress (Cherniss, 1980).

Much of the literature cited above makes a strong case that the stress and burnout model is the key to understanding certain aspects of the human service job experience, and thus to accounting, at least in part, for variations in the quality of care that workers provide. Conspicuous by its absence from most of the discussions of burnout to date, however, is a careful consideration of those characteristics of the human service environment that lead to high levels of worker motivation. The importance of this omission is illustrated by the simple fact that if one focuses only on job stresses, it is difficult if not impossible to explain why individuals initially choose or ultimately decide to remain in human service jobs.

It seems, then, that there are at least two key aspects to the task confronting those human service agencies that attempt to structure work experiences which enhance the quality of care offered to clients. First, as we have seen from the burnout/stress model, jobs need to be designed in such a way that workers are not overwhelmed by job-related stressors. Second, and perhaps of equal importance, jobs need to be structured so as to maximize workers' motivations to perform them effectively. In the remainder of this chapter, we will argue that there are overlapping but distinct characteristics of human service work that lead to worker motivation on the one hand, and to job stress on the other. Moreover, we will attempt to demonstrate that the quality of the relations between workers and clients in a given setting is directly related to the relative presence or absence of these two sets of factors. Toward this end, we first consider the nature of the job characteristics that lead to increased worker motivation in human service settings. We then consider the work demands that lead to higher levels of experienced stress. Finally, we discuss ways of integrating both job stressors and motivators into a broader view of human service burnout.

JOB CHARACTERISTICS AND MOTIVATION

Organizations can create motivation through factors that are either intrinsic or extrinsic to the work itself (Porter, Lawler & Hackman, 1975). An employee's salary is an example of an important extrinsic factor that organizations use to motivate employees. In essence, by paying workers well, an organization may be seen as striking an implicit contract: "you do what we want you to do during work hours, whether or not you find it satisfying or fulfilling, and we will provide you with the financial means for doing what you like during the time you are not at work."

A number of problems exist, however, with relying exclusively on extrinsic factors such as money to motivate human service workers. First, given the current political and economic situation, many human service settings are having increasing difficulty providing adequate pay for their employees (Terrell, 1981; Worland, 1981). Second, most workers do not choose to go into human service professions primarily because of the financial rewards such work offers. Data from our own research illustrate the less than central importance of financial factors as sources of job satisfaction for human service workers. In comparing relative ratings of the importance of a series of possible job satisfactions, workers rated having a high salary and good fringe benefits as relatively less important to them than having a "sense of worthwhile accomplishment in their work" or having adequate "opportunities for personal growth and development" in their jobs.* Yet another problem caused by primary reliance on external factors as motivators of high employee satisfaction and performance is that, by themselves, they simply are not effective. The difficulty Detroit has had turning out a high-quality automobile using highly paid but alienated employees clearly attests to this (Garson, 1972).

The above remarks should not be construed to mean that adequate salaries for workers are not important to the provision of good care. As we have noted previously, adequate funding is a key element impacting on a human service setting's ability to attract and retain qualified staff. It is clear, however, that given the lack of centrality of financial rewards in the constellation of human service workers needs, as well as the generally limited impact of these reinforcers on the day-to-day quality of work performance, intrinsic motivators may be more salient targets of efforts to improve care quality.

A number of studies have attempted to identify intrinsically motivating elements in human service work. Hackman and Oldham (1980) have argued that workers' levels of internal motivation are determined by five characteristics of their jobs. They hypothesize that employees will have higher levels of internal motivation if their jobs utilize a number of workers' skills (i.e., provide task variety), if their jobs have a significant impact on the lives of others, (i.e., provide task significance), and if their jobs allow workers to complete whole and identifiable pieces of work (i.e., provide task identity). Workers' motivational levels will also be increased if their jobs are structured so that they have autonomy in how they perform their work, and if they receive feedback on the results of their efforts from the work itself. Sarason (1971) and

---

*Rating scales and data tables are available from the authors.

Sarata (1972) have suggested two additional job characteristics that may also be important motivators: the extent to which the job provides for the learning of important new skills and the extent to which the job provides for participation in important agency decisions.

The empirical research tends to show that these seven job characteristics are indeed important in motivating human service workers. Studies have consistently shown that human service workers who rate their jobs as higher on skill variety, task significance, task identity, autonomy, feedback, participation, and learning also tend to be more satisfied with their jobs (Cherniss & Egnatios, 1978a; Eisenstat & Felner, 1981a; Sarata, 1972; Sarata & Jeppesen, 1977). In addition, in our research (Eisenstat & Felner, 1981a, 1981b; Eisenstat, Felner, Kennedy, & Blank, 1981), we have found that human service workers who feel that their jobs are relatively high on these job characteristics also tend to be more involved in their jobs, and to feel that they are accomplishing more in their work.

The links between aspects of human service jobs that affect workers' levels of motivation, such as those discussed above, and the quality of the relationships between workers and clients have also been clearly established. Illustratively, in a recent work by Eisenstat and Felner (1981b), human service workers who rated their jobs lower on task significance, or who felt that their jobs offered fewer opportunities for personal learning also felt that they engaged in more dehumanizing behaviors with clients.

In another analysis, we found that human service settings that created a less stimulating job environment for workers tended to create a less stimulating treatment environment for clients as well. That is, in settings where workers reported that their jobs were lower on motivators such as autonomy, task significance or learning, clients also were allowed significantly less autonomy. Similarly, in settings where staff felt that they were learning less, clients were exposed to a less emotionally supportive treatment environment as well.

As may be seen from the foregoing discussion, we have identified a number of aspects of human service jobs that affect both workers' levels of motivation and the quality of their relationships with clients. It would seem then, at first glance, to be relatively simple for agencies to improve both client care and worker satisfaction by designing workers' jobs to maximize the presence of these characteristics. Upon further examination, however, a number of aspects of the human service work environment become apparent which may impede efforts to create internally motivating jobs. We will now briefly highlight a few of the more salient of these barriers.

BARRIERS TO JOB ENRICHMENT

Difficulties for workers in receiving positive feedback on the results of their efforts with clients seem intrinsic to the tasks and goals of human service work. For example, in many human service areas, such as work with the psychiatrically disabled or the mentally retarded, client change, particularly improvement, may be extremely slow and difficult to measure (Sarata, 1974). Indeed, as Maslach (1978) has observed, rather than receiving positive feedback, the worker with direct-care responsibility often becomes "an immediate and visible symbol" of the institutional setting "which is viewed as making the client's life more difficult rather than less" (p. 120). The result is that all too often when the human service worker receives direct feedback at all from clients, it is negative.

Another possible source of feedback for human service workers is from their supervisors. However, even when workers receive positive feedback from supervisors, they may discount it because the administrators' values do not agree with those of the direct service providers. Sarason (1971), for example, has noted that teachers often feel they are being judged by supervisors according to the amount of material they are able to cover in a given amount of time, and by their success in keeping their classes quiet and orderly, rather than by their true ability to promote learning as they might wish. The discounting by staff of feedback received from supervisors may also explain Eisenstat and Felners' (1981a) finding that the degree of feedback from supervisors and other staff is not significantly associated with how much workers feel they are accomplishing in their jobs.

The motivating potential of human service jobs is also reduced in a number of ways by overspecialization. For example, there seems to be an implicit norm in many human service settings that the duties of direct care staff should only involve providing client care while administrators should be given total responsibility for major policy decisions. Consequently, human service workers often report having fewer opportunities to participate in decision making than they desire (Cherniss & Egnatios, 1978a). Functional specialization also decreases the presence of two other job motivators: workers' opportunities to exercise a range of skills on the job and to learn significant new skills. Teachers, for instance, spend year after year teaching children of the same age the same material (Sarason, 1971), and legal aide lawyers find themselves dealing with the same kinds of cases again and again (Cherniss et al., 1979). The division of labor occurs in these human service organizations for the same reasons that it takes place in other work settings; it helps to increase the efficiency with which these organizations are able to accomplish their objectives (Porter et al., 1975). If carried to excess, however, the result may be the creation of boring and routinized work that leads to a loss of worker motivation.

While not exhaustive, the above examples illustrate the difficult problems confronting human service agencies seeking to increase the motivating potential of their workers' jobs. Yet even if an agency is able to overcome these obstacles, creating internally motivating work is not sufficient by itself to decrease the risk of worker burnout. Motivating job characteristics are, as shown above, related to higher levels of worker satisfaction, and to more humane treatment of clients; however, the presence or absence of job motivators does not seem to be directly related to that state of "physical and emotional exhaustion" which Pines and Maslach argue is a key element of burnout. Illustratively, in a study examining a variety of human service settings, including transitional care facilities, schools, and day care centers (Eisenstat & Felner, 1981b), it was found that feedback from staff was the only job motivator that was significantly related to ratings of Emotional Exhaustion on the Maslach Burnout Inventory. Similarly, in a study of staff in community mental health centers, Cherniss and Egnatios (1978b) found that the items that were sources of positive satisfaction for workers were very different from those that workers found dissatisfying. Again, intrinsic or motivating work characteristics, such as opportunities for learning or human development, largely accounted for the sources of job satisfaction, while other aspects of the work environment such as poor communication, lack of organization, inefficiency, and excess amounts of work accounted for the sources of dissatisfaction.

JOB STRESSORS AND EMOTIONAL EXHAUSTION

The job characteristics that Cherniss and Egnatios (1978b) found were related to worker dissatisfaction primarily fall into the category of organizational stressors. These stressors arise in any situation where individuals are confronted with demands at work that threaten to overwhelm their "capabilities and resources" for effective performance (McGrath, 1976, p. 1352). For example, workers may lack the information necessary to perform their jobs successfully, or they may be confronted with so much work that they are unable to function effectively.

The foregoing literature reveals that if workers are placed in nonmotivating jobs the result is a decrease in their levels of job satisfaction and involvement, but not an increase in their level of emotional and physical exhaustion. By contrast, stressful aspects of human service jobs seem to have exactly the opposite effect; that is, job stressors do not appear to affect workers' motivation significantly, but have a very great influence on workers' level of exhaustion. Hence, we have found that variations in the levels of job stressors are unrelated to human service workers' feelings of job involvement, but they are very strongly related to workers' feelings of emotional exhaustion (Eisenstat & Felner, 1981a, 1981b).

These results are of special concern because there is some evidence that human service workers are under more than the usual degree of job stress. In an analysis of the relative impact of job stressors on workers employed in a range of human service settings, the present authors found that workers' ratings of the stressfulness of their jobs were substantially higher than the national average for workers in non-human-service settings. These workers were particularly bothered by the quantity of work they had to perform, feeling that their workload was too heavy to be finished during an ordinary day.

One way in which workers attempt to cope with the highly stressful nature of their jobs is by withdrawing physically and emotionally from their work. Emotionally exhausted workers are more apt to report that they "used to care more about [their] work, but now other things are more important" (Eisenstat & Felner, 1981b). Ironically, however, our findings also revealed that it is just those workers who are most committed to their clients who also show the strongest evidence of exhaustion. For example, workers who report being more "personally involved with [clients'] problems," also tend to feel more emotionally exhausted.

Another disturbing result of job stress is a deterioration in the relationships between human service staff and their clients. Even though the stressors we examined in our research were not caused by clients, but were simply consequences of the ways in which workers' jobs were designed, staff in more stressful jobs reported both acting in more dehumanizing ways and developing more negative attitudes toward clients. Thus, we found that staff who reported being under more job stress also viewed their clients as sadder, more unpleasant, and tenser (Eisenstat & Felner, 1981a).

In summary then, both job motivators and stressors appear significantly to impact on the quality of relations between clients and workers. Stressors and motivators, however, appear to have very different effects on the human service workers themselves. Job stressors are associated with the emotional exhaustion of burnout while job enrichers such as autonomy, skill variety, and task significance are crucial in providing the motivation for human service workers. The research on human service job stress alerts us to the factors that cause workers to withdraw from their jobs either physically or emotionally but it does not tell us how to motivate workers to become committed to their jobs. Focusing on motivators by themselves is also inadequate. Nonmotivating jobs may lead to apathy and alienation, but they don't lead to emotional exhaustion. In a sense, the problem is that nonmotivating jobs never allow workers to "catch fire," much less cause them to burn out. The theoretical implication of these findings is that burnout is a multidimensional phenomenon. Both enrichers and stressors are necessary to understand the human service worker's reactions to his or her job.

CONSULTATION AND INTERVENTION: THE NEED FOR SPECIFICITY

While the distinction between job stressors and motivators may be interesting in theory, what does it mean in a practical sense? If we are confronted with poorly designed human service jobs, is it possible to make the work both less stressful and more motivating, and thus increase both worker satisfaction and the quality of care? As is often true in social science, the answer is "perhaps."

In a number of ways, a job that is more internally motivating can also reduce worker stress. For example, structuring jobs so that workers receive feedback from clients and staff is not only internally motivating, but it also reduces potentially stressful job ambiguity. Also, when workers are given greater autonomy over their immediate working conditions, they should be better able to cope constructively with job stressors.

In a number of other situations, however, the factors that lead workers to feel motivated in their work may also lead to their feeling greater stress. For example, we have found human service workers who report that their jobs are higher on two particular motivators, skill variety and participation in decision making, are also more apt to experience a variety of work stressors, such as "Feeling that [they] have too heavy a work load" and "Feeling that [their] job tends to interfere with [their] family life." These work stressors are, in turn, related to higher levels of emotional exhaustion. This implies that the administrator or consultant who is trying to increase workers' motivation by, for instance, giving them a larger say in agency decisions may also be making their work more stressful. Conversely, a strategy for decreasing work stress, such as decreasing work responsibilities, may only succeed in making an unchallenging job even duller.

In improving the quality of human service work, then, it seems clear that we must show a sensitivity to the demands of individual settings that has been lacking in previous writings in this area. Some human service settings, for example, a hospital emergency room, may be extremely motivating; workers are engaged in important work, have an enormous number of different tasks to perform, and have a great deal of freedom in how they do their jobs. The result, however, may be that they are overloaded with work, and because they care about doing their jobs well, they may become emotionally exhausted or burned out. In another setting, such as a state mental hospital, the work may be extremely routinized, the rules clear, and so on. This job may not put the worker under the same kind of stress as the first setting, but nor does it motivate him or her. In the first setting, an external consultant or internal change agent attempting to combat worker burnout should probably focus his or her efforts on reducing job stressors, while in the second setting, an emphasis on increasing job motivating characteristics might be more advisable.

The differences between these two kinds of job environments can be conceptualized in terms of what Alderfer (1980) has called "underbounded" and "overbounded" settings, respectively. Alderfer has shown that over- and underbounded organizations systematically differ on a variety of dimensions such as authority relations and role definitions. For example:

> Role expectations in overbounded systems tend to be highly precise, detailed and restrictive. Role expectations in underbounded systems tend to be unclear, incomplete and conflicting. . . . In overbounded systems people feel confined and restricted. Incumbents experience a lack of creativity and stimulation, especially at

lower levels in the organization, where the full force of the organizational structure impacts the individual. In underbounded systems people feel fragmented and isolated. . . . There may be a lack of explicit expectations from others or a great diversity of conflicting demands from multiple and uncoordinated sources. [p. 272]

We can see from these definitions that an overbounded human service setting, such as a prison or a state mental hospital, might lead to a very different kind of worker burnout from that prompted in an underbounded system such as a hospital emergency room or a drug-counseling hot line. Overbounded settings, characterized by high rigidity, low worker motivation, and people trapped in alienated roles, could almost be called "burned out systems." In contrast, underbounded systems "burn out people." They are characterized by high stress leading to a state of emotional exhaustion.

In both over- and underbounded human service systems, staff may treat clients in dehumanizing ways, but for very different reasons. In the overbounded system, both provider and client are locked into roles that strip individuals of their full humanity. In contrast, in the underbounded system, the service provider may begin by being almost overly aware of his clients' humanity and needs. Yet, over time, the stresses of the job are so great as to force the worker into more dehumanizing attitudes and behaviors toward clients.

We end this chapter with a plea for differentiation and for integration. The plea for differentiation is that we must not view human service worker burnout as if it were a unidimensional phenomenon. The job characteristics that lead to low worker motivation are not the same as those that lead to high job stress. Further, all human service settings are not alike; in some settings we must be attuned to reducing stress and in others to increasing motivation. The plea for integration is that, in thinking about burnout, we need to acknowledge the inextricable link between the job environment for workers and the service environment for clients. Throughout this chapter we have seen that when we fail to create internally motivating jobs for workers or when we overload them with job stressors, when we treat workers as automata or supermen rather than as human beings, the inevitable result is that the quality of care for clients also becomes less humane.

REFERENCES

Alderfer, C. P. Consulting to underbounded systems. In Alderfer, C. P. & Cooper, C. L. (Eds.), *Advances in experiential social processes.* Vol. 2, New York: Wiley, 1980.

Barton, R. *Institutional neurosis.* 3rd ed. Bristol, England: Wright, 1976.

Cherniss, C. *Staff burnout: Job stress in the human services.* Beverly Hills, Calif.: Sage, 1980.

Cherniss, C. & Egnatios, E. Participation in decision making by staff in community mental health programs. *American Journal of Community Psychology,* 1978, **6**, 171–190. (a)

Cherniss, C. & Egnatios, E. Is there job satisfaction in community mental health? *Community Mental Health Journal,* 1978, **14**, 309–318. (b)

Cherniss, C.; Egnatios, E.; Wacker, S.; & O'Dowd, W. *The professional mystique and burnout in public sector professionals.* Unpublished paper. Ann Arbor: University of Michigan, 1979.

Eisenstat, R. A. & Felner, R. D. *The impact of the human service work environment on job-related attitudes and staff perceptions of clients.* Paper presented at 52nd Annual Convention of the Eastern Psychological Association, New York City, April 25, 1981. (a)

Eisenstat, R. A. & Felner, R. D. *The relationships between job characteristics, work attitudes and human service workers' perceptions of and behaviors towards clients.* Unpublished paper. New Haven: Yale University, 1981. (b)

Eisenstat, R.; Felner, R. D.; Kennedy, M.; & Blank, M. *Job involvement and the quality of care in human service settings.* Paper presented at the 89th Annual Convention of the American Psychological Association, Los Angeles, August 1981.

Freudenberger, H. J. The staff burn-out syndrome in alternative institutions. *Psychotherapy: Theory, Research and Practice* 1975, **12**, 73–82.

Garson, B. Luddites in Lordstown. *Harper's,* June 1972, **244**, 68–73.

Goffman, E. *Asylums.* New York: Doubleday, 1961.

Hackman, J. R. & Oldham, G. R. *Work redesign.* Reading, Mass.: Addison-Wesley, 1980.

Maslach, C. Burned-out. *Human Behavior,* September 1976, 16–22.

Maslach, C. The client role in staff burn-out. *Journal of Social Issues,* 1978, **34**, 111–124.

Maslach, C. The burnout syndrome and patient care. In Garfield, C. A. (Ed.), *Stress and survival: the emotional realities of life-threatening illness.* St. Louis: Moseby, 1979.

McGrath, J. E. Stress and behavior in organizations. In Dunnette, M. D. (Ed.), *Handbook of industrial and organizational psychology.* Chicago: Rand-McNally, 1976.

Pines, A. & Maslach, C. Characteristics of staff burnout in mental health settings. *Hospital and Community Psychiatry,* 1978, **29**, 233–237.

Porter, L. W., Lawler, E. E., & Hackman, J. R. *Behavior in organizations.* New York: McGraw-Hill, 1975.

Sarason, S. B. *The culture of the school and the problem of change.* Boston: Allyn & Bacon, 1971.

Sarason, S. B. *Work, aging and social change.* New York: Free Press, 1977.

Sarason, S. B. & Lorentz, E. *The challenge of the resource exchange network.* San Francisco: Jossey-Bass, 1979.

Sarata, B. P. V. Job satisfactions of individuals working with the mentally retarded. Unpublished doctoral dissertation, Yale University, 1972.

Sarata, B. P. V. Employee satisfactions in agencies serving retarded persons. *American Journal of Mental Deficiency,* 1974, **79**, 434–442.

Sarata, B. P. V. Job characteristics, work satisfactions and task involvement as correlates of service delivery strategies. *American Journal of Community Psychology,* 1977, **5**, 99–109.

Sarata, B. P. V. & Jeppesen, J. C. Job design and staff satisfaction in human service settings. *American Journal of Community Psychology,* 1977, **5**, 229–236.

Terrell, P. Adapting to austerity: Human services after Proposition 13. *Social Work,* 1981, **26**, 275–281.

Vail, P. J. *Dehumanization and the institutional career.* Springfield, Ill.: Thomas, 1966.

Worland, J. Salaries of clinical psychologists employed in APA-approved internship settings: 1979. *Professional Psychology,* 1981, **12**, 453–455.

Part III:

Prevention and Treatment

11

On Burnout and the Buffering Effects of Social Support

Ayala Pines

When human service professionals are asked why they chose their particular profession, the answer invariably has to do with the fact that they perceive themselves as people oriented. Such answers as "I like working with people and helping people," "All my life people came to me to talk about their problems," and "I like interacting with people more than interacting with machines" are the most popular responses.

The nature of occupational tasks acts as a screening device, attracting people with particular kinds of motivation and personality attributes. Most human service professionals are "essentially humanitarians. Their dominant approach is to help people in trouble" (Billingsley et al., 1966, p. 53). They tend to be "oriented more toward people than to things . . . and value themselves most through being sympathetic, understanding, unselfish and helpful to others" (Registt, 1970, p. 11). Rosenberg (1964), in a study of students who aspired to careers in the human services, found that to them the ideal jobs would emphasize working with people rather than things, and would allow opportunities to be helpful to others. Kadushin (1974) has called this a "dedicatory ethic," which elevates service motives to a calling. Because human service professionals care about people, they are particularly sensitive to the social dimension of their work and consequently are particularly vulnerable to the dangers of burnout.

"Burnout," best defined as a state of physical, emotional, and mental exhaustion, typically occurs as a result of long-term involvement with people in situations that are emotionally demanding. Such emotionally demanding situations are characteristic of most human service professions. Burnout is marked by physical depletion and chronic fatigue, by feelings of hopelessness and helplessness, by the development of a negative self-concept and negative attitudes toward work, life, and other people. The negative self-concept is expressed in feelings of guilt, inadequacy, incompetence, and failure. The negative attitude toward work is often expressed in lost idealism. Burnout tends strongly to affect those who enter the field as the most idealistic and caring. As a result of burnout they resent their co-workers, hate their work, and lose concern for the recipients of their services, coming ultimately to treat them in detached and even dehumanized ways.

Our work on burnout (see Maslach & Pines, 1977, 1979; Pines, 1981, 1982; Pines & Aronson, 1980, 1981; Pines & Kafry, 1978, 1981a,b; Pines & Kanner, 1982; Pines & Maslach, 1978, 1980) has involved over 5,000 subjects and more than 100 workshops across the United States and abroad. This research has documented that burnout is significantly correlated to reduced satisfaction from work, life, and oneself, and that it is also correlated with poor physical health and with an increase in sleep disorders, headaches, loss of appetite, nervousness, backaches, and stomachaches. Burnout was also found to be related to hopelessness (and suicidal potential), alcoholism, tardiness, and intention to leave the job. Thus, it is clear that burnout is extremely costly for the individual, the organization in which that individual is working, and society at large.

The present chapter addresses the differential functions of support systems as buffers against burnout. But before we can describe these functions, we need to define "social support" and "social support systems."

SOCIAL SUPPORT

"Social support" has been defined by Cobb (1976) as information that leads individuals to believe that they are cared for and loved, esteemed, and valued, and that they participate in a network of communication and mutual obligation. Cobb reviewed an extensive body of literature documenting that supportive interactions among people effectively immunize them against the detrimental health consequences of life stress. From his review it appears that social support can protect people in crisis from a wide variety of pathological states: from arthritis through tuberculosis to depression, alcoholism, and social breakdown. Furthermore, social support may reduce the amount of medication required and may accelerate recovery. "Social support systems," according to Caplan (1974), consist of enduring interpersonal ties to groups of people who can be relied upon to provide emotional sustenance, assistance, and resources in times of need, who provide feedback, and who share standards and values. By providing emotional sustenance, supportive others help individuals master their own emotional problems by mobilizing their psychological resources. In addition, by providing these people with tangible aid, resources, information, and cognitive guidance, the supporters further enhance the individual's ability to cope with stressful situations. Ideally, according to

Caplan, one belongs to several supportive groups at home and at work, in church and in recreational or avocational sites. Social support systems serve as buffers for the individual; they help maintain the psychological and physical well-being of the individual over time.

Our research on burnout has shown that social support systems at home and at the workplace buffer the individual against burnout. In three different studies (one involving 205 subjects from the San Francisco Bay area, one involving 118 Canadian human service professionals, and one involving 81 Israeli social workers) subjects were asked to describe relationships in their lives and work. As shown in Table 11.1, the quality of these relationships was found in almost all cases to be significantly and negatively correlated with burnout; that is, the better the relationships the less burnout occurred.

Table 11.1.   Correlations between Burnout and Various Social Relationships.

	Super-visors	Subord-inates	Co-workers	Spouse	Family	Friends
205 Americans	− .23*	− .24*	− .26*	− .32*	− .25*	− .28*
118 Canadians	− .23*	− .17*	− .12*	− .25*	ns	− .22*
81 Israelis	− .25*	ns	− .30*	− .32*	− .37*	− .18*

*p < .05

In the sample of 205 Americans it was also found that the availability of support in the work environment and in life outside of work were significantly and negatively correlated with burnout (for work, $r = -.27$; for life, $r = -.29$). Similarly, personal relations, appreciation, and emotional reciprocity—all of which are aspects of a social support system—were also negatively and significantly correlated with burnout (personal relations at work, $r = -.27$; at home, $r = -.32$; appreciation at work, $r = -.32$; at home, $r = -.31$; emotional reciprocity at work, $r = -.18$, at home, $r = -.24$).

THE FUNCTIONS OF A SOCIAL SUPPORT SYSTEM

In the studies cited above, the buffering effects of social support were examined via the people providing the support, i.e., supervisors, subordinates, co-workers, spouse, family, and friends. Actually, one can look at social support from another vantage point: the function it serves for the individual. Social support systems serve a multitude of functions. These can be condensed into six basic support functions: listening; technical support; technical challenge; emotional support; emotional challenge; and the sharing of social reality (Pines & Aronson, 1980, 1981).

Listening. We all need, at least periodically, someone who will actively listen without giving advice or making judgments; someone with whom we can share the joys of success as well as the pain and frustration of failure; someone with whom we can share conflicts as well as trivial everyday incidents. To be a good listener, a person does not need to know us very well or be an expert on the subject we are discussing. Often, all he or she needs is to show interest and concern. Sometimes people find themselves talking openly to another traveler on a long flight in a way they could not talk to their spouse or other relatives, because that person is a good listener. People in the human services tend to be good listeners, especially when active listening is part of the job definition.

Technical Support. To provide technical support and affirm competence, a person must fulfill two important criteria: he or she must be an expert in our field and must be someone whose honesty and integrity we trust. In other words, this person must understand the complexities of the job we do and must be courageous enough to provide honest feedback. If those requirements are met, we can accept support as genuine. Mothers, spouses, or nonexpert friends can provide general encouragement, but that is probably not as meaningful as support from someone who can appreciate the technical intricacies of our job.

Technical Challenge. It can be comforting to be in an environment where we are the experts and where no one challenges that expertise. This comfort might be especially useful and welcome when we are feeling insecure or under stress. Unfortunately, too much comfort of this sort can produce burnout. In other words, if we are not challenged, we run the long-term risk of stagnation and boredom. Contact with a colleague who knows as much or more about the job can keep us from stale or superficial efforts. A critical colleague can challenge our way of thinking, stretch and encourage us to attain greater heights, and lead us to greater creativity, excitement, and involvement in the job. As in the case of technical support, the person who fills this role must have two characteristics: he or she must be good enough at the job to be able to identify what could be improved and he or she must be trustworthy. That is, we must be sure that our colleague's criticism is not intended to humiliate us or to enhance his or her own ego at our expense. The best of colleagues can trust each other to be both emphatic and challenging.

Emotional Support. An important function of an effective support system is emotional support and appreciation. An "emotional supporter" is a person who is willing to be on our side in a difficult situation even if he or she is not in total agreement with what we are doing. Most people need someone who is willing to provide unconditional support, at least occasionally. This can be vital in a stressful situation or in a constantly stressful job. It is often sufficient to have one person who is in our corner; it is marvelous to have this kind of support from four or five people. If this is not present or possible at work, it is essential to have it at home. Unlike technical support and technical challenge for which the person must be an expert in our field, emotional support is something that people at home—parents, spouse, relatives, and friends—can provide. Especially when under stress, we appreciate the people at work and at home who support us under any circumstances.

Emotional Challenge.   People can easily delude themselves into thinking they are doing their best when they are not. It is comforting to convince ourselves that all avenues have been explored when they have not. Occasionally, it is easy to blame someone else rather than take responsibility for problems or crises. These defense mechanisms are useful at times because they keep us from putting excessive emotional pressures on ourselves, but their continual use can block emotional growth and impede the most efficient employment of physical, emotional, and mental energies. At that point, a friend can help by questioning our excuses. To serve in this stretching function, friends can challenge us, questioning if we are really doing our best to fulfill our goals and overcome obstacles. Emotional challenge is different from technical challenge. A friend does not have to be an expert in our particular area of expertise to offer the opportunity to grow emotionally. The friend has merely to say, "Are you sure you are doing all you can?" But trust is still a prerequisite for this function. Any of these social support functions, and especially emotional challenge, can become boring and annoying when used repeatedly and indiscriminately by the same person. Emotional challenge can be very helpful if used sparingly, but when used continually, it becomes nagging. A spouse or coworker can turn into a "nag" simply by developing a strategy of always asking, "Are you sure you are doing your best? Can't you do more?" It is important to temper our resistance to this kind of prodding by remembering that we trust our friends to be doing it in our best interest, and not in theirs.

Sharing Social Reality.   The sixth function, social reality testing and sharing, is an extremely important function of a support system. There are two kinds of reality in the world: physical and social. An example of physical reality is the rain that makes us use an umbrella or a raincoat. Social reality is less obvious and may require external validation of one's perceptions. A friend, for example, can help us interpret social reality and decide on reasonable action. This supportive function is especially important when we think we are losing the ability to evaluate accurately what is happening around us. Eliot Aronson, a colleague of mine, gives as an example an actual situation in which he found himself sitting in a meeting and listening to someone spouting what seemed to him to be utter nonsense. He was sure that everyone else in the meeting was listening intently and he started to think, "My God! I must be going crazy! I'm the only one who's not fascinated." But luckily for him there was one person in that room whose judgment he trusted. He needed only to meet that person's eye and exchange annoyed looks. Then he could relax, realizing that the speaker was indeed talking nonsense and that although everyone else was agreeing with that nonsense or going along with it for reasons of his or her own, he did not need to question his own perceptions. All it usually takes is one other person, not a majority of the people present. In times of stress or confusion when we need sound advice, a person with similar priorities, values, and views can be very helpful. A person who shares our social reality is most likely to give useful advice.

The present study directly investigated the impact of these six support functions on the reported experience of burnout.

METHOD

Subjects

Eighty subjects, all professionals, participated in the study: 48 were Americans, 32 Israelis; 35 were males, 45 females; 35 reported self-fulfillment to be the main motivating force in their lives; 45 reported that people were the main motivation in their lives. The subjects' breakdown in terms of country, sex, and motivation created a $2 \times 2 \times 2$ factorial design. Subjects' professions included psychology, teaching, management, engineering, architecture, chemistry, physics, operation research, computer analysis, weaving, banking, photography, social work, fund raising, theater (directing), medicine, law, song writing, writing, painting, program directing, nursing, counseling, radiology, school administration, geology, business, biology, economics, and ceramics. The average length of involvement in their current jobs was four years and four months, and the average length of involvement in their careers was nine years and eight months. A subjective feeling of burnout was not a criterion for participating in the study. In fact, subjects' average burnout scores was 2.8 (S.D. = .06) on a seven-point scale.

Procedure

Subjects were all recruited individually in the San Francisco Bay Area. Each subject was asked to take part in a short interview in which the relationship between burnout and the availability of social support was investigated. Only subjects who were professionals and fit into the $2 \times 2 \times 2$ factorial design were recruited. Each subject was interviewed individually in interviews lasting anywhere from 15 to 30 minutes. Often, following the interview, subjects were interested in talking further about their particular social network and how it relates to their work stress.

Instruments

The first part of the interview involved the administration of a 21-item burnout measure. The 21 items represent the three components of burnout: physical exhaustion (e.g., feeling weak, tired, rundown); emotional exhaustion (e.g., feeling depressed, trapped, hopeless); and mental exhaustion (e.g., feeling worthless, disillusioned, and resentful). All items were responded to on seven-point frequency scales from 1 = never, to 7 = always. Test-retest reliability of the measure was found to be .89 for a one-month interval, .76 for a two-month interval, and .66 for a four-month interval. Internal consistency was assessed by alpha coefficients for most samples studied; values ranged between .91 and .93. All the correlations between individual items and the composite burnout score were statistically significant at the .001 level of significance. (Validity information is available elsewhere; see, for example, Pines & Aronson, 1981.) The overall mean value of burnout for all samples studied was 3.3. Thus, the mean of the present sample ($\bar{x}$ = 2.9) indicates a relatively low state of burnout.

The second part of the interview included a discussion of the six social support functions. After a short description of the six functions of a support system, subjects were asked to indicate, on a seven-point scale, how important each function was to them personally (1 = not at all important, 4 = somewhat important, and 7 = extremely important). They were then asked to rate the extent to which their need for each one of these forms of support was currently being fulfilled (from 1 = not at all fulfilled to 7 = fulfilled completely); they were also asked to indicate how many people fulfilled each function. At the end of the interview subjects were asked to describe the nature of their work, and to indicate how long they had worked in their current job, and their current career.

RESULTS

From Table 11.2 it appears that all six of the social support functions were rated as very important (the mean of the lowest valued function was 5.3 on the seven-point scale). The two most highly rated functions were listening ($\bar{x}$ = 6.2), and emotional support ($\bar{x}$ = 6.0). It is also noteworthy that the range of standard deviations was very narrow (from 1.2 to 1.5). With the single exception of technical challenge—which was apparently perceived by many subjects as criticism of their work—all of the other support functions were positively and significantly correlated with burnout. That is, the more that subjects experienced burnout, the more important the support was for them. The highest correlation (r = .31, p = .002) was with sharing social reality, thus corroborating earlier research findings (Pines & Aronson, 1981) indicating that the more burned out one is, the most isolated one feels, and consequently the more

Table 11.2.   Social Support Functions:
Means, Standard Deviations, and Correlations with Burnout.

Support Functions	Importance				Current Availability				Number of People Providing Function			
	X̄	S.D	r	P	X̄	S.D	r	P	X̄	S.D	r	P
Listening	6.2	1.2	.18	.059	5.5	1.3	−.29	.005	4.2	2.1	−.21	.033
Technical Support	5.3	1.4	.23	.022	4.9	1.6	−.38	.001	4.6	6.3	.02	.446
Technical Challenge	5.5	1.5	.01	.492	4.4	1.7	−.33	.001	3.2	3.3	−.16	.084
Emotional Support	6.0	1.3	.27	.007	5.2	1.5	−.33	.001	4.1	3.6	−.04	.373
Emotional Challenge	5.4	1.4	.24	.017	5.1	1.4	−.21	.028	3.0	1.8	−.01	.453
Sharing Social Reality	5.6	1.2	.31	.002	5.4	1.2	−.10	.186	5.7	5.4	−.17	.067

importance one attributes to having other people around who share one's social reality. And indeed, the second highest correlation was with emotional support (r = .27, p = .007), again demonstrating the burned out person's sense of helplessness and growing isolation.

While all of the correlations between burnout and the ratings of the importance attributed to the six support functions were positive (i.e., the more burnout, the more importance attributed), all the correlations between burnout and the actual availability of that support were negative (i.e., the more the function was fulfilled for the individual, the less burnout). It is also important to note that all the means of availability were lower than the means of importance.

The highest negative correlation found between availability and burnout was between technical support and burnout (r = −.38, p = .001); the availability of the other work-related function—of technical challenge—was also found to be highly correlated with reduced burnout (r = −.33, p = .001). In another study involving 111 elementary school teachers, a similar pattern of results was found. In that study the correlation between burnout and the availability of technical support was r = −.43, and between burnout and the availability of technical challenge, r = −.50. In the present study, the availability of emotional support and challenge and the availability of a listener were also negatively and significantly correlated with burnout. The availability of people who share one's view of reality was negatively correlated with burnout but the correlation did not reach statistical significance.

In terms of the number of people providing the various support functions, the highest number, on the average, was of people sharing one's social reality ($\bar{x}$ = 5.7). And there were more people, on the average, providing support in the form of encouragement and empathy (technical support, emotional support, sharing social reality, listening) than there were people providing support in the form of challenge (technical challenge, emotional challenge). It is important to note that all of the correlations between number of people providing the support functions and burnout were lower than the correlations between the degree to which subjects perceived the functions to be currently fulfilled and burnout. In fact, only the number of people one had as listeners was found to be significantly and negatively correlated with burnout. What this pattern of results seems to suggest is that the number of people is not crucial in the provision of social support functions. Rather, it is the degree to which these functions are fulfilled which correlates with one's level of burnout.

Subgroup Differences

Tables 11.3 through 11.5 present the correlations with burnout, broken down by country (U.S. versus Israel), sex (males versus females), and motivation (self versus people). Table 11.6 presents the means broken down by country, sex, and motivation and the p values of the F tests that came out statistically significant. Only the main effects are presented because the interactions that were statistically significant were very few and very low.

Americans versus Israelis. As indicated in Table 11.3, the correlations between degree of burnout and the *importance* attributed to the four support functions that provide encouragement and empathy (technical support, emotional support, sharing social reality, and listening) are higher for Israelis than they are for Americans; the reverse is true for the challenge functions. For example, for Americans, the correlation between listening and burnout was .13, for Israelis, it was .25; on the other hand, for Americans the correlation between technical challenge and burnout was .14, for Israelis it was .21. This pattern was almost exactly reversed when examining the actual *availability* of these support functions (Table 11.4). For Americans, the availability of encouragement and empathy was more highly correlated with reduced burnout than it was for Israelis, while for Israelis the availability of challenge was more highly correlated with reduced burnout than it was for Americans. For example, the correlation between technical support and burnout was − .42 for Americans; it was − .33 for Israelis. On the other hand, the correlation between technical challenge and burnout was − .21 for Americans and − .40 for Israelis. In terms of the actual number of people providing the various support functions (Table 11.5): for Israelis, the number of people providing active listening, technical support, and technical challenge was negatively and significantly correlated

Table 11.3. Correlations of Burnout Score with Perceived Importance of Social Support Functions.

	How Important Are The Functions?												
	Total Sample		Country				Sex				Motivation			
			U.S.		Israel		Male		Female		Self		People	
Functions	(n = 80)		(n = 48)		(n = 32)		(n = 35)		(n = 45)		(n = 35)		(n = 45)	
	r	p	r	p	r	p	r	p	r	p	r	p	r	p
Listening	.18	.059	.13	.183	.25	.081	.27	.060	.01	.490	.27	.056	.05	.369
Technical Support	.23	.022	.21	.073	.24	.096	.40	.007	.05	.373	.26	.064	.17	.127
Technical Challenge	.00	.492	.14	.164	-.21	.120	.12	.243	-.06	.357	-.15	.192	.13	.205
Emotional Support	.27	.007	.25	.045	.38	.016	.34	.022	.18	.125	-.30	.040	.23	.061
Emotional Challenge	.24	.017	.23	.059	.16	.188	.23	.096	.20	.096	.34	.022	.14	.187
Sharing Social Reality	.31	.002	.14	.173	.55	.001	.36	.016	.24	.055	.49	.002	.14	.185

Table 11.4. Correlations of Burnout Score with Availability of Social Support Functions.

To What Extent Is The Need For The Functions Fulfilled?
Need Fulfilled

Functions	Total Sample (n = 80)		Country				Sex				Motivation			
			U.S. (n = 48)		Israel (n = 32)		Male (n = 35)		Female (n = 45)		Self (n = 35)		People (n = 45)	
	r	p	r	p	r	p	r	p	r	p	r	p	r	p
Listening	−.29	.005	−.28	.025	−.14	.216	−.27	.058	−.32	.016	−.27	.058	−.31	.015
Technical Support	.38	.001	−.42	.001	−.33	.033	−.43	.005	−.33	.014	−.23	.092	−.50	.001
Technical Challenge	−.33	.002	−.26	.037	−.40	.011	−.48	.002	−.20	.093	−.11	.259	−.54	.001
Emotional Support	−.33	.001	−.27	.030	−.20	.139	−.32	.030	−.33	.013	−.33	.026	−.36	.008
Emotional Challenge	−.21	.028	−.05	.357	−.35	.026	−.33	.025	−.14	.177	.05	.386	−.46	.001
Sharing Social Reality	−.10	.186	−.12	.219	−.16	.196	−.05	.390	−.14	.179	−.04	.404	−.17	.129

Table 11.5. Correlations of Burnout Score with Number of Persons Providing Social Support Functions.

To What Extent Is The Need For The Functions Fulfilled?
Number of People Fulfilling

Functions	Total Sample (n = 80)		Country				Sex				Motivation			
			U.S. (n = 48)		Israel (n = 32)		Male (n = 35)		Female (n = 45)		Self (n = 35)		People (n = 45)	
	r	p	r	p	r	p	r	p	r	p	r	p	r	p
Listening	−.21	.033	−.02	.444	−.42	.009	−.27	.055	−.16	.156	−.14	.217	−.27	.039
Technical Support	.02	.446	.10	.249	−.35	.025	.04	.403	.07	.337	.07	.340	−.01	.476
Technical Challenge	−.16	.084	.13	.192	−.50	.002	−.47	.002	.27	.039	.03	.444	−.30	.022
Emotional Support	−.38	.373	−.02	.459	−.19	.460	−.09	.313	.06	.344	.23	.100	−.13	.198
Emotional Challenge	−.01	.453	.25	.049	−.11	.266	−.16	.175	.17	.140	.33	.029	−.23	.069
Sharing	−.17	.067	.05	.365	−.11	.281	−.01	.474	−.14	.179	−.12	.255	.07	.322

Table 11.6. Means of Support Functions: Subgroup Comparisons.

Support Functions	Variables	Country			Sex			Motivation		
		American		Israeli	Men		Women	Self		People
Listening	Importance	6.2		6.1	5.7	***	6.5	5.9		6.3
	Availability	5.3	*	5.9	5.5		5.6	5.5		5.6
	Number	4.1		4.3	4.2		4.1	4.0		4.3
Technical Support	Importance	5.3		5.2	5.0		5.4	4.9	*	5.6
	Availability	4.9		5.0	5.2		4.7	4.9		5.0
	Number	4.9		4.2	5.9		3.6	4.1		5.0
Technical Challenge	Importance	5.5		5.6	5.6		5.4	5.6		5.4
	Availability	4.3		4.7	4.7		4.2	4.0	*	4.8
	Number	3.1		3.4	3.9		2.7	3.3		3.1
Emotional Support	Importance	6.0		6.1	5.7	*	6.3	5.6	**	6.4
	Availability	4.8	***	5.9	5.3		5.2	5.0		5.4
	Number	3.9		4.5	4.5		3.9	3.7		4.4
Emotional Challenge	Importance	5.6	*	5.1	4.9	*	5.7	5.1		5.6
	Availability	4.8	**	5.5	5.0		5.1	4.9		5.2
	Number	2.6		3.6	3.1		2.9	2.8		3.1
Sharing Social Reality	Importance	5.8		5.5	5.3	*	5.9	5.6		5.7
	Availability	5.4		5.3	5.3		5.4	5.2		5.5
	Number	5.7		5.6	6.0		5.4	5.2		6.1

*** = p < .001
** = p < .01
* = p < .05

with burnout (r = −.42, −.35, and −.50, respectively)—that is, the more people providing the particular function, the less the burnout. No such correlations were found for the Americans. The number of people fulfilling the other social support functions was not correlated with burnout for either Americans or Israelis.

When examining the means of all these variables in Table 11.3, it appears that while there were no statistically significant differences between Israelis and Americans in the mean "importance" of the various support functions, there were significant differences in three of the mean "availability" evaluations, all in the direction of Israelis having more support than the Americans: Israelis had more listening (F = 4.6, p < .035), more emotional support (F = 13.1, p < .001), and more emotional challenge (F = 8.7, p < .004). It is interesting to note that all of the support functions that Israelis experienced to a greater degree than the Americans were in the non-work sphere.

Men versus women. Almost all of the correlations between the importance of the six support functions and burnout (Table 11.3) were significantly and positively correlated for men while none of the correlations was significant for women. For example, for men, listening was correlated with burnout .27, for women .01; for men, technical support was correlated with burnout .40, for women .05. Which is to say, for men the more burned out one is, the more one is likely to value support from one's social environment. For women that relationship does not hold true, possibly because for women support is always important whether or not the woman is burned out. This hypothesis is supported by the data in Table 11.6, in which it is shown that, with the single exception of technical challenge, women value the importance of social support functions more than men.

When examining the extent to which the needs for support were actually met for men and for women (Table 11.4) the results were different only for the listening function: for women the availability of a listener was negatively and significantly correlated with burnout; for men the correlation between the availability of a listener and burnout was somewhat lower. In other words, women who did not have someone whom they could talk to were more likely than men in similar situations to burn out (the correlation between listening and burnout for men was − .27, for women it was − .32). However, in terms of technical support and challenge, and emotional challenge, the negative correlations with burnout were higher for men than for women. It seems that for men, challenges are more effective buffers against burnout than they are for women. This interpretation of the results is supported by the data in Table 11.5 in which the only significant correlation for both men and women is a negative correlation between burnout and the number of people providing technical challenge (r = − .47).

Self-motivated versus people-motivated. People who described themselves as motivated by a need for self-expression and self-fulfillment had consistently higher correlations between burnout and the importance they attributed to the various support functions than did people who described themselves as motivated by people (Table 11.3). For people-motivated people, it seems that support is always important, while for self-motivated people it is more important when they burn out. The pattern of correlations was reversed when the actual availability of support was explored (Table 11.4). Here the negative correlations between the availability of support and burnout were consistently higher for people-motivated people than they were for self-motivated people.

When examining the means in Table 11.6, it appears that for the most part, people-oriented people view the support functions as more important, have more of them available, and have more people fulfilling the function for them. Three of these differences were statistically significant: the importance of technical support (F = 4.2, p < .05); the importance of emotional support (F = 8.1, p < .01); and the availability of technical challenge (F = 6.6, p < .02).

DISCUSSION

Six distinct functions of a social support system were presented: listening, emotional support, emotional challenge, technical support, technical challenge, and the sharing of social reality. Eighty subjects (males and females, Americans and Israelis, self-motivated and people-motivated) were asked to indicate how important these functions were for them, to what extent these functions were fulfilled for them in their work and home, and how many people actually fulfilled the functions.

Results indicated that all six support functions were rated as very important, with "listening" and "emotional support" receiving the highest ratings. In all cases the availability ratings were lower than the importance ratings, indicating that people almost never feel as if they have all the support they want or need.

As burnout correlates, all of the "importance" ratings of the support functions (with the single exception of professional challenge) were correlated positively and significantly with burnout, thus suggesting that the more burned out people were, the more importance they attributed to the support functions. And indeed, those functions with the highest correlations with burnout were shared social reality and emotional support. The more burned out one was, the more one was likely to feel isolated, and consequently to appreciate the presence of supportive people who share one's view of the world. While burnout correlated positively with the importance attributed to all the support functions, it correlated negatively with all the availability ratings of the functions, thus suggesting that people who have social support readily available are less likely to burn out. And, not surprisingly, the most significant negative correlation with burnout was obtained for the availability of technical support.

The number of people providing support, in all but one case, was not correlated with burnout, which seems to suggest that it is not the number of people but rather the quality of the support they provide which determines the effectiveness of the protective buffer they provide for the individual against burnout.

Israelis versus Americans

Since the study employed a 2 × 2 × 2 factorial design, it enabled comparisons to be made between Israelis and Americans, men and women, and self-motivated people and people-motivated people. The cultural comparison is important because it demonstrates the effect of situational factors on the utilization of support factors as buffers against burnout.

While there were no significant differences between Israelis and Americans in terms of the importance they attributed to the various support functions, Israelis had more support available to them than Americans, especially in the nonwork sphere. Previous cross-cultural research in which burnout among Israelis and Americans was compared (Etzion, Kafry, & Pines, 1982; Pines & Etzion, 1982; Pines, Kafry, & Etzion, 1978, 1980; Pines, Etzion, & Kafry, 1982) indicated that social relations among Israelis are better than they are among Americans: Israelis evidenced more emotional reciprocity, sharing, feedback, and mutual influence, and their family relations were significantly better. It was suggested that the social support systems in which Israelis are embedded— because they offer more of those vital functions—may be protecting Israelis better from job stress and tension than do those of their American counterparts. Israelis, more than most Americans, are also part of intimate and stable social systems of family, friends, and neighbors. These social systems protect them from pressure and support them in times of stress and failure (Pines & Zimbardo, 1978). The cohesion and informality that characterize Israeli society may be one of the causes of the good social relationships, the high levels of emotional reciprocity, and the sharing of stresses reported by Israelis (Pines, Etzion, & Kafry, 1980).

While Israelis who burn out are more likely than their American counterparts to attribute their problem to lack of social support, their burnout is much more affected by challenge than by the support provided by encouragement and empathy. For Americans the exact opposite is true, that is, the availability of encouragement and empathy is significantly more effective in terms of reducing burnout than is the availability of challenge. This cross-cultural difference can be explained by the fact that the direct confrontive style is much more popular among Israelis as a strategy for combating burnout than it is among Americans. This difference between Israelis and Americans was documented in previous research conducted in collaboration with the Israeli psychologist Dalia Etzion (Pines, Etzion, & Kafry, 1980). In that research, it was found that Israelis tended to report more frequent use of direct-active strategies and less frequent use of inactive strategies than Americans. It was noted also that the use of active techniques by Israelis may imply a cultural difference in regard to the value attached to active coping with the environment. Israelis seem to value it for its own sake, independent of its outcome, while Americans value active coping only when it proves successful. Living in the shadow of the Holocaust, Israelis developed a resistance to the perceived inactivity of generations of Jews in the Diaspora. They emphasize the isolated incidents of resistance during the Holocaust, such as the rebellion of the Warsaw Ghetto, because the rebels, unlike six million other Jews, did not go as "sheep to the slaughterhouse," but actively fought to their deaths. The value of active confrontation and the importance of taking one's own fate in one's hands, regardless of the risk of failure, is crucial for the understanding of how Israelis deal with the security and political problems of their country as well as with their own personal everyday stress. In the present chapter, the other side of confrontation—namely, challenge—was addressed. And, very characteristically, Israelis reported challenge to be an extremely effective buffer against burnout, much more so than Americans.

Men versus Women

For men there was a higher positive correlation between burnout and the importance attributed to various support systems than there was for women. This result was interpreted as indicating that only when men burn out do they attribute importance to social support (especially technical support in their work) while to women the various support functions are always important. And, indeed, it was shown that with the single exception of technical challenge, which some women interpreted as criticism, all the other support functions were evaluated as much more important by women than they were by men. Unfortunately, the discrepancy between the importance and availability of the various support functions was greater for women than it was for men, indicating that, at least in the work sphere, women receive less support than men.

Another interesting result was the finding that challenge was a more effective buffer against burnout for men than it was for women. This finding is supported by previous research (Pines & Aronson, 1981) in which it was found that women tended to use, more frequently than men, indirect coping strategies such as talking about the stress, getting ill, or collapsing. Men, on the other hand, tended more than women to use the direct strategies of changing the source of stress and confronting the source of stress.

Self-Motivated People versus People-Motivated People

Self-motivated people, in comparison to people-motivated people, had consistently higher positive correlations between burnout and the importance they attributed to the various support functions. This pattern of results was interpreted as indicating that for self-motivated people, support is important only when they burn out, while for people-motivated people, support is always important. This interpretation was supported by the analysis of the means in which it was shown that, with almost no exception, people-oriented people viewed the support functions as more important, had more support available, and were receiving that support from more people.

When the availability of support functions was examined, it was clear that, with no exception, all of the negative correlations between burnout and the availability of support were higher for the people-motivated people than they were for the self-motivated people. This suggests that for people-motivated people, the availability of support proves a more effective buffer than it does for self-motivated people.

The Importance of Social Support

The data of the present study suggest that people differ significantly in terms of the importance they attribute to social support, the support available to them, and the effectiveness of that support as protection against burnout. The data suggest, too, that it is important to differentiate between the six support functions. This conclusion is supported by extensive group work done in collaboration with Elliot Aronson in which we found that the varied use of social support systems provided effective prevention against burnout. Unfortunately, we also found that most people do not make adequate use of potential social support systems; rather, they squander these valuable resources out of a lack of awareness of their importance, of their different and distinct functions, and of how best to utilize them.

In that group work, we found that people who burn out in their professions often begin to put pressure on their marriages. Those who lack social support systems at work often begin to demand that their spouses fulfill the functions that are not being met by people at work. Unfortunately, most people, especially when under stress, do not make the effort to discriminate the various functions that a social support system can serve and are consequently left with a vague feeling that they are not getting what they need. Frequently, this sense of disappointment is not verbalized but becomes associated with home life. The atmosphere of regret and disappointment may begin to erode the marriage and the family; the result is burnout at home.

In this chapter, six basic functions of a social support system were presented. There may be variations on these functions, but these six are essential. It is important to discriminate one function from another, to be able to think of social support not in a global sense but as functionally divisible. While some people in our environment may be able to fulfill some of these functions, others may not. Without realizing it, we may expect our best friend or spouse to fulfill all of these functions—a nearly impossible task. While different people have different needs for support, and different people can and should serve different support functions for each another, one cannot err by concluding that social support is an extremely important buffer against burnout.

REFERENCES

Billingsley, A., Streshinsky, N., & Gurgin, V. *Social work practice in child protective services.* Berkeley: University of California, School of Social Welfare, 1966.

Caplan, G. *Support systems and community mental health.* New York: Behavioral Publication, 1974.

Cobb, S. Social support as a moderate of life stress. *Psychosomatic Medicine,* 1976, 5 (38), 300–317.

Etzion, D., Kafry, D., & Pines, A. Tedium among managers: A cross-cultural American-Israeli comparison. *Journal of Psychology and Judaism,* 1978, 3, 81–101.

Kafry, D. & Pines, A. The experience of tedium in life and work. *Human Relations,* 1980, 33 (7), 477–503.

Kanner, A., Kafry, D., & Pines, A. Conspicuous in its absence: The lack of positive conditions as a source of stress. *Journal of Human Stress,* 1978, 4 (4), 33–39.

Maslach, C. Burned out. *Human Behavior,* September 1976.

Maslach, C. & Pines, A. The burnout syndrome in day care settings. *Child Care Quarterly,* 1977, 6 (2), 100–113.

Maslach, C. & Pines, A. "Burn out," the loss of human caring. In Pines, A. & Maslach, C. (Eds.), *Experiencing social psychology.* New York: Random House, 1979.

Pines, A. Burnout: A current problem in pediatrics. *Current Problems in Pediatrics,* April 1981.

Pines, A. & Aronson, E. *Burnout.* Schiller Park, Ill.: MTI Teleprograms, 1980.

Pines A., & Aronson, E. *Burnout: From tedium to personal growth.* New York: Free Press, 1981.

Pines, A. & Etzion, D. Burnout and coping with its antecedents: A cross-cultural cross-sexual comparison (women vs. men, Israelis vs. Americans). Paper presented at the International Interdisciplinary Congress on Women, Haifa, Israel, January 1982.

Pines, A., Etzion, D., & Kafry, D. Job stress from a cross cultural perspective. In Reid, K. (Ed.), *Burnout in the helping profession.* Ann Arbor: Michigan University Press, 1980.

Pines, A. & Kafry, D. Occupational tedium in social service professionals. *Social Work,* November 1978, 23 (6), 499–507.

Pines, A. & Kafry, D. The experience of life tedium in three generations of professional women. *Sex Roles,* 1981. 7 (2), 117–134. (a)

Pines, A. & Kafry, D. Coping with burnout. In Jones, J. (Ed.), *The burnout syndrome.* Park Ridge, Ill.: London House Press, 1981. (b)

Pines, A. & Kafry, D. Tedium in the life and work of professional women as compared with men. *Sex Roles,* 1981, 7, 963–977. (b)

Pines, A., Kafry, D., & Etzion, D. A cross-cultural comparison between Israelis and Americans in the experience of tedium and ways of coping with it. Paper presented at the Annual Convention of the Western Psychological Association, April 1979, San Diego, CA.

Pines, A. & Maslach, C. Characteristics of staff burnout in mental health settings. *Hospital and Community Psychiatry,* 1978, 29 (4), 233–237.

Pines, A. & Maslach, C. Combatting staff burnout in a child care center: A case study. *Child Care Quarterly,* 1980, **9** (1), 5–16.

Pines, A. & Silbert, M. *Burnout of police officers.* Unpublished paper, 1981.

Pines, A. & Zimbardo, P. The personal and cultural dynamics of shyness: A comparison between Israelis, American Jews, & Americans. *Journal of Psychology and Judaism,* 1978, **3**, 81–101.

Registt, W. *The occupational culture of policemen and social workers.* Washington, D.C.: American Psychological Association, 1970.

Rosenberg, M. *Occupational values and occupational choice.* Unpublished doctoral dissertation, Columbia University, 1964.

12

Organizing Helping Settings to Reduce Burnout

William L. Fibkins

Schools are analogous to families in both structure and function. For teachers, "caring" schools can be nourishing, supportive environments that create a sense of belonging and recognition of unique contributions. They can be places where teachers feel cared for by their colleagues, even when classes are tough, discipline measures backfire, and lesson plans fail. In caring schools, like caring families, teachers can have bad days and make mistakes, but they will still be encouraged to "keep going" and seek different solutions to the inevitable problems they face.

But schools, like families, can also be abusive settings for teachers. Schools can be lonely places and teachers can feel alienated from their colleagues and community, and ultimately from themselves as well. In such settings, teachers appear lethargic; they come in later, leave earlier, and work less. They also make extensive use of sick days, particularly on Mondays and Fridays. Their anxiety and sense of worthlessness may be heightened by or manifested in the drinking of too much coffee and the smoking of too many cigarettes. Outside of school there is often increased use of alcohol to help buffer the lack of fulfillment at work. The anxiety of teachers in abusive schools is also heightened by the troubles in the world around them, e.g., the energy crisis, problems with the economy, and public resentment toward teachers. In abusive schools, teachers spend their free time seeking ways to "escape." There is much talk of summer trips, second jobs, baseball pools—anything to dissipate the feeling that colleagues, supervisors, and parents seem to care so little for their contribution. These teachers perceive the community as increasingly hostile and not appreciative of their efforts. They see the administration as enmeshed in its own set of problems and not available as a source of support. During their coffee and lunch breaks these teachers form small "survival groups" whose main purpose is to help members get through the day. In short, these teachers perceive the environment as hostile, with little hope for change; they feel stuck, locked into an abusive organization for the lifetime of their professional career. Ultimately, these feelings affect the children. Teachers who feel unnourished cannot draw on any sustenance to help children. Teachers who work in abusive settings for many years gradually begin to ignore some children; they increasingly talk about children "not being the way they used to be" and of the decline of "standards." Teachers in abusive schools, like children who are physically or emotionally abused, eventually burn out. Their maintenance of professional appearances is belied by a sense of despair, of giving up.

Yet burnout does not have to be the fate of all teachers. Teachers have the choice to make their schools either nourishing or abusive "families." Unfortunately, many teachers, like many abused children, settle for less and choose not to confront and change their settings. They see themselves as alone and powerless, blaming others for their situation—the principal, parents, government, university, union, or children. Teachers are often aware of what is missing but are reluctant to ask for what they need: colleagues who care about them both personally and professionally, a time and place during the school day to share successes and failures with colleagues in a nonjudgmental environment, and an opportunity for positive involvement with parents, administrators, and teachers from other schools in the district. Burnout cannot be averted by temporary measures such as in-service courses or weekend retreats. Burnout is the result of the school organization's lack of responsiveness to the complicated and increasingly pressurized aspects of teachers' work. Burnout, like abuse in a family, means that the support system for help in the "family" has broken down; there is no longer stability and safety in the environment.

To begin to change the burnout conditions in our abusive schools, teachers must first assess those aspects of their work that are abusive and counterproductive. For example, teachers' work often lacks the status of other professions; it is both a lonely and a little understood occupation that often leaves the teacher defensive and drained at the end of the workday. Yet, in attempting to tease out the more complex aspects of teachers' work, we have limited our understanding by confusing the *product* of teachers' work with the actual *experience* of their work (Dewey, 1934). Teachers' work in most settings is often defined by the unit taught—a teacher of fourth grade, a teacher of the handicapped, a biology teacher. Moreover, we often define the success of a teacher's work in this unit by attaching production markers to the unit. A teacher's success in biology is defined by the percentage of students who pass the state's Regents exam in biology; a teacher's success in fourth grade is defined by the scores of the class on reading and arithmetic achievement tests. By describing teachers' work in terms of production, we have failed adequately to describe and measure the day-to-day experience of school teachers, both for teachers themselves and for the members of the larger community. The teacher's role has undergone changes that are not represented in current assumptions and role definitions held by laypeople and teachers alike. At present, teachers and community groups are locked into an adversarial relationship because both groups lack the opportunity to recognize that their struggles to educate "their" children often follow parallel paths. Indeed, active involvement of community members in schools may create increased opportunities for positive exchanges between teachers and community groups. Such involvement might reduce the isolation of educators fostered by abusive schools, as well as heighten the esteem in which educators are held.

MAKING SCHOOLS REWARDING SETTINGS

To assist teachers in organizing new ways of working in schools, I believe it would be helpful to utilize Dewey's (1934) notion that in order for work to contribute to an "expanding and enriched life," it must be rewarding at an individual, a developmental, and a social level. Teachers, administrators, and school support staff must see that their individual efforts make a difference to the lives of the children with whom they work. In addition, they must clearly see that their individual efforts to educate children interface with those of parents, community members, and colleagues in other schools. Teachers need to experience their common bond with others.

Teachers, administrators, and support staff must also see their work as developmental. That is, they must be afforded opportunities for change and growth. Opportunities for teaching at different grade levels, for community service, for team teaching, and for research and writing must be accessible and ongoing. In addition, opportunities must be created for parents and teachers to exchange fears and hopes for "their" children. Parents and teachers need to share feelings common to their work with children—their fears of failure, their pain in observing a child's difficulties, their frustrations in trying to teach a slower child to read and write, their anxiety in dealing with various stages of adolescent rebellion. Parents and teachers need to know that each sometimes feels unable to cope, overwhelmed by the enormous responsibility that accompanies parenting and teaching. What really is the difference in their work? Teachers are cautioned by the school organization to mask love and anger when talking with parents. Parents hesitate to share their seemingly irrational and bizarre thoughts and worries about their children at parent-teacher conferences. Yet the children "belong" to both groups, and both need to begin to "talk out loud" to each other about realities of child education. Each developmental stage ushers in a unique set of problems and opportunities in working with children. Teachers can help parents better understand what behavior is expected at each stage of development, and parents can help teachers appreciate the unique qualities and skills of their child.

In a real sense, teachers, administrators, parents, and children all find themselves in the same dilemma in our school settings. All feel the need for positive human contact, novelty, and intellectual stimulation in their daily efforts. All long for others to recognize their own special talents and to feel that their presence does indeed make a difference. Teachers know what they need in order to feel fulfilled but they become entangled in a web of grades, departments, groupings, curriculum edicts, and regulations that limit their understanding and respect for the "other," whether he or she be administrator, secretary, parent, student, or fellow teacher. Concern for children and other teachers thus becomes replaced by a malaise that speaks of retirement, lack of hope, and things never changing.

Choice is always there for teachers to alter this destructive process. Perhaps this is the most frightening and optimistic aspect of the teacher burnout phenomenon. For the most part, teachers know what they need, but verbalizing the specific nature of their discontent means facing the risk and uncertainty of change. Teachers have had little experience with "speaking out loud" about issues of work. They are not accustomed to asking for what they need, and when they do, it is usually associated with salary and contract negotiations. They seldom ask for recognition, understanding, and respect for their contributions to the community. Yet the continual absence of success and feelings of well-being in teaching has moved teachers "over the edge." Teachers are beginning to voice their concerns over conditions that are causing burnout in the schools. Teachers are beginning to realize that problems of staff morale, financing of schools, discipline, leadership, and control of curriculum are all beyond the patch-up efforts of one-day superintendent's conferences and after-school in-service education programs. In psychotherapy, an important part of the therapeutic process is to allow the patient to "hit bottom"—that is, to allow him to focus on his own pain until he finally begins to take responsibility for and control over his own behavior. Teachers have experienced despair for so long, they have been deprived of positive human contact with colleagues, autonomy in their work, and recognition from the community to the point that they are saying "enough is enough." Literally millions of teachers throughout the country are describing themselves as "burned out," and, in effect, looking for change. They have destroyed the myth that schools are really like the model they present on open-house night—clean, organized, controlled, staffed by a flower-wearing, satisfied, professional and support staff. For the first time, teachers are telling parents and community members the truth—the sweat, the stink, the frustration of the job and their need to hear more about the positive effects of their efforts. Like members of an abusive family, teachers have finally decided to tell the neighbors the way it really is, and what they are saying isn't always pleasant.

Yet, as in therapy, teachers must do more than talk if they are to change the situation. They must develop a process within their school organizations that helps them to look critically at the causes of their own burnout and to develop a positive support system in their school "families" that encourages growth and development. School settings, like "families," need to become places where teachers, administrators, and support staff have ongoing opportunities for renewal throughout the lifetime of their service. Schools need to become places where parents and other community members can better understand teachers' work and contribute their own resources and knowledge to the education process. Schools need to become places where children see their teachers, parents, and community members as having equal status in the education process.

Yet none of this will be easy. The work of helping teachers reduce burnout is linked, I believe, to increased involvement of teachers and parents in shaping their own school setting. As such, this effort represents a major effort to change our schools. This effort will be lengthy and will include a great many setbacks. Teachers must find within themselves the capacity to look critically at their work and to plan a support system that encourages professional and personal development. They must find within themselves the capacity to open up classrooms to colleagues and parents and to learn to use creative resources that these individuals can offer them and their children. And teachers must face up to the fact that they haven't had much practice at sharing ideas and resources. Traditionally, teachers have been loners and are used to operating on a system of reward and punishment based solely on the achievement of students in their classrooms. Yet teachers must learn to share resources. And teachers must learn also to see *individuals* and their unique resources as the key to renewal, rather than institutions and large, bureaucratic agencies. To accomplish this task, a great deal of coordination is necessary. Fellow teachers, teacher unions, administrators, school board members, and parent groups must all be convinced that a renewal process based on individual needs and resources can be a source of new life for all sectors of the school community. At the same time, it is critical that this process maintain an essentially neutral political posture in the face of the increasing legalistic and bureaucratic nature of school business. Teachers cannot presume to solve administrative, union, or community problems. The business of teachers in this context is to propose a new process of interaction based on mutual respect and contributions. The goal of teachers is not to destroy the existing system of reward and punishment; rather, it is to suggest an alternative that allows and encourages a free flow of resources and ideas among all staff and community members—each person a resource, each person a learner.

A useful starting point for those groups interested in solving burnout in the schools would be to examine the ailing United States auto industry and the attempts being made to emulate successful Japanese management procedures. In fact, there are many parallels between our ailing educational system and auto industries. In both cases the consumers have opted for other "products."

In the schools, the parents are increasingly choosing private schools. In the auto industry, the car owners are choosing Japanese and other foreign cars (in record numbers—foreign car sales were up 28 percent in June 1981). Simultaneously, the workers and leaders in both the education and auto industries are subject to the fear of layoffs and they experience little community affirmation for their products. The auto consumers talk of poor workmanship and constant need for repairs. The education consumers talk of thousands of graduates who cannot read or follow simple directions. However, while the education leaders tinker with alternatives to the present system, some auto leaders, like Buick, are taking an entirely different approach based on the constructive maneuvers of the Japanese system: Buick is building a management and employee system that emphasizes a work value system involving categorical commitment to serve society, a spirit of cooperation, and group decision making.

The Buick Work Life Program emphasizes training in "active listening," "problem solving," and group and individual psychology. Workers selected for the program are trained for a half-dozen jobs on the assembly line. The ultimate goal of the program is to link the quality of the Buick product with worker participation. Groups interested in Burnout Prevention Programs may wish to look at the Buick program as one example of new management systems that emphasize lifetime employment for workers, collective decision making, and nonspecialized career ladders so that people are trained to work in many phases of the enterprise. For example, Japanese executives do not specialize, and regularly move from one department to the next. Given the disastrous state of conditions in our schools, parent groups may begin to negotiate with teacher unions and Boards of Education for pilot school sites that can experiment with lifetime employment for teachers and principals, and nonspecialized career ladders where colleges of education and State Departments of Education create differing forms of certification. For example, a teacher might teach junior high school social studies for five years, language arts for three years, serve as a counselor for children for five years, serve as assistant principal for three years, and spend the last ten years of his career in community education. In this way a teacher has differing career options, and he or she can be of service in varied ways to children and community members. Moreover, such a person has some guarantees of continued work and can be reasonably certain of community support.

A STRATEGY FOR INTERVENTION

It has been my experience in helping develop teacher support centers to reduce teacher burnout that this process is in itself developmental and can only emerge when a significant cadre of change agents from the school and community decide to alter their professional and personal relationships in the direction of mutual support and regard. In this section I will attempt to demonstrate for the reader how a six-stage process to reduce burnout emerged from the development of the Bay Shore Teacher Support Center at Bay Shore Junior High School on Long Island (Fibkins, 1974, 1977, 1980a, 1980b). I was director of the center from its inception in 1971 through 1980. I believe the evolution of the Bay Shore Teacher Support Center is important to study for those interested in teacher renewal programs because the center represents one of the earliest efforts by a local cadre of teachers, administrators, and support staff to develop a setting that could meet their own needs for professional and personal renewal. It is also important to study the emergence of this setting because this cadre of change agents was eventually able to expand its support process to include parents and community members. Why were these change agents— teachers, administrators, secretaries, custodians, and department chairpersons—able to translate the struggles and frustration so commonplace in the late 1960s into a meaningful six-point process for renewal that eventually led to every staff member at Bay Shore Junior High School presenting burnout prevention workshops at the center (125 staff members), while staff members in neighboring schools were still caught in the malaise that set in as a reaction to the reform movement of the 1960s? What was so unique and special about these change agents and this setting that encouraged teachers, administrators, support staff, parents, and students to utilize each other's resources in positive and creative ways to help resolve their professional and personal problems?

In reading this case study I strongly urge the reader to keep in mind that the burnout prevention process always begins with an individual or small group who start out in an amorphous way to change the work setting and who quickly learn that professional and personal discontent, once verbalized, can lead to positive professional and personal change for the individual and the entire school community.

Stage I: Understanding the History of the Setting

It is important for those change agents attempting to start a burnout prevention program to understand the history of the setting (see Sarason, 1971, 1972). What have been the positive contributions of the setting? What leaders have helped the setting to function in an effective way? How has the community perceived the setting? What internal and external factors have led to the feeling of burnout among the staff? When and how did the beginning "missionary" excitement fade? Facilitators for staff development programs should pay close attention to those past contributions that have enabled the setting to be useful to both the staff and the people they have served. There is a positive history to build on. A close examination of what went wrong for staff should begin with what went right.

In 1971, Bay Shore Junior High School (grades 7–9 with a population of 2,200 students) was the largest junior high school in Suffolk County, New

York. Once a leader in public education on Long Island, the district had been under steady attack by the community during the days of student unrest in the late 1960s and early 1970s. There was increasing friction among white and minority students and staff seemed unable to deal effectively with a new set of discipline and curriculum problems. The organization of the junior high into departments and teams, while an aid in the management of curriculum, increased the isolation of staff into cliques and self-interest groups and added to the notion held by many staff and community members that "we're not the school district we used to be." When staff did meet at faculty meetings, most of the issues were concerned with discipline and control. Community interest centered on rumors about racial conflict and teacher apathy. What was once considered to be the "best school district in Suffolk County" was now seen by both staff and community as unsure of its mission and unable to return to the position of educational leadership it once held.

Stage II: Identifying Appropriate Facilitators for Staff Development

Who are the facilitators for staff development who will provide the leadership to develop a burnout prevention program? Do they understand the real needs of the staff? Can they mobilize the different constituencies in the setting for such a program? What are the facilitators getting out of the process? Do they have enough of the "will to win" to overcome the resistance that will clearly emerge early in the project? It is essential that a project have facilitators who have credibility with staff and who can translate the renewal needs of staff into program.

I had returned to Bay Shore in 1971 after completing a Ph.D. degree in Counseling at Syracuse University. I had previously worked as a counselor at Bay Shore High School from 1966 to 1969 and had been active in teacher training and leading student groups. Upon returning to Bay Shore, I was assigned to the junior high school as part of a grade reorganization plan. It was not a move I desired and I spent the first months at the junior high wanting to be somewhere else. However, I soon saw opportunities to utilize my skills in teaching in-service courses in the areas of discipline and student counseling. In this process I was able to align myself with 40 other teachers who were enthusiastic about new approaches to their own training. Most of these staff members had been out of the university for at least ten years and were now in their middle or late 30s. They believed they could create school-based training for themselves and their colleagues. Their enthusiasm was also supported by the school principal who encouraged any kind of initiative among the staff and was reaching for all the support he could get to deal with the ambiguity and unrest that characterized the early 1970s. This setting and this place in time provided me the opportunity to implement my ideas for a teacher support center and make connections with the State University of New York at Stony Brook Teacher Education program—a program that was, in fact, seeking to establish a teacher support center in a secondary school. I was designated as the facilitator for this program because of my training in counseling, the need in the school for training opportunities with a counseling emphasis, and the need on the part of the university to pilot school-based renewal programs. It was here, in the early days of the 1970s, that the issues related to burnout first began to emerge.

Stage III: Acknowledging that the Development of a Burnout Prevention Program Takes Time

The development of a burnout prevention program requires identification of past contributions, assessment of current needs for renewal, a survey of existing resources to meet these needs, and development of ongoing renewal programs. In this process all staff members become involved and each person is seen as a contributor and receiver in the process. However, while most teachers and human service workers are experienced at giving to clients, they have little practice at giving to or receiving from colleagues. Long-held grievances cause early resistance in any burnout prevention program based on full and equal staff participation. The building of trust and avenues for staff affirmation is not a task that can be accomplished in a month or a year in most settings. Leadership in burnout prevention projects must be prepared for a long-term battle with staff resistance. It is not a task for those with thin skin!

In our initial efforts to begin a renewal program at Bay Shore Junior High School, two issues immediately became very clear. First, renewal programs would have to be held during the work day and be accessible to administrators, secretaries, and custodians, as well as teachers. If we isolated any group, we would not be fulfilling our intended mission of helping "all people who work with children" to have renewal opportunities. Second, we had to use our own staff to provide leadership for training opportunities. A way would have to be found to release staff to teach "each other." We would also have to find a comfortable place in the school to hold our sessions. It took us two years of missionary work to find and decorate a center, develop a weekly series of workshops based on staff needs, encourage, cajole, and manipulate fellow staff members to lead workshops, and, most difficult of all, encourage staff to give up old habits and grievances so that they would participate in these sessions. Most of the staff relationships were based on departmental and grade lines. Most meetings they attended centered on problems and focused on what was not done and what went wrong. Participating in activities that were not problem-centered and were not arranged along departmental lines was new and threatening. The job of the facilitator was to learn each person's skills and needs and connect that person with like-minded staff in activities that were affirming and worthwhile. This process of trust building, need assessment, resource identification, and program development took months. We met with many failures that were personally and professionally discouraging. Nevertheless, after two years we had a daily program for staff renewal built on a system of releasing teacher leaders—through utilizing substitute money—who would offer training throughout the day whenever staff could voluntarily participate.

Stage IV: Creating a Process That Provides Opportunity for Staff to Focus on Work Dilemmas

Local teacher and community groups must create opportunities for teachers and others involved in the schooling of children to reflect on their vision for the school setting. How do they envision the value of their unique contribution? How do they see themselves as being of value to their colleagues, the children, the community over the lifetime of their service? This process is intended to help staff understand that career dissatisfaction and job change are positive aspects of the adult developmental cycle.

In developing the Bay Shore Teacher Burnout Center, each morning some of my colleagues and I would go around the school talking informally with each staff member. We were able to develop a sense of the school and the individual and collective needs of staff. We found that discipline, retirement, health, clear avenues for recognition from peers, administration, community, and students were high among staff needs. Through programs at the center we were able to create workshops that helped participants practice their reactions to a variety of conflict situations, talk openly about their plans for retirement and career alternatives, learn how to care for themselves with better nutrition and exercise, and seek affirmation for their projects. Participation in many of these programs included all the staff in the building. Members were able to see each other, talk, reflect on their work, and be affirmed for their contribution to the workplace.

Stage V: Developing New Areas for Professional Growth

Local teacher and community groups must actively negotiate to help teachers and others in the schools to have easily accessible opportunities for job change both within the school structure and in community service. The opportunity to participate in renewal programs that offer positive human contact, intellectual stimulation, resource exchange, and novelty must be available in each school.

As the Bay Shore Teacher Burnout Center developed through the mid-1970s, we increasingly received requests for staff to talk about our renewal center at state and national conventions. Staff was also asked to help set up renewal centers at other schools in the district and in the communities' parochial schools. This process created additional opportunities and novelty for the staff. They were leaders in their own renewal effort, and not only worked at teaching children and their local colleagues but were now "teaching teachers" throughout the country. In turn, we invited teachers from other public and private schools in the district and neighboring schools to offer workshops at the center, thus providing an opportunity not only to expand our learning but also to enable our colleagues in other settings to begin developing career alternatives and renewal systems of their own. The passage of federal support for teacher centers at the national level in 1976 also enabled our pioneer effort to have a national base. Finally, members of the center began to publish descriptions of the center renewal programs which appeared in many national professional journals. Owing to the help of Kathleen DeVaney of the Teacher Center Exchange in San Francisco, visitors from all over the United States and the United Kingdom visited the center and contributed additional resources and opportunities. Our effort to solve our renewal problems was in itself a vehicle for growth and change.

Stage VI: Developing Opportunities for Exchange of Resources Between Community and School Groups

Local teacher and community groups must actively exchange their resources to help create a competent school setting and community. Those engaged in trying to reduce teacher burnout must be prepared to reach out to other professionals in medicine, police work, clergy, social service, and academia, whose resources and talents are hidden behind parochial institutional structures. A competent community must utilize all its resources to help professionals and community members, indeed the entire community structure, from becoming over-whelmed by its daily problems. The utilization of all community members in projects to reduce professional burnout and improve community life provides an exciting opportunity to utilize students themselves as important members of this process.

In developing the Bay Shore Teacher Burnout Center we began to learn that members of the renewal center must continually extend their hands to other members of the broader community and enlist their resources in the daily battle to make our schools and communities better places in which to live. In our work at the Bay Shore Teacher Burnout Center, we began to realize that community needs could be handled if we could somehow overcome the ways we limited our perspectives on solutions to community problems. Problems related to energy, social service, senior citizens, drug abuse, and the like required new areas of cooperation among parents, clergy, and social services. Through center programs, teachers and others in the schools became more aware of the many resources of staff and children that could be mobilized for worthwhile community projects. We found that children learn to become good citizens by contributing to their community in real projects, not sitting in a school room isolated from the pressing concerns in the everyday environment. We discovered that teachers could be used as resources to train and teach adults in the community (new immigrants, those without reading and math skills, unwed mothers, etc.). In turn, parents, senior citizens, and other community members became more involved in the schools where they could share their resources and be known for their community contributions. During the late 1970s, the Bay Shore Teacher Center emerged as a major forum for community members to help solve pressing community issues related to energy, housing, recreation for adolescents, and the establishment of a community network. The schools and staff, only eight years before beseiged by uncertainty and burnout, created a new base for community support by acknowledging and putting to work the skills of their school staff.

FUTURE PROSPECTS

There is a unique and fascinating array of factors at work in communities today. This array generally involves overburdened taxpayers, limited resources, aging and burned out teachers, deterioration of downtown business sections, and an energy panic—all of which have left many Americans skeptical about the ability of institutions to provide the quality of leadership necessary at this time. Yet we are beginning to see that for communities to survive, they need to begin to use the resources of all groups.

There are unique alternatives present in which the schools, by joining with local business and community groups, can become model programs for demonstrating how cooperative production and decision making can be carried out. Teachers and other staff members, because they are experiencing some of the same frustrations and boredom of the workers in the broader community, can be instructive in helping others to create alternative work futures, decision-making procedures based on mutual interest and solidarity, and opportunities for worker renewal throughout their careers. The ways in which teachers deal with their own burnout can be models for workers in the larger community. Teacher-centering, a process that attempts to involve all segments of the educational community in an effort to improve the quality of functioning for all those involved in working with students, can be equally effective if utilized by community groups to help solve pressing community problems. If Teacher Centers are effective in improving the work life of teachers, administrators, and secretaries in the schools, then similar centers might be created in hospitals, social service agencies, police departments, universities, and any other human service agencies that provide continuous care and service to those in need. Linkages might be established between various centers in the community (hospitals, social service, universities, police, for example) in which various groups could both identify and share resources needed to solve critical community problems.

Schools are truly a microcosm of society. Like other workers in the larger society, teachers have become alienated and estranged from larger sectors of their own interests, needs, and capacities. They are often people who entered teaching after World War II, experiencing the great expectations that characterized the period between 1946 and 1974. They thought that they could solve all social problems: racial conflict, poverty, lack of education, and so on. Careers were built on the "great expectations" theme. They thought that they could help everyone do everything. Yet, years later, they find their great expectations drowning in the reality that social change is much more difficult and complicated than was originally expected. Teachers now find that their careers retain little of their original excitement and hope. They feel a loss of human spirit, a malaise that is the dark mood of the times. They are affected in their work by distant events and people. Yet these changing conditions may themselves be a potential impetus for teachers. Through Teacher Centers, teachers may be provided with significant opportunities to influence events and people far removed, enabling them to change the way education, work, and community life interrelate in America. The very mission of the school in our society may be about to change.

REFERENCES

Dewey, J. *Art as experience*. New York: Minton, Balch & Co., 1934.

Fibkins, W. The whys and hows of teacher centers. *Phi Delta Kappan,* April 1974, 567–569.

Fibkins, W. Ownership and dialogue in transforming teachers' work. In DeVaney, K. (Ed.), *Essays on teachers' centers*. San Francisco: Far West Laboratory, 1977.

Fibkins, W. Teacher centering to reduce burnout and isolation. *Action in Teacher Education Journal,* Spring 1980, 31–36. (a)

Fibkins, W. *The work experience of teachers and professional burnout*. Fairfield, Conn.: Teacher Center, Inc. 1980. (b)

Sarason, S. *The culture of the school and the problem of change*. Boston: Allyn & Bacon, 1971.

Sarason, S. *The creation of settings and the future societies*. San Francisco: Jossey-Bass, 1972.

13

The Work-Setting Support Group: A Means of Preventing Burnout

Rosemarie Scully

It is 2 P.M. The nurses on the general unit drift, one by one, into the conference room. The atmosphere is tense. They sit rigidly in their chairs. They stare into space or at the floor, consciously avoiding eye contact with each other. Each of them is acutely aware that Jenny, the 26-year-old woman down the hall, is dying. She cries out with pain that the nurses cannot seem to alleviate. She has defied each of the medical profession's attempts to save her. And now there is nothing left but death. Slowly, each of the nurses reveals her feelings—sadness, frustration, anger, helplessness, guilt, hopelessness. One of the nurses cries. She's doing the best she can but nothing she does is good enough. The nurses start realistically to examine what they can do for Jenny. They cannot save her but they can spend time with her, try to ease her fears, try to comfort her family. And these things can help Jenny to die more peacefully. This *is* something positive they can do, they decide. And those few positive actions they can take will help them to deal with the anguish they feel about the loss of a patient so close to them. They go away still feeling sad, but no longer overwhelmed. They also go away with a greater sense of community. Sharing the sorrow somehow brings a closeness and lightens the burden.

You've just had a glimpse of a support group for nurses. The support group is a staff development approach designed to help members deal with stressful work situations. In structure, the support group resembles a discussion group. The goal of the support group is to increase staff effectiveness and to build a sense of competence; to help participants feel that they can deal with the stresses they encounter in their work situation. Staff will function most effectively if they can reach a "psychological middle ground" somewhere between feeling stripped of defenses and feeling so defensive that they have no sensitivity to those around them. Helping staff find this "middle ground" is the aim of support groups.

The method for reaching this goal is a problem-solving one. When situations are brought to group by a staff member, they are examined in this way: Why is this a problem? What are the feelings associated with this situation? What are the factors that contribute to this situation? What is the real issue? What can be done about the situation? What will be the likely consequences of various interventions? How will one know when the problem is solved?

This is very different from the interpretive approach most often associated with group work. Motives, personality deficiencies, and intrapsychic conflicts should not be explored in a staff support group. The clients are professionals, not patients, and the group leader is acting as a consultant/facilitator, not as a therapist. Hence, the responsibility for dealing with a situation remains with the staff member who raises it as an issue. Sometimes the staff member will choose to do nothing about a problem presented in group, and that freedom of choice must be respected by the support group leader. In addition, the group leader should believe in the staff members' ability to deal with the problem. This sense of respect is essential to the enabling philosophy on which that support group is based.

In keeping with the consultation nature of the support group, content discussed must be work-related. Discussion of personal issues would violate the goal of increasing the staff's effectiveness because it would, in reality, increase their vulnerability. Exposing personality deficiencies removes the focus from the patient and work and shifts the support group into the realm of therapy. Anxiety would be increased, and because the group cannot fulfill therapy goals, the nurse would leave feeling less competent instead of strengthened. Thus, the focus should remain on patient care and staff relationships. Topics such as how to help families in crisis, how to ease the stress of death for patients, how to care for demanding patients, how to handle conflict between staff members, how to approach abrasive staff members, how to offer each other support are all appropriate and can lead to useful practical suggestions for reducing the stress levels at work. Most often, support groups are structured to include only staff from a given hospital unit. Meeting times are set, usually on a weekly basis, and staff "rotate" in as their schedules and patient loads permit. This format may build in resistance, which means that staff can avoid dealing with sensitive issues by pleading "short staffing" and not attending the meeting; or, a nurse may begin to deal with an issue in one group meeting, then not attend the following meetings because of scheduling problems and subsequently not resolve the issue in group. But the reality of the hospital setting is that nurses do change shifts and workdays and that patient needs may preempt scheduled meetings. In addition, this structure is in keeping with the consultative nature of the support group.

A cross-section support group is an alternative design. Staff from various hospital units contract to attend a given number of meetings. With this format, membership is consistent and the structure more closely adheres to group

Table 13.1.   The Differences between Therapy and Support Groups.

	Therapy	Support
Goal:	personality change	staff effectiveness
Method:	interpretation	problem solving
Clients:	patients	professionals
Content:	intrapsychic	work problems
Leader:	therapist	consultant
Members:	consistent	rotating

treatment principles. However, the function of this group is different from the one-unit group. The one-unit group can alter patterns of relating and group norms, thus changing the work milieu. The cross-sectional group can assist individuals in dealing with stress, but can change the work environment only to the extent that the one who attended can affect the work group. Thus, if a powerful, influential member attends a cross-sectional support group, work-group relationships may change; if an important work-group member attends, relationships will probably change little.

To provide an atmosphere conducive to discussion, the group is led by a mental health professional skilled in group dynamics, but tangential to the work group. A leader from outside of the organization will be more able to help staff identify their perceptual ruts and nonproductive patterns of relating; one working from a staff (as opposed to line) position within the organization will have greater knowledge of the system and resources for problem solving within that system. Ideally, the support group will have two co-leaders—one from outside the organization and one from inside. Although they do not provide leadership for the support group, it is often helpful if authority figures do attend, at least occasionally. The organizational changes that members sometimes formulate require administrative support. If authority figures participate in the problem solving they will have a greater investment in seeing the change accomplished. There may be times when the group needs to meet without authority figures present, and this need should be respected. For example, nurses might need to work through and examine some anger toward an authority figure, or some situation in which they are embarrassed by their inadequacy. But a group that consistently wants to exclude administrators obviously has a problem relating to authority figures and needs to work out rather than avoid difficulties. For the group leader to try to establish a supportive environment without involving the administrator would be like a family therapist trying to treat a family while excluding the parents.

Support groups, then, though based on a model of group treatment, are very different from therapy. As illustrated in Table 13.1, group therapy involves a stable group led by a therapist and is directed toward personality change through interpretation of intrapsychic material; the support group, on the other hand, has a rotating membership led by a consultant and aims for increased staff effectiveness through problem solving of work-related difficulties.

HOW SUPPORT GROUPS WORK

Support networks have been identified as a primary tool in preventing burnout (Farber & Miller, 1981; Maslach, 1976; Pines & Aronson, 1981; Mullins & Barstow, 1979; Shubin, 1979). Support networks are the organization's way of formalizing and assuring support for staff. It is the organization's attempt to offset the occupational stress present in the human services environment.

Each profession has inherent stressors. Group process, if mobilized constructively, can mediate many of these. Nurses, for example, identify stress as stemming from four sources: patient care, tensions inside the work group, forces outside the work group, and unrealistic self-expectations. Caring for patients can be distressing when nurses feel inadequate to assist the person through a crisis. If their efforts cannot resolve the situation for the patient—cannot help him to cope with his illness, or worse, cannot save him from a painful or untimely death—they feel they have failed. Patient care, particularly when it involves newly researched or high-risk procedures, can arouse ethical questions for nurses, such as: "Is this treatment I am administering worth the suffering it is causing the patient? Should I add to his pain when I know he's going to die anyway?" These haunting concerns can be very stressful for nurses.

Becoming too involved with a patient may cause stress for the nurse; in sympathy, the nurse suffers with the patient and loses her sense of self and her ability to help. Becoming too distant may also cause stress; the resulting guilt and cynicism do not allow the nurse to develop any positive feelings about her work and herself.

The support group can provide a mechanism for dealing with these patient-care stressors. First of all, the group provides a safe place to ventilate the feelings of anger, helplessness, and sadness that caring for critically ill patients can induce. Once catharsis has occurred, staff can more realistically examine the sources of their feelings. The group can provide a linking function as well: as staff share their feelings, they realize that they are not alone in their anger or sadness. This sense of commonality can reassure the individual and strengthen the group. After some of the emotion in the stressful situation has been diffused, the group can search for alternative ways to deal with patient-care stressors.

Tensions within the work group are another stressor in the workplace, particularly for nurses. Competition for positions of power or influence, interpersonal friction, and destructive group norms are all facets of this source of stress. For example, one group of nurses revealed that there was a growing schism between the older staff members and the newer staff members. As the group explored the issue and talked about willingness to help each other with work tasks, one senior staff member said, "I'll help people, but they'd better have really tried to complete their work and have good reason for asking for help." This norm of having to prove oneself before being accepted by the group put new people in a bind. Younger staff needed the help of senior staff in order to become competent, yet older members wanted to know that newer staff were competent before they would extend help. The support group helped to mediate this source of stress by first bringing this norm to the conscious awareness of the group. After the norm was identified, the support group could clarify the effect that adherence to this unwritten rule was having on the work group. This created some cognitive dissonance for the members: "We have caused ourselves a lot of stress by buying into this rule." They could then problem-solve alternative ways to meet the need that the norm was established to satisfy.

The support group can also help to alleviate tensions in the work group indirectly. When one member offers help to another, via suggestion or simply via acknowledgment, an empathic bond may be created. This process can build cohesiveness and decrease the incidence of interpersonal conflict. In addition, the support group can deal directly with work-group tensions by providing a "safe" place for staff to disagree. With the leader providing some measure of control—monitoring the level of tension, preventing scapegoating of members, and keeping discussion focused on the issue at hand—group members can learn to work a conflict through to resolution.

Forces external to the work group, such as lack of staff, lack of supplies, lack of administrative support, or ineffective communication with other professionals in the work setting, may also engender stress in nurses. Support groups often begin by dealing with issues such as these. These concerns, because they are perceived as being outside the participants' control are perhaps the easiest to talk about. Ironically, the support group helps staff to deal with these by challenging their perceived lack of control and the "one-sidedness" of these stressors. Assuming some responsibility for changing these situations can be frightening at first, but is facilitated by the problem-solving approach and by the input of varied perceptions from staff members. In dealing with external stressors in the support group, nurses have initiated plans for alternate staffing patterns, decided on how to approach abrasive physicians, and explored possibilities for gaining the administrative support they needed.

Unrealistic self-expectations are perhaps the greatest source of stress for those in the helping professions (see Cherniss, 1980). This source often interacts with other sources of stress, exacerbating the effect of patient crises, interpersonal conflicts, and environmental conditions. This stressor is so pervasive because it has its roots in the professional's identity. Helpers give help in certain prescribed ways, with certain expected outcomes. Adoption of this belief is a necessary part of socialization into the role of the helping professional. Thus, when the helper cannot feel helpful in an expected or desired way, the result is stress. Nurses report that they experience this stressor in the form of intense guilt and self-chastisement and in feelings of anger, hopelessness, and helplessness. The support group helps staff to deal with these feelings by fostering increased self-awareness. For example, nurses may begin to explore a problematic patient situation. As they work in retrospect to identify the central issue, they realize that the root of the problem is that the patient is not responding in a way that will allow them to feel successful. This self-awareness is a crucial step in mediating this stressor, and one not easily arrived at, for unrealistic self-expectations are often confounded by a denial of the desire to meet one's own needs through work with clients. It is the sense of acceptance and empathy that the support group engenders that allows acknowledgment of this threat to the professional's self-esteem. Once staff is aware that the problem is with them, rather than with the patient, the support group can help them design more attainable goals for their work with this patient. They can then derive some sense of partial success instead of total failure.

THE SUPPORT GROUP PROCESS AND ORGANIZATIONAL CHANGE

As described to this point, the support group provides a direct service for professionals experiencing stress. Content-level interventions help individuals with work-problem analysis and formulation of alternatives, refocusing of perspectives, and reality testing for perceptions. Content interventions also help the group: as individuals share their varying perceptions, concerns, and alternatives, they identify more closely with each other and develop a sense of altruism and group cohesion. The support-group leader also makes process-level interventions that aim at fortifying the group: identifying and examining work-group norms, noting incongruities between what the group says and what the group does. Figure 13.1 illustrates these levels of intervention and targets for these levels.

Direct services are only part of a support group's potential impact, however. The support group is generally a microcosm of the entire work group; although the leader may see only a segment of the group for limited periods, he or she can

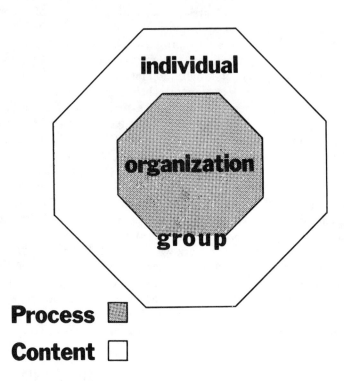

Figure 13.1. Two levels of support-group intevention: content interventions aim at assisting the individual and the work group. Process interventions can alter the work group and the organization.

make a fairly accurate assessment of work-group functioning based on support group meetings. In addition, the group consultant, often regarded as an expert on group dynamics and as an objective observer, has the opportunity to influence the system. Hence, the support-group leader has the information and the position to provide process consultation to the hierarchy while providing service to the work group. This feedback to administration can facilitate organizational change in the direction of creating a system that mediates stress instead of inducing it. What does this process-consultation intervention con- sist of, then? Generally, it involves making higher-level administration aware of how the system contributes to stress or ineffective group functioning. This may mean identifying destructive norms which the organization is reinforcing (or originating); elucidating poor intergroup communication flows; and providing feedback about how the leadership can help mitigate stress. It is important that this intervention be at the process level rather than the content level, i.e., the consultant does not go to administration to share specific problem situations or names of individuals involved in conflicts. Revelations of this nature will undermine trust that the work group has in the consultant, and render the support group ineffective. In addition, relaying this type of information to the hierarchy would indicate a lack of trust in the work group's ability to solve its own problems, and would be clearly destructive of the competency building that the support group aims for.

An example from a nursing support group may help to clarify how process consultation is used. This group of nurses worked on a research unit. They utilized experimental, but medically aggressive procedures in an attempt to treat terminally ill people who resisted traditional therapies. As might be expected, their patient population had a very high mortality rate: approximately 70 percent of the patients did not survive the treatment. The nurses' request for the group stemmed from intense interpersonal conflicts and feelings of paranoia. Figure 13.2 depicts the problem segmentation and analysis at which the nurses arrived in the support group setting. The root issue identified was the nurses' frequent inability to effect a positive patient outcome. The administration had not realized that consistently assigning all these high-risk patients to one group of nurses would be so stressful. The nurses were caught in the dilemma of feeling unable to help patients get well or even to help them to die a comfortable death (in fact they were inducing pain and suffering with the treatments they administered). Yet because this was so at odds with their professional identities, intense guilt would not allow them to choose any intervention that they perceived as abandoning the patients. In other words, the organization was not providing opportunity for positive reinforcement which could offset the pain nurses induced and the death nurses had to stand by and witness. Process consultation to nursing administration, in this instance, consisted of clarifying the organizational deficits and their effects on group functioning. The administration then decided to rotate staff out of this unit on a regular basis to an area where they could see positive outcomes of their actions. When these staff members returned, it was with a more positive sense of self and an increased ability to deal with the lack of reinforcement on the research unit.

Certain observations will help the consultant to give process feedback to administrators. The support-group leader should note: Who requested the initiation of the support group? What is this person's position? Power? Is the designated team leader involved? What are the initiator's goals and expectations for the group? Are they synonymous with participants' goals and expec-

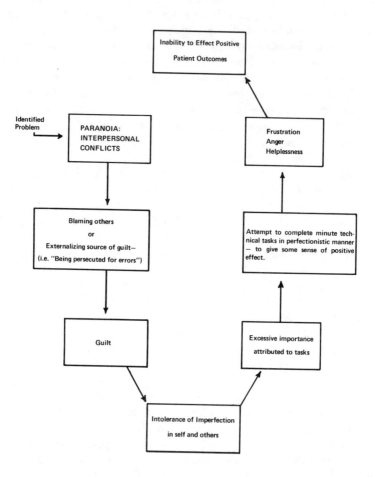

Figure 13.2.   Problem analysis of nurses in a support group.

tations? In the group, who talks to whom? About what? What are safe topics?
How are negative feelings dealt with? What are the implicit or unwritten rules?
Can group members assume affective group maintenance roles as well as task
roles? Does the designated leader contribute anything to the group (e.g., time
allotment for support group meetings, presence at the meetings)? What kind of
relations does this staff group have with other staff groups in the organization?

SUMMARY

The support group provides human services professionals with a three-faceted alternative for preventing burnout. The support-group leader can influence the individual, the work group, and the organization via content- and process-level interventions. In striving to assist organizations to develop an optimum environment for stress management, the group consultant can set forth these goals:

1. The work group should have norms that permit: talking about stressful events; admitting feeling inadequate, fallible, depressed, angry and guilty; giving interpersonal feedback; making suggestions to improve group functioning; thorough problem analysis; and offering and accepting of help.
2. The work group should have leaders who model and encourage empathy, are congruent in word and action, and have sufficient administrative support.
3. The work group should have members who can move in and out of affective group maintenance roles and have the ability and willingness to look at themselves and their behavior.
4. The work group should function within an organizational structure that facilitates attainment of the group's goals by providing the leader and the staff with needed resources.

REFERENCES

Alexander, C. J. Counteracting burnout. *AORN Journal,* 1980, **32**(4), 597–604.

Cherniss, C. *Professional burnout in human service organizations.* New York: Praeger, 1980.

Eisendrath, S. J. Psychiatric liaison support groups for general hospital staff. *Psychosomatics,* 1980, **22**(8), 685–694.

Farber, B. A. & Miller, J. Teacher burnout: A psychoeducational perspective. *Teachers College Record,* 1981, **83**(2), 235–243.

Maslach, C. Burned-out. *Human Behavior,* 1976, **5**(9), 16–22.

Mullins, A. C. & Barstow, R. E. Care for the caretakers. *American Journal of Nursing,* 1979, **9**(9), 1425–1427.

Pines, A. & Aronson, E. Combatting burnout. *Children and Youth Services Review,* 1981.

Schein, E. *Process consultation: It's role in organization development.* Reading Mass.: Addison-Wesley, 1969.

Scully, R. Stress in nursing. *American Journal of Nursing,* 1980, **5**, 912–915.

Scully, R. Staff support groups: Helping nurses to help themselves. *Journal of Nursing Administration,* March 1981, **11**(3), 48–51.

Selye, H. *The stress of life.* New York: McGraw-Hill, 1978.

Shubin, S. RX for stress—YOUR stress. *Nursing,* January 1979, **9**(1), 52–55.

14

The Ideological Community as an Antidote to Burnout in the Human Services

Cary Cherniss
and
David L. Krantz

A basic premise of this chapter is that most of the previous research and theory on burnout in the human services has been misguided by certain theoretical and philosophical biases. More specifically, the field has overlooked some important lessons of the past concerning burnout and its prevention because we have failed to recognize that the most important precursor of burnout is the loss of commitment. In recognizing this, and in studying how commitment is generated and sustained in social systems, some new and powerful insights about how to prevent burnout emerge.

Although there are many different definitions and formulations of burnout in the literature, almost all incorporate the notion that burnout is a response to stress encountered on the job. One especially popular version of this theory, promoted by Freudenberger and Richelsen (1980), is that burnout is a "disease of over-commitment." Those people who are most prone to burnout are excessively involved in their careers, psychologically as well as physically. Those in the human services tend to burn out more, according to this view, because it is so easy to become totally absorbed in the care of others and because the human services attract people who tend to be highly committed. Those suffering from burnout are counseled to reduce their involvement in the job, to push themselves less, and to develop other interests and commitments in their lives. In other words, they are told to reduce their commitment. We shall suggest in this chapter that this advice is not only wrong, it probably increases the potential for burnout.

We began to question the wisdom of this prevailing stress-overload-over-commitment theory of burnout when we visited a residential setting for mentally retarded people operated by a Catholic religious order. The sisters who work in this setting violate almost every prescription that has been offered by the burnout experts. Their work is not simply a large part of their lives; it is their whole life. In fact, they literally have no life outside of the religious order and their work with retarded people. They are in contact with their "clients" seven days a week, 52 weeks a year, year after year. Of course, they do spend some time away from the clients and the setting, and not every minute is spent working; there is time for recreation, prayer, and so on. However, there is much greater involvement and continuous contact with clients than one usually finds in a human service program.

The prevailing view would predict that staff burnout would be rampant in this residential program, yet many of the sisters have maintained a high level of care and commitment for years. (One person we interviewed had been doing this kind of work for over 30 years.) As we talked to these people, we began to realize that burnout ultimately is not caused by overcommitment, working too long or too hard. Long hours, hard work, and the other stresses often cited as causes of burnout only lead to burnout when there is an absence of meaning in work. The burnout process thus begins not with *stress* but with the *loss of commitment and moral purpose in work*. The focus of research, theory, and especially intervention thus should be on how to strengthen and sustain commitment.

There is a large amount of scholarship on what generates commitment in social systems. Research on communes, social movements, and religious orders, as well as on more conventional organizations, offers many ideas germane to this topic. One of the most important conclusions to emerge from a review of this literature is that commitment tends to be greatest in ideological communities. In such settings, there is a clear, explicit, official ideology. The ideology may be secular or religious. It may be a political ideology or a philosophy of treatment such as psychoanalysis or normalization. Another important characteristic of an ideological community is that membership in the system is contingent upon identification with and adherence to the ideology. In other words, everyone is expected to "buy into" the ideology. This does not mean, of course, that apostates are burned at the stake. However, those who cannot work within the official doctrine usually are encouraged to find another place to live or work. Thus, in an ideological community, people share a commitment to an external frame of reference, which provides a strong commonality of belief.

To clarify our subsequent discussion we will refer to two examples of ideological communities in the human services which we observed. The first is the residential setting for mentally retarded people operated by a Catholic religious order, which we have already mentioned. The sisters who belong to the order live and work at the facility. Thus, the setting is both a convent and a human service program. Although there are staff working at the facility who are not members of the order (and some who are not even Catholic), the sisters represent the largest and most central staff group.

The other example of an ideological community is a Montessori school for mentally retarded and emotionally disturbed children who have been excluded from the public schools. About five years ago, the administration of the school decided to adopt Montessori as their formal teaching method and all staff working there were first encouraged and then required to obtain training and certification as Montessori teachers. New staff now are required to obtain the necessary training and certification soon after being hired if they are not already Montessori teachers. Thus, the formal ideology is the Montessori method, and most of the staff identify with and are certified in this particular approach.

HOW DOES IDENTIFICATION WITH A FORMAL IDEOLOGY HELP REDUCE BURNOUT?

Embracing a formal ideology helps alleviate burnout first by reducing the ambiguity and internal conflict inherent in human service work (Hasenfeld & English, 1974). A formal ideology such as psychoanalysis, behaviorism, or existentialism literally provides "moral support" for difficult decisions that human service providers must make every day. To know that the Catholic church or Montessori sanctions a particular action is to reduce much of the self-doubt that can impede a sense of competence and contribute to burnout, provided, of course, that one accepts the Catholic church or Montessori as the most legitimate authority.

Sonya, a teacher at a Montessori school for mentally retarded and emotionally disturbed children, provides a good example of how a formal ideology can reduce conflict and ambiguity. When Sonya started teaching, she did not follow a formal ideology. She had her own values and ideas, but they were vague, general, simplistic, and not based on any external "authority." For instance, she felt that it was wrong to stress academic subjects too much with her students, but this was not based on any particular, formal system of teaching. She said that at the time she felt much pressure from parents and from "society" to stress academics rather than "start where the children were." When she was introduced to Montessori after three years of frustration in the classroom, she felt a sense of relief, for the approach gave her the moral support to reject certain competing demands and expectations once and for all and to use a consistent approach that made sense to her.

Another Montessori teacher had a similar experience. Like Sonya, she had taught for three years before "finding" Montessori. She said that when she finished her training and began teaching, she just was not sure how she wanted to approach the teaching process. Her ideas seemed to be even more vague and uncertain than Sonya's. The Montessori approach now provides her with the structure and direction that she previously lacked. She believes that Montessori has made her "stronger" and more effective in her interactions with children.

According to Sonya, the children are the ultimate beneficiaries of the new sense of confidence and security provided by the ideology. She said that when she adopted Montessori, she found herself becoming more relaxed. As she felt more confident and relaxed, her attitudes toward the children became more positive. As this happened, the children seemed to respond. They became happier, more motivated, and easier to teach. They learned more. As they did so, Sonya became even more relaxed and self-confident. The previous vicious cycle of self-doubt, failure, and frustration was replaced by a positive cycle of confidence, competence, and success.

Before these teachers adopted Montessori, they worked in settings that had clear goals. The problem did not lie in the formal goals of the program. The goals told the teachers *what* to do, but not *how* to do it or *why* they should do it in a particular way. The Montessori ideology provided the "how" and "why" that had been missing.

Thus, finding an appealing ideology and following it made these teachers more sure about what they were doing and more sure of themselves. Teaching in an ideological community helped resolve the "crisis of competence," a major cause of burnout in the human services (Cherniss, 1980a). In most schools, however, there is no ideological community and thus no *consistent* support or validation for the teacher's approach. Consequently, teachers usually are less sure of themselves and less sure of their competence. The "rightness" of what they are doing is constantly in question.

A formal ideology also can help sustain commitment by emphasizing the importance of intrinsic rewards and by conferring a special status on the more routine, physically unpleasant, or other potentially aversive aspects of the work. The religious order we visited provides a vivid example. At one point during an interview, one of the sisters said: "We're here primarily for the spiritual life. Of course, we're also here for the children, but first we're here to get closer to God. The children help us at the same time that we help them. They help us become closer to God." Another sister said with a wry smile, "You get your paycheck now; we feel that we're going to get it when we get up to heaven. Of course, you'll get yours up there too, but we feel that we're going to get a bigger one."

For these sisters, the religious ideology that guided their efforts helped them achieve a greater balance between "giving" and "getting." People in the human services burn out when they feel that they are giving much of themselves and getting little in return (Cherniss, 1980b). The sisters we interviewed did not feel this way about their work. Even on "bad" days when a sister might feel that she was not accomplishing anything with the children or when the work was especially arduous, she still felt that she was accomplishing something in terms of her religious goals. In fact, one may well achieve the greatest rewards on the most depressing and frustrating days, for such days can be seen as trials. They help these sisters to remain humble, test their faith, and come closer to God. Thus, what would be a totally negative experience for one who does not embrace this religious ideology is positive for one who does. Because their work is a means for achieving personal salvation, these sisters believed that they were getting back as much as they were giving.

Even in the most lofty of ideological settings there will be many tasks that are dull and unpleasant. Over a long period of time, performing these tasks could become a source of burnout unless there is a formal ideology that confers special status on performing them. In fact, in many ideological communities, all invidious distinctions between different tasks and roles are muted. There is a tendency to confer equal value on each task in the caring process. According to Marks (1977, 1980), role strain (and thus burnout) will be minimal in such a setting. He calls such a setting a "sacralizing" cultural system and uses the Bruderhoff community as an example. In Bruderhoff societies, there is no such thing as a "good" or a "bad" job. Every task, no matter how menial or routine, is considered to be blessed and marked by the divine. There is dignity and purpose in everything that one does.

The Catholic religious order referred to above appears to be based on a sacralizing ideology. In this order, every member is regarded as equally impor-tant and every task that contributes to helping children and serving God is deemed to be equally worthy. Everyone is expected to do anything that needs to be done; professional title or educational background does not exempt one from doing maintenance, or cleaning, or working in the kitchen. When we asked why the facility was unusually clean, one of the sisters replied, "We don't belong to a union here. There's not a rigid line of demarcation—this is your job, this is my job. We do a variety of things every day, and we're all willing to pick up garbage or clean the floors when it needs to be done." In a setting where there is an ideology that discourages invidious distinctions on the basis of role, function, or professional credential, an ideology that confers honor and dignity on any effort that contributes to the larger goal of helping the needy, burnout caused by "role strain" is less likely to occur.

Thus, in such ideological communities, the careerist rewards associated with professional status tend to be minimized; and this, as the following analysis suggests, helps reduce burnout. Many new professionals in the human services are enticed by the professional mystique; they go into this kind of work because they desire status, autonomy, varied and interesting work, and the like. Those working in human service settings rarely find such rewards, and this frustration can lead to burnout (Cherniss, 1980b). But those who work in ideological communities are constantly encouraged to be less interested in such rewards. As Montessori (1967) wrote:

[The teacher] used to feel that her task was a noble one, but she was glad when the holidays came and hoped, like all human beings who work for others, that her working hours would be reduced and her salary raised. Her satisfactions were, perhaps, to exert authority and to have the feeling of being an ideal to which the children looked up and tried to emulate. It would make her happy to become a headmistress, or even an inspectress. But to go from this level to the higher one is to understand that true happiness does not lie in these things. One who has drunk at the fountain of spiritual happiness says goodby of his own accord to the satisfactions that come from a higher professional status, and this is shown by the many heads of schools and inspectors who have abandoned their careers to dedicate themselves to small children, and to become what others call contemptuously "infant teachers" [p. 87].

ENHANCING THE POWER OF IDEOLOGY THROUGH COMMUNITY

When ideologically committed individuals unite and become a community, the benefits of ideology in reducing burnout are greatly enhanced and sustained. The community reinforces commitment in several ways. First, it buffers members from assaults on their ideology that would occur if they were working alone in an indifferent or hostile environment. This is the lesson that many idealistic new teachers learn when they begin teaching in the public schools. Public school systems are a good example of human service systems that usually are not ideological communities. There is an ideology, to be sure, but political pressures and the socially diverse community that schools serve force them to minimize this aspect as much as possible. It is rare that principals are educational leaders who espouse a particular ideology, select teachers based on it, and constantly reinforce it. Instead, they maintain certain general standards (such as classroom control) and allow each individual teacher to follow his or her own approach, whether it be the open classroom, Montessori, or a more traditional "three Rs" approach. An ideologically committed teacher in such an environment receives no official sanction for his or her approach and is constantly reminded that there are other methods that can work just as well if not better. Unless the provider is unusually myopic or rigid, the initial ideological commitment will weaken and as it does, the growing uncertainty and conflict contribute to stress and burnout.

A shared commitment to an ideology also can reduce conflicts between administration and staff, a major source of burnout (Cherniss, 1980b). Administrators in ideological communities should have more trust in their staff, knowing that the staff follow a particular approach and feel a strong identification with it. The administrators should see close supervision and control as unnecessary because staff have internalized a normative system in which the administrators believe. In such a situation, staff are likely to experience more autonomy in day-to-day activities. There also should be more trust and rapport between supervisory personnel and line staff.

The advantages for administrators in such a system are suggested by the work of French and Raven (1959). They identified several different bases of power that exist in a social system, including normative, utilitarian, expert, and so on. In ideological communities, normative power prevails—i.e., control through internalization of a set of norms. Thus, administrators need not rely on utilitarian or coercive methods of motivating and controlling staff. In human service programs, this is especially advantageous because utilitarian and coercive power ultimately are limited. Utilitarian control is problematic because it is difficult to link valued rewards (such as pay raises or job security) with performance outcomes. Coercive methods also are increasingly limited by the growth of unionization, civil service regulations, and other worker safeguards.

Thus, the ideological community provides a setting in which "humanistic" approaches to management are more viable. Modern organizational theory has espoused the virtues of participative, democratic management for some time. It remains difficult, however, to convince managers to adopt such an approach in their own jobs. Even if they overtly endorse a participative approach, their actual behavior is likely to be very different (Argyris & Schon, 1974). Perhaps the problem is that the more progressive approaches to management require a high level of trust in the subordinate, a willingness to delegate authority downward while remaining accountable for the results. Normally, it is difficult to truly convince managers that their workers can be trusted with this authority, that they will not abuse it or fail to perform. However, in an ideological community where workers and managers strongly identify with a well developed, formal set of beliefs and procedures, such trust is more likely to occur. Thus, the practice of modern, participative management methods may occur most easily in ideological communities.

What we have said about relations between managers and workers in ideological communities also applies to relations among peers. When most of the staff in a program share an ideology, a major barrier to collegiality and social support among workers is removed. Writers on the burnout problem have consistently favored the use of "social support groups" or "networks" as a way of helping people cope with stress and maintain their commitment to the work. But it is often difficult to create such groups in human service settings (Cherniss, 1979; Grzsiak, 1981). One problem that organizers of such groups frequently encounter is lack of trust among members and interpersonal and intergroup conflicts caused by differences in professional status or theoretical persuasion.

The value of a shared ideological commitment in enhancing social support was demonstrated by one of the Montessori teachers we interviewed. She had taught at two other schools before coming to the one where she now worked. The other schools were not ideological communities. In comparing the three settings where she had worked, she said that the Montessori school is a better place to work because the teachers help each other more. There is less isolation, less "loneliness" in the classroom. "They're alive, involved, interested, and concerned about each other," this teacher said at one point. "Other teachers will come right into your room to help if things start falling apart. There's so much togetherness here, so much of people watching out for each other." In other words, there is strong social support and a psychological sense of community in this school.

This teacher went on to say that sharing a common external framework contributes to the high level of social support: "Because there is a sameness in the philosophy and everyone knows what we're trying to do and how we're trying to go about it, we can help each other much more. We have a common bond. Montessori is a common ground. . . . It's an area of communication that's safe. You can discuss the work and feel relaxed on that level. It makes the whole atmosphere less tense." This teacher concluded by noting that because she gets so much support and "nurturance" at work, she does not feel as needy. Thus, she is less likely to take advantage of or fight the administration. She feels less greedy, selfish, and self-preoccupied because she feels that others are looking out for her. "When you feel that others are concerned about you, you don't have to be as concerned about yourself."

Writers on burnout have noted that goal and value conflicts are a major source of burnout in the human services (Cherniss, 1980b; Harvey, 1981). Another virtue of the ideological community is that it helps brings about a self-selection process that leads to a better match between the values of the worker and those of the setting. If a program is explicitly Montessori (or psychoanalytic or behavioral), then potential staff who disagree with such an approach are less likely to take a job in such a program. And if staff with a discrepant viewpoint do become employed in such a program, it is likely that they will either convert or leave within a short period of time, minimizing the goal and value conflict experienced by all. Thus, the consistency in belief that prevails in an ideological community helps reduce burnout in a number of ways.

WHAT CHARACTERISTICS MAKE AN IDEOLOGY MORE EFFECTIVE AT PREVENTING BURNOUT?

Ideologies and ideological communities differ greatly in many respects, and some are clearly more effective than others in maintaining commitment and preventing burnout. In certain cases, the nature of the ideology might even increase rather than alleviate burnout. An important task for future research is to study different kinds of ideological communities in the human services in order to determine the important variables. To illustrate what we mean, we shall cite two potentially important factors.

The first is the political focus of the ideology. Previous work has suggested that those who identify with a radical social action ideology may be more prone to burnout (Cherniss, 1980a). The goals of the social change ideology are more difficult to achieve, and failure to achieve them is all-apparent. Of course, the goal of salvation found in religious ideologies may be even more unlikely, but since it usually is supposed to follow death in a place that the living never can see, it is more resistant to skepticism and discouragement. Also, because the social action ideology challenges the political status quo, it will probably be regarded as more deviant. Those who are part of the prevailing power structure will strongly discredit it in many different ways, and these constant attacks will undermine the commitment of potential adherents. For these reasons, a radical social action ideology ultimately may be a weaker buffer against burnout than a more conservative, individual-oriented one.

A second difference in ideological communities that may be important is the degree to which the general, abstract ideology is translated into specific guidelines for day-to-day work (Reppucci, 1973). Montessori is a good example of this concept. The method is based on a clear set of values concerning living and education; values such as curiosity, experience, independence, and avoidance of drill are constantly stressed. However, there also is an elaborate, standardized curriculum that specifies the materials to be used in teaching certain concepts or abilities, the arrangement of the classroom, and directions concerning the role of the teacher. Furthermore, each teaching unit is broken down into small, predetermined steps. A teacher merely determines each child's current level and then begins doing what the curriculum prescribes to move the child to the next level. The levels are so numerous and close together that it is possible to move a child through many levels in a relatively short period of time. This not only reduces ambiguity for the teachers but also gives them frequent positive feedback and a strong sense of accomplishment. Although this standardized system might seem overly rigid and confining to many of us, the teachers I interviewed who use it claim that it leaves much room for individual creativity and flexibility on the part of the teacher while reducing some of the undesirable ambiguity and uncertainty that characterized the teaching process before they used Montessori. Also, because the curriculum is part of an ideology, a belief system that the teachers have embraced, following it provides a sense of meaning, purpose, and fulfillment that helps maintain commitment and prevents burnout.

The "open classroom" is an example of an ideology that lacks the level of operational specificity found in Montessori. Both systems begin with a generally positive, humanistic philosophy, but open-classroom advocates usually eschew the enunciation of specific, fixed goals and curriculum found in Montessori. Not surprisingly, one of the Montessori teachers we interviewed said that she preferred Montessori to the open classroom approach for this reason.

SOME POTENTIAL DANGERS AND PITFALLS OF IDEOLOGICAL COMMUNITIES

The ideological community should not be seen as a panacea for burnout. There are a number of dynamics that can occur in ideological communities that not only adversely affect service delivery but even increase burnout among staff. Even if the ideological community stresses a relatively noncontroversial ideology which is translated into concrete guidelines for action, there are potential dangers inherent in this form of social organization.

An obvious danger is that it will foster intolerance of other viewpoints. There always is the possibility that ideological communities will become repressive, authoritarian systems in which the "tyranny of the majority" makes life especially miserable for the deviant. In the Montessori school referred to above, I was told of a teacher who had "burned out" in only three months. According to my informant, this teacher was someone who "had her own ideas." She had an unusually strong background in the area of special education—a master's degree, some training toward a Ph.D., and considerable professional experience in other settings. She was not a Montessorian and apparently did not want to become one. She would not go to any of the other teachers for support or help when she had problems with her class, and if she had, they "would have found it difficult to help her, given her feelings about Montessori." She became more and more isolated, her class deteriorated rapidly, and after three months she resigned with much bitterness. Although teaching always is "a lonely profession," for the deviant in an ideological community it can be especially so.

A related problem that might be more pervasive in ideological communities is that passivity, dependency, and uncritical acceptance of tradition may become overly valued. The ideological community is always in danger of becoming stagnant. Initiative and innovation may wither. But such an outcome is not inevitable. In fact, many students of the creative process have argued that creativity thrives when there is a certain degree of structure (cf. May, 1975). In an ambiguous, unstructured milieu, the artist and innovator can be distracted in a way that inhibits creativity. In this regard, it is interesting to note that the Montessori teachers we talked to claimed that the system allowed endless possibilities for innovation, challenge, and creativity. For instance, a teacher can develop new materials to supplement the regular Montessori ones as long as the new material or exercise implements Montessori principles. The teacher also is free to conduct supplementary activities that are not part of the regular Montessori curriculum, such as group singing, arts and crafts, a second language, poetry, games, and so on. A teacher who had worked in a setting that was not tied to a particular ideology said that in the Montessori setting she felt more stimulated and creative than she had in her previous job. She also was learning more. The structure provided by the ideological community seemed to reduce the role ambiguity that had inhibited learning and creativity in her previous job. Thus, ideological communities may lead to passive dependency and stagnation, although under certain conditions, they may stimulate creativity and learning rather than inhibit them.

Ideological communities, however, may also be especially susceptible to "goal displacement." Ultimately, the ideology should be seen only as a means to an end. The most important goal in any human service program is to provide relevant, effective help to those who need it. But in the ideological community, following the ideology may become the sole objective. Over time, the ends and the means may even diverge so that ideological purity becomes antithetical to high-quality care, while members of the setting may not even realize that this is occurring.

The need to maintain an ideology in the face of a hostile or complex environment also can add to the frustrations involved in human service work, increasing burnout rather than preventing it. The need to compromise in response to external pressure can be painful for ideologically committed providers. An illustration of how ideological commitment can lead to perplexing self-contradictions is found in the observations of Gatz, Siegler, and Dibner (1979). They studied the creation of a therapeutic community in a state mental hospital. The staff were a highly committed, idealistic group embracing a formal, well articulated ideology. The ideology valued participation in decision making by staff and patients, patients were seen as responsible and self-sufficient, and discharge from the hospital was a primary goal. However, as the demands for efficiency, the paucity of community resources, and the need to maintain political favor with external groups began to impinge on the new setting, the staff found themselves making many compromises. In order to minimize deviation from their ideology, they had to work harder and longer than anyone had expected. In other words, the staff had to pay a heavy cost for ideological purity. Work overload and value conflicts probably were greater in this setting than they would have been in a less ideological one. On the other hand, Gatz et al. point out that the problem was caused primarily by the nature of the ideology and the program. The ideology, according to the authors, was unrealistic for that particular setting and for the patients they worked with; the time frame and the program structure were also impractical. Thus, the problem was not simply strong ideological commitment, but commitment to that particular ideology in that particular setting.

Ultimately, perhaps the greatest pitfall to overcome in creating an ideological community concerns the difficulty of finding a valid and meaningful ideology in the human services today. For the religious sisters and the Montessori teachers we interviewed, this is not a problem. They have found a moral system—a philosophy of care and of teaching—to which they can commit themselves. For many of us, however, there currently is no valid formal ideology with which we can identify. Those that exist are not meaningful or compelling, or perhaps there are too many competing systems from which to choose. As service providers, we may have certain values and ideas that we follow and techniques that we routinely use which seem to be effective some of the time. But we have discovered no formal *system* that we can totally believe in, and we have found no ideological community in which we could comfortably feel a part. In fact, for many of use who have been exposed to the professional socialization of contemporary social science, the idea of ideological commitment itself makes us uncomfortable. We have been taught that it is good to think but it is bad to believe.

THE BIAS AGAINST IDEOLOGICAL COMMUNITIES

Advocating the ideological community before an audience of human service professionals and social scientists is like preaching heresy. Personally, some of us may have a strong religious commitment, we may believe in particular political ideals, and we may work for certain causes outside of our work. But in our professional roles, we strive to be neutral, objective, and value-free. Also, the professional world view places a high value on freedom, autonomy, and individualism. Conformity is anathema. Willing obedience to a particular system of thought is considered a sign of immaturity or psychopathology. Strong belief in an ideology leads to cultism and even to the atrocities of the mass suicide at Jonestown. The true believer symbolizes everything that contemporary Western social science attempts to overcome: prejudice, irrationality, blind conformity, and violence. We are more comfortable with technology than with moral belief, at least within the context of our work roles.

As Lasch (1979) and Krantz (1981) have pointed out, behavioral scientists have not simply replaced the religious and familial authorities of the past with a new system of authority. The new "religion" in the "Age of Psychology" (Sarason, 1977) is essentially antireligious and antiauthority. As Krantz (1981) notes:

> The moral guides of the past, the religious leaders and family heads who provided recipes for living with a truth bred from an embeddedness in authority, are now suspect. In their place, a clergy of apparent and actual social scientists has arisen in a truly modern fashion; in their claimed authority of science and professionalism, they preach that all authority is suspect and ultimately to be dismissed for the sake of unfettered expression [p. 93].

In the human services, there have been two general sources of authority and their correlated approaches to intervention: the moral and the scientific-technical. In the early 19th century, the moral approach prevailed, especially in mental health (Bockoven, 1963; Grob, 1966). This approach emphasized the service provider's values and zeal as key factors in effective helping. The moral approach gradually gave way to the scientific-technical approach, which was influenced strongly by the medical model. In psychology, behaviorism is a good example of this dominance by the scientific-technical approach. Although Skinner is a moralist at heart (as revealed in works such as *Walden Two* and *Beyond Freedom and Dignity*), behavioral psychology is usually applied to a human service context in a nonemotional, mechanistic fashion. The behaviorist mistrusts ideology and moral fervor. The solution to any social or psychological problem is seen as technological in nature. The ideal helper is not a member of an ideological community but an isolated "engineer": apply the proper technique, set up the appropriate reward contingencies, and positive change will surely follow.

The other dominant contemporary theoretical perspective in the helping profession is humanism. Although humanists take issue with behaviorists on many fronts, they share the behaviorists' disdain for ideological commitment and fervor. Modern organizational theorists such as Argyris and Bennis, and clinicians such as Perls (Gestalt Therapy), Berne (Transactional Analysis), and Glaser (Reality Therapy) all emphasize self-direction, openness, experimentation, and liberation from formal authority. The Freudians, with whom contemporary humanists often do battle, similarly define self-reliance and freedom from irrational dependency on authority figures as the epitome of mental health.

The ultimate effectiveness of these different approaches as change methods is not relevant to the main point we have tried to make in this chapter. We are proposing that burnout is likely to be reduced in a setting where there is strong commitment to an official ideology and that using a technology based only on "empirical support," or a mere endorsement of a vague humanistic philosophy, may actually increase the potential for burnout. To inspire the level of sustained commitment in the face of hardship necessary for effective work in the human services, there should be a guiding framework based on a "higher," more absolute and certain authority than mere scientific verification. Even if the ideology begins with a set of more or less scientific observations and conclusions, these should be integrated into a grand and moving vision of what is and should be. Anything less is a poor foundation for work in the human services. In short, a renewal of the moral tradition in the human services may prove a significant antidote to burnout.

Unfortunately, many students in human service training programs are discouraged from embracing a particular moral ideology or philosophy as a guide in their work. Instead, they are exposed to a variety of "viewpoints" and given the message that no single approach has all the answers. The ideal service provider is depicted as an informed "eclectic," able to use a variety of approaches, selecting the best one on the basis of a careful assessment of each situation. This ideal is appealing because it is consistent with our cultural values of pluralism, autonomy, rationality, and individualism. However, it undermines commitment and exposes the new provider to the stresses that contribute to burnout in the human services.

Thus, the notion that ideological commitment and community can reduce burnout seems to go against the dominant belief systems found in the social sciences today. However, the emotional and intellectual resistance that the idea of an ideological community raises among us cannot easily be dismissed as narrow-minded dogmatism. As we noted above, there clearly are dangers and pitfalls associated with forming ideological communities. We are sure that many of us can point to ideological communities in the human services where commitment became excessive, irrational, and ultimately destructive. Perhaps some of these negative features associated with ideological communities can be reduced by incorporating into the ideology values such as innovation, flexibility, rationality, and personal freedom. But even this would not be enough for many of us, for we are successful products of the modern system. We are skeptics at heart. We become depressed and confused by the relativism in which we seem to be mired, at the same time that we take pride and solace in the fact that we are intellectually "independent" and "free"; we have not become captured by a particular ideological framework. We cannot escape the tension between belief and freedom. Ernest Becker (1973) described the situation well:

> He [man] wants to expand by merging with the powerful beyond that transcends him, yet he wants while merging with it to remain individual and aloof, working out his own private and smaller scale self-expansion. But this feat is impossible because it belies the real tension of the dualism. One obviously can't have merger in the power of another thing and the development of one's personal power at the same time at any rate without ambivalence and a degree of self-deception [p. 155].

And not believing is no solution; this antiideology in the human services is itself an ideology, and one that does not work very well when we become engaged in a helping role.

Ultimately, what Krantz (1978, 1981) wrote about the "mid-life crisis" may be equally true of this phenomenon we call burnout: "It is inextricably tied to collapsing frames of reference in our culture at this particular historical juncture." In other words, burnout is not a problem of individual coping or adaptation. It is a cultural and historical phenomenon. Burnout results from the loss of moral purpose and commitment in work. And when so many individuals in a society reveal a loss of moral purpose, when so few can become morally committed to an overarching frame of reference in their work lives, then we are dealing with a social problem. And any action for remedying the distress directed at the individual is misplaced. We cannot prevent burnout simply by asking individuals to "believe" in something. Individual belief and commitment in a culture characterized by anomie and relativism, in a culture that explicitly values nonbelief, is absurd. Before we can help individuals to overcome their loss of moral purpose in work, our *culture* must overcome *its* loss of moral purpose. And this will only occur when we support the development of ideological communities, in the human services and in other social institutions.

REFERENCES

Argyris, C. & Schon, D. A. *Theory in practice: Increasing professional effectiveness.* San Francisco: Jossey-Bass, 1974.

Becker, E. *The denial of death.* New York: Free Press, 1973.

Bockoven, J. S. *Moral treatment in American psychiatry.* New York: Springer, 1963.

Cherniss, C. Institutional barriers to social support among human service staff. In Reid, K. A., Quinlan, R. A. (Eds.), *Burnout in the helping professions.* Kalamazoo, Mich.: Western Michigan University, 1979.

Cherniss, C. *Professional burnout in human service organizations.* New York: Praeger, 1980. (a)

Cherniss, C. *Staff burnout: Job stress in the human services.* Beverly Hills, Calif.: Sage, 1980. (b)

French, J. R. P. & Raven, B. The bases of social power. In Cartwright, D. (Ed.), *Studies in social power.* Ann Arbor: University of Michigan Press, 1959.

Freudenberger, H. J. & Richelsen, G. *Burn-out: The high cost of high achievement.* New York: Anchor Press/Doubleday, 1980.

Gatz, M., Siegler, I. C., & Dibner, S. S. Individual and community: Normative conflicts in the development of a new therapeutic community for older persons. *International Journal of Aging and Human Development,* 1979, **10,** 249–263.

Grob, G. N. The state mental hospital in mid-nineteenth century America: A social analysis. *American Pyshcologist,* 1966, **21,** 510–523.

Grzsiak, R. C. *Support groups for preventing burnout in rehabilitation staff.* Paper presented at Annual Convention, American Psychological Association, Los Angeles, 1981.

Harvey, S. B. *Staff burnout and coping in mental health programs.* Unpublished doctoral dissertation, University of Michigan, 1981.

Hasenfield, Y. & English, R. A. (Eds.). *Human service organizations: A book of readings.* Ann Arbor: University of Michigan Press, 1974.

Krantz, D. *Radical career change.* New York: Free Press, 1978.

Krantz, D. L. *The psychologist as moralist.* Unpublished manuscript, Lake Forest College, 1981.

Lasch, C. *The culture of narcissism.* New York: Warner Books, 1979.

Marks, S. Multiple roles and role strain: Some notes on human energy, time, and commitment. *American Sociological Review,* 1977, **42,** 921–936.

Marks, S. Culture, human energy, and self-actualization: A sociological offering to humanistic psychology. *Journal of Humanistic Psychology,* Summer 1979, **19**(3), 27–42.

May, R. *The courage to create.* New York: Norton, 1975.

Montessori, M. *The absorbent mind.* New York: Dell, 1967.

Reppucci, N. D. Social psychology of institutional change: General principles for intervention. *American Journal of Community Psychology,* 1973, **1,** 330–341.

Sarason, S. B. *Work, aging, and social change.* New York: Free Press, 1977.

15

Social Policy Issues in the Prevention of Burnout: A Case Study

J. Lawrence Aber

When presented with multiple indicators that a human service agency is failing, in part because of worker burnout, how does the policy-making process respond? In this chapter, I ask this question for several interrelated reasons.

Several authors have decried the scapegoating of individuals for the high burnout role among human service professionals. As Farber and Miller (1981) note, "While the symptoms of . . . burnout form an observable clinical profile, their origins must be properly located in a social-environmental context" (p. 240). Cherniss (1980) warns us not to blame professionals or their clients for the causes of burnout, but to view burnout among human service professionals as part of the social conditions under which both professionals and clients live. Such recent expansions in the conceptualization of the causes of burnout are very important antidotes to an individual psychopathology model of the causes of burnout. In turn, they raise the issues of what these social conditions are that lead to burnout and how these social conditions are created, perpetuated, and maintained. If we are ever to prevent burnout, we must have a better understanding of the system that creates the social conditions that lead to burnout. For human service workers, that system is the public policy-making process because the policy-making process is the major source, direct or indirect, for creating, funding, and maintaining human service programs. Similarly, if we fail to understand how this system responds to crises related to worker burnout, we may fail to discover how the solutions to old crises can often create the conditions for new crises related to burnout.

In this chapter, I shall attempt explicitly to describe some aspects of public policy making that bear directly upon the creation of the social conditions that lead to burnout among human service professionals. I shall describe how the demise of an old child welfare agency within Massachusetts state government was due in part to the agency's inability to deal with the kinds of problems that lead to worker burnout. I shall then describe the creation of a new successor state agency that was explicitly designed to solve many of the problems of the old agency which were thought to be major sources of worker burnout. Finally, I shall attempt to explain why, despite the new agency's success at identifying and dealing with many of the component parts of the problem of worker burnout, its solutions to the old problems entailed assumptions that in turn set the stage for new problems of burnout in the new agency. Through such an analysis, I hope to convince the reader that the main problem for the new agency was the failure of its planners to anticipate events which, had the task of planning the new agency been viewed from a political-economic and historical perspective, could and perhaps should have been anticipated.

In one sense, this is a case study of the type one would expect to find in a casebook used by graduate schools of business or public administration. The chapter presents the organizational history of a problem, describes how the problem was perceived and defined by decision makers within the organization who were in a position to do something about the problem, outlines the perceived options for solving the problem, and offers the reader the opportunity to consider other options that were not considered or acted upon by the decision makers the first time around. This chapter may differ, however, from many such case studies because it is the report of a participant observer. The author participated in the entire process described, first as a legislative lobbyist and child advocate working to eliminate the old agency and start a new agency, second as a consultant to the executive branch of government in the design and creation of the new agency. Thus, this chapter suffers from all the potential weaknesses (e.g., selective memory) and strengths (e.g., access to private deliberations) of the participant-observer method.

THE ROLE OF WORKER BURNOUT IN THE DEMISE OF A CHILD WELFARE AGENCY

In the late 1960s, the state of Massachusetts passed legislation that created a new agency within state government, the Department of Public Welfare (DPW), to administer the two major components of the state's public welfare mandate: assistance payments (AP) programs which delivered financial services such as Aid to Families with Dependent Children and Medicaid, and social services (SS) programs which delivered such child welfare programs as protective service, foster care, and day care. Previously, responsibility for AP programs rested with the 300-plus municipal governments in the state and responsibility for public child welfare services lay with a state agency known as the Division of Child Guardianship (DCG). (At this point in the state's history, more child welfare services were provided by private rather than public agencies.) At first, AP and SS functions were administered by DPW separately at both the state and local level. The AP portion of DPW's budget always dwarfed the SS portion of the budget (90 percent as opposed to 10 percent) and consequently little attention was paid by top DPW administrators to the unique problems associated with the funding and delivery of child welfare services. In the early 1970s, however, in an effort to integrate and coordinate fiscal and social services, DPW reorganized its local offices and merged AP and SS functions at the community level.

Because of the state's civil service laws and regulations, the merging of AP and SS functions within the agency led to the situation where many clerical workers from AP (classified in the state employment system as social workers of a sort) became eligible to work as child welfare workers. In short, many secretaries who used to complete the paperwork necessary to distribute welfare checks and therefore had little or no training or interest in human service work were placed in a position of either beginning to provide child welfare services or losing promotional or employment opportunities.

At the same time, the demand for child welfare services began to grow at an astonishing rate. For example, the number of cases of suspected child abuse or neglect reported to DPW under state law in 1970 was approximately 2,000. By 1980, this number had swelled to nearly 20,000. While there was a significant increase in the number of child welfare workers, these work force increases could not keep pace with the growth in the number of cases. Therefore, the caseloads mushroomed from 10 or 15 cases to 25 or 30 cases per worker, a caseload level of abusive/neglectful, chaotic families much too high to serve effectively according to recommendations of professional groups like the National Association of Social Workers. Consequently, many cases of child abuse/neglect went "uncovered"—either no social worker was assigned to the case or if a worker was assigned, he or she had so many cases that the worker could not really serve the case.

In 1974, the widely publicized death of a child who had been reported as abused to school authorities and to private child welfare specialists but not to public agency child welfare workers initiated within government a process of reform of the child welfare component of DPW which was to last until the end of the decade. Early on in this process of reform, consensus existed both inside and outside state government about some of the basic elements of real reform. The Department of Public Welfare was advised to:

1. Clarify the unique responsibilities of public and private child welfare agencies in handling child-abuse cases;
2. Hire more social workers to reduce the size of the caseloads of the child welfare workers;
3. Employ only properly trained and supervised social workers to serve high risk caseloads;

4. Fund more support services for families at risk (e.g., counseling, protective day care, homemaker services);
5. Manage its limited resources to address social service problems in a more effective manner.

Despite this consensus on the elements of a solution to DPW's child welfare problems, over the next several years very few of the reform measures were actually implemented.

Civil service laws and regulations made it nearly impossible to shift clerically trained caseworkers out of child welfare positions. State budget problems made it extremely difficult to hire additional workers or to increase support services. And the administration of DPW showed very little inclination to make significant changes in the management structure or process to increase the efficiency of resource allocation. To outside observers, the reform recommendations seemed to be trapped by massive governmental inertia.

Consequently, a bad situation within the agency rapidly became worse. Under the continual scrutiny of advocacy groups, the media, and even the state administration, with fewer and fewer resources available to serve growing caseloads, the child welfare workers within DPW increasingly evidenced the "soft" signs of worker burnout. Absenteeism increased, morale sank to an all-time low, professional relations between public child welfare workers and other human service workers deteriorated. Most important, the child welfare workers began to withdraw from or blame their clients for the difficulties of their jobs.

On May 7, 1978, a major newspaper article was published in the *Boston Globe* which documented the lack of the state's progress over the previous four years in reforming the child welfare system. The article warned that other children would die unnecessarily because of various failures of the state's service system unless earlier recommendations for reform were enacted. Just two weeks after this article appeared, the death of another child who had been reported to the state as abused received extensive media coverage. Although the exact circumstances of the two cases differed, this new tragedy brought to the surface a similar group of problems with the child welfare system. Earlier, this child had actually been removed from her home by state social workers and placed in a foster home. But then, based on recommendations to the court by state social workers and over the objections of the child's foster parents who insisted that she was still being abused during weekend visits to her natural parents, the child was returned home permanently. Only a few months after the court's final action, the child was discovered dead.

In response to the May 7th newspaper article and the new tragedy, both the state legislature and child advocates increased the pressure on the executive branch of government to "do something already." An investigation by top state child welfare administrators into the events surrounding the decision to return the child to her home led to the highly publicized and controversial dismissal by DPW officials of two social workers and two supervisors for professional negligence in the case (Office for Children, 1978). The final report of the investigation stated that the social workers violated departmental regulations by visiting the child too infrequently and by withholding from the court information about suspected reinjury of the child by the natural parents. The supervisors and administrators were found to be negligent because they failed adequately to review the clinical judgments of the workers under their supervision. In return, the public employees union that represented the workers argued that the workers could not visit the child more frequently because of the prevailing caseload levels in the agency and that the workers withheld the information about suspected reinjury because of the department's failure to train its workers adequately in legal procedures. The union charged that the state was scapegoating workers for its own repeated failures to devote sufficient fiscal and administrative resources to the reform of the entire child welfare system.

On the basis of the public controversy surrounding this most recent tragedy, the governor and a faction of liberal legislators drafted and proposed legislation to eliminate the social service function in DPW and to create a new state agency (to be named the Department of Social Services—DSS) with its own goals and unique management structure for the planning, delivery, and administration of social services. This legislative proposal seemed to stem from a growing conviction shared by both the governor and the legislature that it was no longer possible to reform the child welfare portion of the old agency because the top management of the agency was geared to the provision of assistance payments services, not social services, and because the child welfare workers in the old agency were irreversibly "burnt out." Because the top decision makers in state government were convinced that the majority of child welfare workers in DPW were no longer capable of adequate performance in their jobs, they decided not to include a "grandfather" clause in the legislation to create the new agency. Child welfare workers in DPW would be required to apply for employment with DSS or lose their jobs. To state workers, it appeared that the executive and legislative branches of government were conspiring to create a new state agency in order to circumvent civil service laws and labor agreements and to gain the power required forcibly to change the nature of the public child welfare work force.

The proposed legislation generated intensive lobbying on both sides of the bill. The public-sector labor union representing DPW's child welfare workers, Local 509 of the Service Employee International Union (SEIU), tried very hard either to block the legislation completely or to introduce a grandfather clause. Most professional and child advocacy groups who had been lobbying the state for four years to reform the child welfare system supported the bill as the only vehicle that was likely to improve the system sufficiently to protect the lives of vulnerable children in the state. They felt that the fate of abused/neglected and foster children should not be held hostage to state government employment problems and that DPW should have to figure out what to do with workers who were not able to secure jobs in the new agency. The way the issue unfolded, professionals, advocates, and child welfare workers were forced to take positions against potential allies in the reform of the child welfare system.

As is true of many pieces of controversial state legislation, this particular bill was decided in the wee hours of the morning at the very end of a legislative session. In July 1978, owing to a political deadlock in passing a permanent state budget for the new fiscal year, a bill to create a temporary state budget to pay all state employees and welfare recipients was proposed. Obviously, a temporary budget enjoyed the backing of most state employees. Just before the temporary budget was voted upon, the bill to create DSS was attached to it by the legislative allies of the governor. This maneuver served to isolate the state's child welfare workers from the rest of the state employee labor force enough to win final legislative approval. The bill was then signed into law by the governor as Chapter 552 of the Acts of 1978.

This history of the role of the worker burnout issue in the creation of a new state agency illustrates a fundamental point. The larger systemic forces that create the social conditions that lead to worker burnout cannot be properly understood outside of the context of public-sector labor-management disputes. Therefore, it would be a mistake to approach the problem of burnout among child welfare workers in Massachusetts as if it were solely a psychological, technical, or bureaucratic problem with no real political-economic history. Without an understanding of the history of labor-management conflict, the roots of worker burnout are invisible and incomprehensible. Even the brief history presented here in no way adequately captures the complexity of public-sector labor-management conflict which forms the backdrop against which the problem of worker burnout should be viewed.

For nearly a decade, historical developments such as state adoption of new civil rights and affirmative action policies, evolution in the structure and a reduction in the number of collective-bargaining agents (unions) for state employees, statutory and court-mandated changes in civil service laws and regulations and growth in the tendency for state government to purchase services from private organizations rather than hire public employees all contributed to rapid changes in the nature of state labor-management relations. Perhaps it was under the pressure of needing to influence so many factors in order to reform the state's child welfare system that the solution of creating a new agency began to appear to state executives and legislators alike as a more attractive approach.

THE ROLE OF WORKER BURNOUT IN THE DESIGN
OF A NEW CHILD WELFARE AGENCY

The bill creating the new Department of Social Services stipulated that the governor appoint a five-member commission to make plans for and oversee the implementation of the legislation and the creation of the new agency. In turn, the commission hired a group of consultants to draw up the concrete plans to transfer authority and responsibility for the delivery of social services from DPW to DSS.

The commission and its consultants were very much influenced by four interrelated "guiding principles" in creating the plans for the new agency. Because of their relationship to the problem of worker burnout, these principles are worth describing in some detail.

1. *Confronting limited resources.* During the late 1970s, social theorists (see Sarason et al., 1977) began to describe, and governments began to recognize, the reality of limited fiscal and human resources. The commission decided consciously to confront the reality of limited resources in their design of this new social service system. They concluded that there simply were not sufficient fiscal or human resources (at least as those resources were conventionally defined) for the state to address every social service need of its citizens. In fact, the commission felt that the failure to establish clear priorities among the many competing claims to social services had led to many of the difficulties of the old agency. Too many cases were eligible for services, so professional resources were spread too thin and burned out too quickly.

A corollary to this principle of confronting limited resources is Sarason's notion that if a social problem is defined in such a way that the only solution to the problem involves an increase in the number of professionals needed to address the problem, then the problem has been rendered unsolvable. Based on these principles, the commission decided that, while a modest increase in the number of child welfare workers in the new agency was desirable and feasible, a reconceptualization of state social service priorities would also be necessary to effect real reform in the child welfare system.

2. *Establishing service priorities.* Legal scholars like Wald (1976) and Goldstein (Goldstein, Freud, & Solnit, 1973, 1979), and professional groups like the Juvenile Justice Standards Project (1977) were converging on a common idea. State governments, they believed, were not doing a good job of intervening in an increasingly greater number of child maltreatment cases. In fact, state governments actually may be doing harm in overintervening in the lives of some families. Therefore, these scholars reasoned, coercive intervention by the state into private family lives should be restricted to cases in which actual or imminent serious harm to the child can be documented. The commission

concurred with this civil libertarian construction of the role of the state in child-abuse cases and also noticed that the adoption of such a standard would reduce the number of new cases for which the new agency would become responsible.

3. *Encouraging permanency planning.* The commission was also influenced by the most recent critiques of the nation's foster care system (Children's Defense Fund, 1979). Foster care, the placement of abused/neglected or abandoned children in out-of-home care, even when it is intended to be a temporary solution to a temporary problem, instead tends to take on a life of its own. The state ends up supporting thousands of children for years on end as they are shuttled from one foster home to the next. Such practices both harm the children by depriving them of stable homes and "psychological parents" and drains the state of valuable resources that could be used for other needed services.

On the basis of such an analysis, the commission concluded that the new state agency should develop a "permanency planning system" which would guarantee children a permanent home by either returning the children to their natural families in a timely fashion through the intensive provision of services to the family or freeing children for a permanent placement (e.g., adoption) within one to two years where return to the natural parents is not feasible.

4. *Reducing worker stress and burnout.* In keeping with the conclusion of both the legislature and the governor, the commission and its consultants firmly believed that the last agency failed in part because of the problem of worker burnout. They therefore felt that the new agency should address this problem at its roots by beginning with new, well qualified, appropriately trained child welfare workers and by designing "work environments" for the new workers that would help prevent (or at least reduce) worker burnout.

The commission believed it had won the ability to start with new workers when the bill creating the new agency was passed without the inclusion of a grandfather clause. Therefore, they turned their attention to the issue of the design of work environments in the new agency. What would an environment that reduced stress and burnout among child welfare workers look like? In order to answer this question, the commission's staff of consultants read the meager literature available at the time on the causes, treatment, and prevention of worker burnout and the effects of job stress on human service professionals, held discussions with authorities in other states who were attempting to deal with this issue, and above all, conducted extensive interviews with child welfare workers from DPW to collect their ideas about how to improve their work environments in a way that would reduce stress and burnout. Based upon these efforts, the consultants recommended to the commission the following steps in order to reduce stress and prevent worker burnout in the new agency:

a. Reduce the unmanageable caseload levels of child welfare workers with high-risk cases.

b. Draft and adopt clearer decision-making standards for the highly stress-inducing decisions that must be made by child welfare workers (for example, the decision to remove an abused/neglected child from his or her home or the decision to petition the court to terminate parental rights to the custody of their maltreated child permanently).
c. Improve the quality of clinical supervision of the child welfare workers.
d. Increase the child welfare worker's sense of autonomy by reducing unnecessary regulations and paperwork; decrease the worker's sense of isolation by organizing service units into teams that share caseloads.
e. Improve the worker's pay scale to enhance worker self-esteem and to improve the quality of applicants.
f. Implement a career development program and career that encouraged advanced training and professional growth.
g. Improve the physical condition of the child welfare worker's offices (for example, provide private rooms to interview clients on sensitive matters, ensure that clients are able to reach workers by phone, etc.)

These guiding principles became the theoretical bases for the concrete proposals for action in the planning and design of the new agency (Social Services Implementation Committee, 1979). I believe that each of these four principles is based on insights that are fundamentally accurate when each principle is considered separately and ideally. This does not imply, however, that these principles are mutually compatible when considered together and practically. How specific policies based upon these guiding principles interacted with other historical developments became a test of the ultimate compatibility of this set of guiding principles. Not surprisingly, the goal of reducing stress and burnout among child caseworkers became the most expendable principle.

The first three principles—confronting limited resources, establishing service priorities, and encouraging permanency planning—converged on a political idea that was becoming increasingly attractive to a large segment of the state and national electorate at that point in history. Each of these principles implied that the new agency (like government in general) should try to do fewer things but make sure it does a top-rate job at what it does do. In short, the idea gaining favor was that government should *do less better.* The rise and fall of Democratic and Republican administrations since the New Deal (linked in part to their positions on this issue) provide concrete evidence that the American electorate's view of this idea changes over time as their perceptions of whether the economy is expanding or contracting changes. During the last half of the 1970s, a heated ideological debate developed over whether to continue to expand or to contract the growth of the human service sector. In Massachusetts a growing number of state politicians who had earlier argued for increases in human services now argued for the need to reduce services in order to reduce state taxes and to strengthen the state's economy.

Against the backdrop of this debate, the first three guiding principles together seemed to imply a reduction in the state's human services labor force. As unions perceived these first three principles, they meant something entirely different from what they meant to the commission, consultants, state administration, and legislature. The unions read the principles to mean the following: "The state is in a budget crunch (confront limited resources), therefore the administration wants to provide fewer services to fewer clients (establish service priorities) for a shorter period of time (encourage permanency planning). They think that this will help them with the budget crunch because it will require that they pay fewer human services workers. In other words, they want to sacrifice our jobs and our clients' welfare to solve the state's budget problems." The unions were raising the possibility that the political philosophy that government "do less better" was really a smokescreen to hide the true ideological intent of the philosophy that government simply "do less."

Public-sector labor unions were the newest and fastest-growing kids on the block of the organized labor movement in America. But despite their youth, they could still recognize a bread-and-butter issue when they saw one. Given the history of the state administration's refusal to grandfather child welfare workers from DPW into DSS, the public employee labor union viewed the plans of the implementation commission and its staff as continued threats to the job security of a large number of human service workers. Even the implementation commission's plans for modest increases in the number of child welfare workers in the new agency were viewed with skepticism.

It is ironic that the implementation commission never gained the opportunity to disprove the union's fears of planned reductions in the human services labor force. Just as the commission completed the first draft of its extensive plan (including all the elements to reduce stress and prevent burnout in human service workers) to submit to the governor, he went down to a surprising defeat in the Democratic primary to a fiscally conservative candidate who campaigned on the Massachusetts version of California's sweeping tax cut referendum, Proposition 13. This conservative candidate later won the general election and interpreted his victory as a mandate to get government off the backs and out of the lives of private citizens and to reduce state government spending in order to increase local aid and provide the state's taxpayers with some property tax relief.

In reviewing the work of the implementation commission when they came into office, the new governor and his top administrators agreed to accept those plans for the new agency that were based upon the first three guiding principles because they perceived these principles to be consistent with their philosophy of a reduced role for government in the provision of human services. But they were not willing to implement the many recommendations based upon the fourth principle of reducing worker burnout because these recommendations seemed to entail additional expenditures at a time when the new administration was attempting dramatically to reduce the size of the state budget in order to support the promised tax relief. Therefore, the new administration flatly rejected the modest increases in the number of social work positions, the increases in social worker pay scales, and many of the other plans for upgrading the work environments of child welfare workers proposed by the implementation commission. In fact, the fervor to cut the operating costs of all human service agencies led the new administration to relax many of the standards that were to be used to screen qualified child welfare workers from DPW for employment in DSS. Thus, when the Department of Social Services opened in 1979, most of the basic elements for reform of the child welfare system had not been implemented. The new agency was new in name but not in substance.

CONCLUSION

A movement to reform a child welfare system through increasing and upgrading social worker positions in order to prevent worker burnout became caught in the crunch of a major historical shift in state budget policy that was created by the political-economic conditions that led to the election of a fiscally conservative governor. Given the spiraling politics of tax cuts and service cuts that came to prevail at both the state and national levels in the late 1970s, Massachusetts service employee unions felt increasingly powerless to mount an effective fight against work-force reductions.

No union ever wishes to accept reductions in work-force levels as management's solutions to fiscal problems. But the late 1970s witnessed an increasing willingness on the part of labor to do just that. In the private sector, work-force reductions were rationalized by labor as necessary to keep their industry alive and/or competitive with foreign rivals. In the public sector, unions seemed to accept the necessity of some reductions in work-force levels in order to cut government budgets enough to prevent a tax revolt.

During the debates on the bill to create DSS, the child welfare workers were viewed by many child advocates and professionals as well as the general public as more interested in protecting their jobs than in working for what is in the best interests of the state's most vulnerable children. Thus, child welfare workers found themselves in the tremendously demoralizing position of feeling powerless to fight against work-force reductions and severely criticized for even trying to do so. This position resembles the position of public school teachers when they are faced with the options of striking or settling for inadequate wage agreements. For both teachers and child welfare workers who enter their professions in large measure out of the motivation to serve children, the public view of their disputes with management which seems to pit workers' interests against children's interests has a powerfully demoralizing effect.

Finally, as long as the issue of work-force reductions figured so prominently in the public policy debate over human services in general and child welfare services in particular, the unions also felt powerless to raise issues of work conditions. Public employee unions and their members, like all organizations, worry about first things first. You can't fight to improve a job unless you have a job to improve. Thus, the extensive plans to create new "work environments" to reduce job stress and prevent worker burnout elaborated in the implementation commission recommendations remained largely on paper. Now, in addition to burdensome caseloads and poor work environments, another potential source of worker burnout was added: a deterioration in the public employee union's ability to protect its members' job security.

From a perspective of several years, it is possible to ask what went wrong with the state's efforts to reform the child welfare system and to address the problem of worker burnout. One popular explanation for the state's failure is that a downturn in the state and national economy led to the election of a fiscally conservative governor who stopped many of the reform measures dead in their tracks because they entailed the additional expenditure of funds. It is true that the new governor would not make a commitment to a policy of improving the work environments of child welfare workers because many of the elements of such a policy seemed to conflict with his major policy initiative of reducing the cost of state government. But such an explanation for the failure of the reform efforts is too simple. Cyclical variation in our economy has long been a part of our country's economic life. And the fact that politicians respond to the tax concerns of upper- and middle-class citizens is part of the fundamental nature of our political life. Perhaps the designers of human service systems should be able to anticipate some of the common barriers to reform of the human service workplace and not fall into the trap of making improvements in the work conditions of human service employees totally dependent upon economic upswings. In other words, designers of human service systems must come to understand more fully how prevailing political, economic, and historical conditions influence the policy-making process which in turn determines the work-force levels and work conditions that affect burnout among human service workers.

Given the present state of fiscal conservatism in the country, are there viable alternative strategies for addressing the problem of human service worker burnout? It is clear that there are no easy answers to this question but one approach strikes me as particularly promising because it doesn't place the worker's fate solely in the hands of administrators and politicians who necessarily respond to downturns in the economy with budget reductions. Human service workers may wish to rethink how they themselves conceptualize the nature of their jobs. For instance, is it possible to think of human service workers as greatly expanding their "productivity" and "effectiveness" by being the organizers, conveners, trainers, and coordinators of voluntary resource networks (Sarason et al., 1977)? Are there ways, in other words, that human service workers can organize to make the issue of increased effectiveness their own issue, thus breaking both the public's and the state administration's conceptions of them as motivated largely by the desire to protect their "do-nothing" jobs? If so, might such increases in productivity be offered by public-sector unions as their part of an exchange with state administrators who in turn would guarantee job security? The fiscal crisis of the country in the last year has led to several such historical arrangements between labor and management in the private sector. Clearly, the problems in labor-management relations are different in the private and public sectors. It is harder to define the productivity of a child welfare worker than that of an assembly-line worker. And for all the reasons detailed above in the history of the legislative proposal to create a new child welfare agency, it is more difficult to extract a consistent labor agreement from a state government whose chief executive officer changes every two to four years than from a corporation whose chief executives enjoy longer terms in office. Nonetheless, the point is worth considering because it illustrates how differently one might approach the root causes of burnout among human service workers if one were to adopt a historical and political-economic perspective on the problem rather than (or in addition to) an architectural-bureaucratic approach that is based on notions of the proper design of work environments. If worker burnout is understood in the context of enduring structural problems in public-sector labor-state-management disputes, then a plan to solve the problems created by worker burnout by creating a new state agency and getting rid of all old workers may appear a lot less attractive to the designers of human service systems.

REFERENCES

Center Research Associates. *Work environment report.* Unpublished report to the Social Services Implementation Committee, Executive Office of Human Services, Commonwealth of Massachusetts, 1979.

Cherniss, C. *Professional burnout in human service organizations.* New York: Praeger, 1980.

Children's Defense Fund. *Children without homes: An examination of public responsibility to children in out-of-home care.* Washington, D.C.: Children's Defense Fund, 1979.

Farber, B. & Miller, J. Teacher burnout: A psychoeducational perspective. *Teachers College Record,* 1981, **83**, 235–243.

Goldstein, J., Freud, A., & Solnit, A. *Beyond the best interests of the child.* New York: Free Press, 1973.

Goldstein, J., Freud, A., & Solnit, A. *Before the best interests of the child.* New York: Free Press, 1979.

Juvenile Justice Standards Project, Institute for Judicial Administration/American Bar Association. *Standards relating to abuse and neglect.* Cambridge, Mass.: Ballinger, 1977.

Office for Children and Department of Public Welfare. *Child abuse and neglect fact-finding commission final report*. Office for Children, Commonwealth of Massachusetts, 1978.

Sarason, S. B.; Carroll, C. F.; Maton, K.; Cohen, S.; & Lorentz, E. *Human services and resource networks*. San Francisco: Jossey-Bass, 1977.

Social Services Implementation Committee. *Implementation plan*. Executive Office of Human Services, Commonwealth of Massachusetts, 1979.

Wald, M. State intervention on behalf of "neglected" children: Standards for removal of children from their homes, monitoring the status of children in foster care, and termination of parental rights. *Stanford Law Review*, 1976, **28**, 626.

16

A Tripartite Model of Coping
with Burnout*

Marybeth Shinn
and
Hanne Mørch

Several of the other chapters in this book deal with the causes of burnout among human service workers. Our topic is how to cope with it. We will argue that, just as burnout is more than an individual problem, coping can and should occur at more than just the individual level. We will propose a tripartite model of coping involving strategies used by individual workers, strategies undertaken by groups of workers to aid one another, and strategies initiated by human service agencies.

At each level, coping can attempt to remove a source of stress (problem-focused strategies) or to relieve workers' emotional distress without altering the original stressor (emotion-focused strategies). For example, a worker whose job demands are excessive could talk to the supervisor about which tasks might be postponed or dropped (individual problem-focused coping) or might meet with co-workers to commiserate about the problem (group emotion-focused coping). The agency might try to restructure the job so that the demands are more reasonable (agency problem-focused coping) or might tell workers that the demands are unavoidable for now, but offer them moral support and reassurance that their efforts are genuinely appreciated (agency emotion-focused coping). We will examine the relative effectiveness of these different forms of coping with burnout in two samples of human service workers. But first let us examine the literature on coping more generally.

*Research reported here was supported by the National Science Foundation Grant # DAR-8011824 and a Biomedical Research Support Grant from the National Institute of Health; # RR 07062.

THE COPING LITERATURE

There is surprisingly little empirical research on the effects of coping in natural settings. Much work in the field is theoretical (e.g., Lazarus, Averill, & Opton, 1974; Mechanic, 1974; White, 1974) or based on retrospective self-reports or clinical data (e.g., Cohen & Lazarus, 1973; Murphy, 1974). Laboratory studies in which subjects are led to or instructed to employ specific strategies in response to an experimental stressor (e.g., Houston & Holmes, 1974; Monat, Averill, & Lazarus, 1972) offer little information about ways that people typically select coping strategies (see Lazarus & Launier, 1978). Folkman and Lazarus (1980) answer this question for a sample of middle-aged people, but do not evaluate the effects of coping on strain.

An important exception is Pearlin and Schooler's (1978) sample survey of the effectiveness of coping in four realms: marriage, parenting, household economics, and work. They found that coping works in the sense of reducing psychological strain* in the first three realms, but has little effect on strain resulting from work. We believe that this is not simply a statistical accident. In the workplace, where many stress factors are beyond an individual's control, the individual coping strategies that Pearlin and Schooler (1978) studied may be less potent than those we will call higher-level strategies involving groups of workers or entire organizations.

Job stressors may be among those that, according to Mechanic (1974) "are not amenable to individual solutions, but depend on highly organized cooperative efforts that transcend those of any individual ... no matter how well developed his personal resources" (p. 34).

Newman and Beehr (1979) outline a number of adaptive responses that organizations can use to reduce stress. These include redesigning jobs, altering the organizational structure, changing the evaluation or reward system, changing schedules, providing feedback for role clarification, refining selection and placement criteria, introducing human relations training, marking career paths and promotions, improving communications, and improving benefits such as health services. Unfortunately, very little research has been conducted on these organizational coping strategies.

Newman and Beehr's (1979) coping responses require the active involvement of the organization in efforts to reduce job stress or resulting psychological strain. Group strategies for mutual aid can be undertaken by workers without the organization's participation, and may involve others such as friends or family who are not organizational members. Primary among these group coping strategies is social support.

---

*Pearlin and Schooler (1978) would say, "reducing stress." Their use of strain as the external cause and stress as the psychological reaction is the opposite of the terminology here. Our nomenclature is derived from the occupational stress literature.

G. Caplan (1974) and G. Caplan and Killilea (1976) suggest that support systems may aid members to mobilize their psychological resources, master strain, share tasks, and obtain necessary supplies such as information and skills. Lenrow (1978a, 1978b) calls for developing networks of mutual aid among helping professionals, Cherniss (1980) describes both the importance and the difficulty of establishing social supports in human service agencies, and Pines presents data elsewhere in this volume showing the importance of different types of social support in reducing burnout. Several recent reviews have shown the benefits of social support for psychological and physical health in the face of general life stress (Cobb, 1976; Dean & Lin, 1977; Kaplan, Cassel, & Gore, 1977) and for occupational stress in particular (LaRocco, House, & French, 1980).

The two studies described here asked respondents to identify group and organizational coping strategies as well as individual strategies to reduce stress and strain. We predicted that individual coping strategies would have little impact on job-related strain, as in Pearlin and Schooler's (1978) analysis, but that group and organizational strategies would prove effective.

Although we expected little variance in strain to be explained by individual coping strategies, we were curious about the relative effects of problem-focused and emotion-focused strategies. Lazarus, who originally made the distinction between problem-focused or instrumental strategies and emotion-focused or palliative strategies at the individual level (e.g., Lazarus & Launier, 1978), specifically warns against assuming that instrumental strategies are the more effective. He argues (Lazarus, 1980) that defenses, such as denial, avoidance, or intellectualization, attempts to avoid negative thoughts, and even activities such as taking drugs, can be adaptive, especially in situations where little can be done to remove sources of stress. On the other hand, several researchers using modified versions of the scale developed by Lazarus and his colleagues or other instruments have found emotion-focused strategies to be less useful than problem-focused strategies, and in some cases actually associated with increased strain.

Chiriboga, Pierce, and Bierton (1980) found self-blame and wish-fulfilling fantasy to be associated with somatic symptoms among their sample of divorced men and women. Active mastery was associated with more positive outcomes. They also compared outcomes for people categorized by a cluster analysis into coping types. Active copers, who were high on both active mastery and help seeking had the lowest amounts of reported symptoms, loneliness, and depression. Imaginative escapers, who were especially apt to use self-blame and wish-fulfilling fantasy had the worst outcomes.

Felton, Revenson, and Hinrichsen (1981) found that the emotion-focused strategies of wish-fulfilling fantasy, emotional expression, and self-blaming denial were related to low levels of health self-esteem and high levels of negative affect in their sample of older adults coping with chronic illnesses. Cognitive restructuring and the problem-focused strategy of information seeking were associated with positive affect.

Pines and Aronson (1981) reported that two of six "active" coping strategies such as confronting the problem were reliably associated with low tedium (a measure of physical, emotional, and mental exhaustion or burnout) in an unspecified sample. Five of six "inactive" strategies, such as drinking or use of drugs, were reliably associated with high tedium.

Pearlin and Schooler (1978) found that the most effective coping strategies varied across situational domains. In marriage and parenting, where coping explained the most variance in strain, active coping and self-reliance rather than avoidance, ignoring, and emotional discharge were helpful. In household economics, more palliative strategies, such as devaluing money and selective ignoring, reduced strain. Although Pearlin and Schooler's (1978) work shows that successful coping is likely to be domain-specific, a preponderance of evidence suggests that problem-focused coping may be associated with better outcomes than emotion-focused coping across a variety of domains.

Other interesting questions concern the range of strategies individuals, groups of workers, and organizations use to cope with burnout, and the strategies they do not actually use but believe might be helpful. Here the literature is rather sparse. Existing coping inventories (e.g., Folkman & Lazarus, 1980; Pearlin & Schooler, 1978) deal only with individual strategies and were not developed with human service agencies in mind. Thus, they are unlikely to cover the universe of possible strategies for coping with burnout. In Chapter 11, Pines presents a useful typology of social support, but this does not include many instrumental actions that workers can take to aid one another (e.g., filling in for a co-worker who needs relief). Moreover, no inventories for organizational coping are currently available.

To answer some of these questions, we conducted two studies of coping with burnout in different samples of human service workers. Both were designed to test the tripartite model of coping by cataloging the types of strategies individuals, groups of workers, and agencies used, and examining their success. The second study additionally distinguished between problem-focused and emotion-focused coping at all three levels. Both studies asked in different ways about additional strategies that could have been used to cope with job stress and strain. (Each also collected a variety of other data beyond the scope of this chapter.)

Method

Study 1. The first study was a mail survey of 141 members of a statewide professional society for group therapists and other group workers, including psychologists, social workers, psychiatrists, pastoral counselors, nurses, and others. Respondents worked in a variety of human service settings, including private practice (n = 30), mental health centers or university counseling centers (n = 26), universities (n = 24), school systems (n = 15), social service agencies (n = 10), and in smaller numbers, in psychiatric and medical hospitals, alcohol and drug programs, residential treatment programs for adults and children, religious organizations, and so on.

Respondents answered a six-page anonymous questionnaire that included four open-ended questions on coping with stresses they had described previously. The domain of individual coping responses available to workers and those actually employed were assessed with the questions, "How do you think human service professionals cope with the feeling of being burned out?" and "What do you do to cope with the stress and strain of your particular job?"

Two raters independently coded the presence or absence of six individual coping strategies from responses to these questions. Interrater agreement ranged from .91 to .98 and remained above .8 in all cases when corrected for chance using Cohen's κ (Cohen, 1968).

Potential and actual group and organizational coping responses were elicited with the questions, "What sorts of things can agencies, or groups of human service professionals, do to keep workers from burning out?" and "What do your agency and your co-workers do to keep you from burning out?" Two raters independently coded four levels of group coping, or social support, and three levels of agency coping. Interrater reliability (Pearson's r) was .94 for social support and .90 for agency coping.

Because burnout is multifaceted and has been variously defined and operationalized (Maslach, 1981; Shinn, 1981), we chose to use four more specific indices of psychological strain as our outcomes. Alienation (Berkeley Planning Associates, 1977) had been used previously as a measure of burnout. Sample items include "I feel optimistic about my clients," and "I am disenchanted with my job." Job Satisfaction (*Michigan Organizational Assessment Package,* 1975) assessed satisfaction with particular job facets such as "your pay," "the way other staff members treat you," and "the opportunity to develop your skills and abilities." Psychological Symptoms (Caplan et al., 1975) asked respondents how often they felt "sad," "nervous," "angry," etc. Somatic Symptoms (Caplan et al., 1975) asked for the frequency with which the respondent had experienced specific symptoms such as headaches or loss of appetite in the previous month. Internal consistency reliability (Cronbach's α) ranged from .71 for Somatic Symptoms to .93 for Alienation.

Study 2. The second study involved in-depth (two- to four-hour) interviews with 82 child care workers in residential programs for youths. Workers were asked to describe a stressful incident and an ongoing source of job stress. For each they were asked how they, their co-workers, their supervisor, and their agency had coped and what else each could have done. Interviewers probed for coping with the causes and with their feelings in each situation so that both problem- and emotion-focused coping could be assessed.

Two raters independently scored the amount of actual and potential problem- and emotion-focused coping reported at each level across these and several additional questions (e.g., "What do you do to relieve tension [associated with work]?"; "In what ways do your co-workers help and support you?"; "If you wanted to change this agency so as to reduce burnout and turnover, what would you do?"). Supervisor coping was included with agency strategies. Interrater reliability (Pearson's *r*) ranged from .71 for co-worker emotion-focused coping to .89 for agency problem-focused coping. After all disagreements were resolved by consensus, one rater rescored all protocols, raising the range of correlations between her ratings and the consensual ratings from .77 to .94.

The same outcomes were used as in the previous study. This time internal consistency reliability (Cronbach's α) ranged from .78 for Somatic Symptoms to .90 for Psychological Symptoms

Results

Table 16.1 shows the percentage of respondents in the first study who indicated they actually used each of the coping strategies and the percentage mentioning each as a potential strategy that was used by other individuals or that could be used by groups of workers and agencies. On the individual level, respondents suggested a plethora of coping strategies that they actually used to combat stress on their own jobs. The most common coping response, reported by 64 percent of respondents, involved focusing on activities or family and friends outside the job. Other strategies mentioned by about a third of the sample each were building competence, primarily by attending workshops and conferences; changing one's approach to the job, as, for example, by setting realistic limits on one's activities; taking breaks or vacations; using cognitive or emotional strategies, such as withdrawal and alienation; focusing on positive aspects of work; feeling depressed or blaming oneself; or getting angry. About a fifth of the sample reported changing the job itself, for example, by introducing greater variety into the work.

Respondents were somewhat less apt to report that other workers used active strategies such as changing their approach to the job or changing the job itself. They reported that others used cognitive and emotional strategies more frequently. They saw others as focusing on activities outside the job less frequently than they themselves did and were more apt to describe these activities in negative terms (e.g., "use of drugs and alcohol") for others. In short, respondents painted a somewhat more favorable picture of their own coping responses than of those they saw around them.

The situation is reversed for agency coping. Respondents suggested a variety of strategies that agencies could use to help workers avoid burnout. These

Table 16.1.   Percentage of Workers Reporting Actual and
Potential Coping Strategies in Study 1.

Individual Strategies	Actually Used	Used by Others
Build Competence	30	27
Change Approach to Job	30	14
Change Job Design	22	7
Cognitive/Emotional Strategies	32	51
Focus Outside Job	64	32
Take Breaks	31	24
Group Strategies	Actually Used	Could be Used
Social Support	64	40
Agency Strategies	Actually Used	Could be Used
Build Competence	18	33
Change Job Design	10	38
Improve Supervision/Communication	8	23
Increase Rewards	4	13
Encourage Recreation	7	8
Give Breaks	16	20

included building competence by offering training programs, making consultants available, or sending workers to conferences; changing the job design by limiting caseloads, increasing variety, or making goals clearer and more realistic; improving supervision, communication, and participation in decisions; increasing both monetary rewards and recognition; encouraging recreation and offering breaks and vacations. But in response to the question, "What do your agency and your co-workers do to keep you from burning out?" most workers mentioned only social support.

Many answers were bitter, especially with reference to the agency (e.g., "Not a damn thing"; "When someone really freaks out [cries, gets angry, etc.] brief attention is paid to that person's pain. Otherwise it's ignored"; "Provide peer support. The agency itself is the major stressor"). Because so few agency strategies were actually employed, all were combined for predictive purposes into a single three-point index.

Answers on social support ranged even more widely on an intensity dimension, and thus were coded on a four-point scale from "none" to "much" for predictive purposes. For example, "Occasional reinforcement, some support, mostly nothing" was coded as a low level of support (2 on the four-point scale). Much support is shown in the answer, "In private practice many of us are in the same office park complex. Touching base, hugs, lunch, health clubbing together, and in general good cooperative and loving spirit help a lot. I can turn to a colleague on a bad day and get support and whatever else I may need." The latter response also demonstrates the possibility of group coping in private practice.

Table 16.2.   Percentage of Workers Reporting Actual and Potential Coping Strategies and the Mean Number of Strategies Used within Categories in Study 2.

	Actually Used	$\overline{X}$	Also Could Have Been Used
INDIVIDUAL STRATEGIES			
Problem-Focused			
Seek Help/Information	43		23
Change Approach to Job/Situation	68		44
Take Action With Youths	39		16
Mean Number of Strategies Used		2.1	
Emotion-Focused			
Cognitive/Emotional Strategies	65		13
Focus: Outside Job			
Active	46		2
Quiet	74		1
Family/Friends	40		0
Eat/Drink/Smoke	39		4
Take Breaks	17		4
Mean Number of Strategies Used		3.3	
CO-WORKER STRATEGIES			
Problem-Focused			
Take Action	87		38
Give Advice/Information	76		12
Mean Number of Strategies Used		2.9	
Emotion-Focused			
Give Support	84		7
Mean Number of Strategies Used		1.4	
AGENCY STRATEGIES			
Problem-Focused			
Change Job Design:			
Workload/Schedule/Pay/Benefits	30		66
Training/Job Ladder/Information	10		54
Emergency Procedures	15		7
Give/Receive Advice/Information	54		65
Take Action with Youths	23		34
Mean Number of Strategies Used		1.9	
Emotion-Focused			
Give Support/Recognition	52		32
Mean Number of Strategies Used		.8	

Table 16.2 shows the parallel descriptive results for the sample of child care workers. Again, individual strategies were employed more frequently (mean of 5.4 per worker) than group strategies (mean of 4.3) and twice as often as agency strategies (mean of 2.7).

The strategies used most frequently by individuals fall into the emotion-focused category, "Focus Outside the Job." Three-quarters of the sample engaged in quiet attention-diverting activities, such as sleeping, reading, and watching television; close to half took part in dancing, sports, exercise, and other active pursuits. Two-fifths focused on family and friends, and a similar number ate, drank, or smoked various substances.

Two-thirds of the sample mentioned Cognitive or Emotional Strategies such as "making the best of it," resignation, controlling feelings, joking, or getting angry. Close to one-fifth took breaks or vacations to "get away from it all." Only a handful of respondents indicated that they could have done more than they did in the way of emotion-focused coping.

Of the individual problem-focused strategies, "Change Approach to Job or Situation" was mentioned most frequently (by two-thirds of the sample). This included confronting or ignoring a situation or person, changing a working style, or switching positions, for example, to an administrative job. Two-fifths sought help or information, and a similar number took action with their young clients—counseling, threatening, or punishing them. When asked what else they could have done, respondents were apt to mention additional problem-focused rather than emotion-focused strategies.

The child care workers identified three ways their co-workers helped them to cope, each with high frequency. Almost 90 percent listed some sort of action—pinch hitting to give the worker some relief, sharing tasks (e.g., "they'll take one [kid] and I'll take the other"), shifting schedules to accommodate the respondent, or backing the worker up (e.g., "in confrontation with [a] kid, [you] will be backed by others; they will back your authority"). Three-quarters mentioned discussion of problems or alternative ways of dealing with situations. All of these were classified as problem-focused strategies. Four-fifths of respondents also mentioned emotion-focused support from co-workers, such as "share and diffuse most of feelings"; "joke and laugh it off"; or "counsel me not to get upset about these girls." Hardly any workers mentioned emotional support as something more their co-workers could have done, nor was there much need for advice. However, almost two-fifths of the sample saw a need for some additional action on the part of their co-workers.

As in the first study, respondents suggested a variety of strategies that could have been used by the agency, especially in the area of job design. These included changing schedules, increasing pay and benefits, augmenting the staff, increasing time off, and providing more training. Relative to the large number of respondents suggesting what more the agency could do, the actual number of strategies used was small.

More than half of the sample reported that their agency gave or received advice or information by allowing participation in decision making, facilitating two-way communication, or offering supervision, feedback or flexibility. However, two-thirds of the sample felt that more could have been done, e.g., "give child care workers more input into decisions regarding kids and programming." About a quarter of the sample mentioned actions the agency took with youths, such as removing or not accepting inappropriate youths or enforcing rules. Again the need was greater than the supply: one-third of the sample mentioned additional actions that the agency could have taken.

Half the sample reported receiving emotion-focused support or recognition from the agency, e.g., "they take care of you, make you feel wanted, everybody's close, little family" or "supervisor is part of the tears and laughter." About a third wanted additional support or recognition from the agency.

Next we explored the effects of the various coping strategies on respondents' reported levels of strain in the two samples. In the first study, we used a set multiple regression framework.* As predicted from Pearlin and Schooler's (1978) and Mechanic's (1974) work, the set of individual coping variables was not reliably related to any of the four strain measures after stress was accounted for. (It was marginally related to Somatic Symptoms, $F[6,109] = 2.04, p < .1$).

The set of higher-level (group and agency) strategies *was* reliably associated with reduced strain in the two areas most closely related to the job, i.e., Job Satisfaction, $F(2,105) = 5.94, p < .01$, and Alienation, $F(2,83) = 4.15$, $p < .05$. Analyses within the set showed that these effects were largely due to social support, which uniquely accounted for significant proportions of variance in both variables. Agency coping was only marginally related to each. It may not have received a fair test, however, since so little agency coping was actually used.

Although individual coping strategies as a set did not reliably predict strain, the pattern of relationships within the set was of interest. Of the three strategies in Table 16.1, classified as problem-focused (Building Competence, Changing Approach to the Job, and Changing Job Design), two were consistently, although nonreliably associated with reduced strain. All the remaining strategies, including the emotion-focused responses of Cognitive and Emotional Strategies, Focusing Outside the Job, and Taking Breaks, were associated (nonreliably) with increased strain. These findings are consistent with previous empirical literature (cited above) suggesting that instrumental coping is more efficacious than palliative coping, however they must be interpreted cautiously, since none reached conventional levels (.05) of statistical significance.

Table 16.3 shows the relationships between coping and strain in the second sample. Relationships between coping and the two symptom scales again were weak. No measure of coping predicted Somatic Symptoms, and Psychological

---

*For each dependent variable, sets of independent variables were entered into the equation hierarchically with the set of (previously identified) stressors first, the set of individual coping strategies second, the set of group and agency strategies third, and a set of theoretically meaningful interaction terms last. For more details of this and other analyses, see Shinn, Rosario, Mørch, and Chestnut, 1982.

Table 16.3.   Zero-Order Correlations between Coping and Outcomes in Study 2.

| | | Outcomes | | |
Coping	Somatic Symptoms	Psychological Symptoms	Alienation	Job Satisfaction
Agency Problem	−.02	−.02	−.36***	.37***
Agency Emotion	−.03	−.17+	−.35***	.40***
Group Problem	−.07	−.22*	−.44***	.31**
Group Emotion	.11	.12	−.04	.12
Individual Problem	−.17+	−.21*	−.21*	.23*
Individual Emotion	−.03	.11	.00	.14

$+p < .1.$
$*p < .05.$
$**p < .01.$
$***p < .001.$
$N = 73–77.$

Symptoms were reliably reduced only by group and individual problem-focused coping.

Relationships for the job attitudes of Alienation and Satisfaction were again stronger. In this sample, which had more variance than the first in levels of agency coping, both problem-focused and emotion-focused coping by the agency predicted decreased Alienation and increased Satisfaction at the .001 level. At the group and individual level, only problem-focused coping had an ameliorative effect (on both outcomes). Group and individual emotion-focused coping were not related reliably to any outcome measure.

SUMMARY AND IMPLICATIONS OF FINDINGS

Taken together, the results of these two studies provide considerable support for the tripartite model of coping with burnout among human service workers. Both professional group workers in a vareity of service delivery settings and child care workers in residential programs for youths could identify coping responses that they, their co-workers, and their agencies used to combat job stress and burnout. Where coping strategies were sparsest, at the agency level, workers identified a number of additional responses their agencies could make.

Group and agency coping made substantial contributions toward workers' favorable attitudes toward their jobs. Coping of all sorts had less effect on self-reported symptoms, although individual and group problem-focused coping were related to low levels of Psychological Symptoms in the second study.

Individual coping was not as ineffective as we had supposed. It was reliably related to three strain measures in the second study and marginally related to the fourth (Somatic Symptoms) in both studies. However, the proportions of variance explained by individual coping were uniformly small. This, along with

Pearlin and Schooler's (1978) parallel finding that individual coping had little impact on job-related strain, suggests that individuals should not be held responsible by themselves for combatting burnout. We do not advocate that workers give up individual efforts to cope, rather that the more powerful weapons in the arsenal, the group and agency strategies, be given more attention.

Also interesting was the second study's finding that, whereas problem-focused strategies at the individual and especially the group level were effective in coping with burnout, emotion-focused strategies were not. (The first study found a nonsignificant trend in the same direction for individual coping and failed to subdivide group coping owing to insufficient detail in the answers.) Perhaps emotion-focused coping at these levels is simply ineffective. Or perhaps high levels of strain differentially lead to emotion-focused coping strategies such as having a drink or getting together with co-workers to ventilate feelings. If these strategies in turn make one feel better, the two causal effects would cancel out, leading to weak relationships between coping and strain. Still, our research and other studies cited previously give us little reason to advocate emotion-focused coping at the individual or group levels.

Emotion-focused coping at the agency level is another story. Although we identified only one such strategy, giving emotional support and recognition, and the mean and variance were the lowest of all the coping categories, agency emotion-focused coping explained substantial portions of variance in child care workers' job attitudes. Apparently workers are committed to and satisfied with agencies that are supportive and committed to them.

Workers may not be unaware of the sorts of coping that are most effective. When asked in the second study about what more could have been done in particular situations or to reduce burnout more generally, child care workers listed problem-focused strategies at all three levels and emotion-focused strategies at the agency level—precisely the types of coping that were related to job satisfaction, alienation, and, to a lesser extent, psychological symptoms. Very few workers mentioned the ineffective individual and group emotion-focused strategies.

We close by translating these findings into recommendations for coping with burnout. Much responsibility for reducing burnout rests with the agency, which can improve job design, offer workers opportunities to participate in decision making, provide appropriate supervision and training, and give workers emotional support and recognition. Fostering instrumental support among co-workers is also important.

Simply ventilating feelings alone or with co-workers or cultivating outside interests does not appear to be effective, but taking action on one's own or another's behalf, discussing problems and potential solutions with co-workers, and seeking help or information elsewhere can be useful. Such actions can make one feel less depressed, angry, or anxious as well as reduce alienation or increase job satisfaction. Coping at all three levels is important. It is especially needed at the group and agency levels where, despite its effectiveness, it is often lacking.

REFERENCES

Berkeley Planning Associates. *Evaluation of child abuse and neglect demonstration projects 1974-1977. Volume IX: Project management and worker burnout; final report.* Springfield, Va.: National Technical Information Service, 1977.

Caplan, G. *Support systems and community mental health: Lectures on concept development.* New York: Behavioral Publications, 1974.

Caplan, G. & Killilea, M. (Eds.). *Support systems and mutual help: Multidisciplinary explorations.* New York: Grune & Stratton, 1976.

Caplan, R. D.; Cobb, S.; French, J. R. P., Jr.; Harrison, R. V.; & Pinneau, S. R., Jr. *Job demands and worker health.* Washington, D.C.: U.S. Government Printing Office, 1975, HEW Publications No. (NIOSH) 75-160.

Cherniss, C. *Staff burnout: Job stress in the human services.* Beverly Hills, Calif.: Sage, 1980.

Chiriboga, D. A., Pierce, R., & Bierton, P. *Stress and coping among the divorced.* Paper presented at the Annual Meeting of the Gerontological Society, San Diego, November 1980.

Cobb, S. Social support as a moderator of life stress. *Psychosomatic Medicine,* 1976, **38**, 300-314.

Cohen, F. & Lazarus, R. S. Active coping processes, coping dispositions, and recovery from surgery. *Psychosomatic Medicine,* 1973, **35**, 375-389.

Cohen, J. Weighted kappa: Nominal scale agreement with provision for scaled disagreement or partial credit. *Psychological Bulletin,* 1968, **70**, 213-220.

Dean, A. & Lin, N. The stress-buffering role of social support. *The Journal of Nervous and Mental Disease,* 1977. **165**, 403-417.

Felton, B. J., Revenson, T. A., & Hinrichsen, G. A. *Stress, coping, and psychological adjustment among chronically ill adults.* Unpublished manuscript, New York University, 1981.

Folkman, S. & Lazarus, R. S. An analysis of coping in a middle-aged community sample. *Journal of Health and Social Behavior,* 1980, **21**, 219-239.

Houston, B. K. & Holmes, D. S. Effect of avoidant thinking and reappraisal for coping with threat involving temporal uncertainty. *Journal of Personality and Social Psychology,* 1974, **30**, 382-388.

Kaplan, B. H., Cassel, J. C., & Gore, S. Social support and health. *Medical Care,* 1977, **25** (5), Supplement, 47-58.

LaRocco, J. M., House, J. S., & French, J. R. P., Jr. Social support, occupational stress, and health. *Journal of Health and Social Behavior,* 1980, **21**, 202-218.

Lazarus, R. S. The stress and coping paradigm. In Eisdorfer, C.; Cohen, D.; Kleinman, A.; & Maxim, P. (Eds.), *Theoretical bases for psychopathology.* New York: Spectrum, 1980.

Lazarus, R. S., Averill, J. R., & Opton, E. M. The psychology of coping: Issues of research and assessment. In Coelho, G. V., Hamburg, D. A., & Adams, J. E. (Eds.), *Coping and adaptation.* New York: Basic Books, 1974.

Lazarus, R. S. & Launier, R. Stress-related transactions between person and environment. In Pervin, L. A. & Lewis, M. (Eds.), *Internal and external determinants of behavior.* New York: Plenum, 1978.

Lenrow, P. B. Dilemmas of professional helping: Continuities and discontinuities with folk helping roles. In Wispe, L. (Ed.), *Altruism, sympathy, and helping.* New York: Academic Press, 1978. (a)

Lenrow, P. B. The work of helping strangers. *American Journal of Community Psychology,* 1978, **6**, 555–571. (b)

Maslach, C. Understanding burnout: Problems, progress, and promise. In Paine, W. S., (Ed.), *Proceedings of the First National Conference on Burnout.* Philadelphia: Mercy Catholic Medical Center, 1981.

Mechanic, D. Social structure and personal adaptation: Some neglected dimensions. In Coelho, G. V., Hamburg, D. A., & Adams, J. E. (Eds.), *Coping and adaptation.* New York: Basic Books, 1974.

Michigan organizational assessment package. Ann Arbor, Michigan: Institute for Social Research, 1975.

Monat, A., Averill, J. R., & Lazarus, R. S. Anticipatory stress and coping reactions under various conditions of uncertainty. *Journal of Personality and Social Psychology,* 1972, **24**, 237–253.

Murphy, L. B. Coping, vulnerability, and resilience in childhood. In Coelho, G. V., Hamburg, D. A., & Adams, J. E. (Eds.), *Coping and adaptation.* New York: Basic Books, 1974.

Newman, J. E. & Beehr, T. A. Personal and organizational strategies for handling job stress: A review of research and opinion. *Personnel Psychology,* 1979, **32**, 1–43.

Pearlin, L. I. & Schooler, C. The structure of coping. *Journal of Health and Social Behavior,* 1978, **19**, 2–21.

Pines, A. M. & Aronson, E. *Burnout: From tedium to personal growth.* New York: Free Press, 1981.

Shinn, M. Caveat Emptor: Potential problems in using information on burnout. In Paine, W. S. (Ed.), *Proceedings of the First National Conference on Burnout.* Philadelphia: Mercy Catholic Medical Center, 1981.

Shinn, M.; Rosario, M.; Mørch, H.; & Chestnut, D. *Coping with job stress and burnout in the human services.* Unpublished manuscript, New York University, 1981.

White, R. W. Strategies of adaptation: An attempt at systematic description. In Coelho, G. V., Hamburg, D. A., & Adams, J. E. (Eds.), *Coping and adaptation.* New York: Basic Books, 1974.

CONCLUSION
Current Trends, Future Directions
Barry A. Farber

Our knowledge of burnout has increased considerably over the last decade. Conceptual models no longer suggest a linear relationship between stress and burnout, nor do they attribute burnout exclusively to intrapsychic factors. The chapters in the present volume reflect the growing awareness that burnout is not a simple, unidimensional problem with easily grasped causes and solutions, but rather a complex issue with roots in intrapsychic, interpersonal, occupational, organizational, historical, and social phenomena.

What have these chapters contributed specifically to our understanding of stress and burnout? Several chapters have addressed theoretical issues, suggesting new ways to order old data. Fischer, for example, by adhering to an internally consistent psychoanalytic model of burnout, convincingly demonstrates that the field has, over the years, gradually come to confuse a small class of truly burned out workers from a large and growing class of worn out workers. Fischer points out that those workers originally described by Freudenberger as burned out strove to maintain their high self-esteem by working even *harder* in the face of impossible demands. These people, claims Fischer, "idealize their work," and use it to cling to a "compensatory illusion of grandiosity." On the other hand, according to Fischer, worn out workers (who are frequently and mistakenly described as burned out) use the burnout label as an "excuse for poor performance and as a justification for both easier working conditions and higher pay." Fischer not only adds to our knowledge of the intrapsychic factors underlying burnout (i.e., that it is a response to "narcissistic trauma"), but forces us also to recognize the importance of carefully defining the phenomena that we are addressing.

Fischer's perspective emphasizes the importance of self-esteem as a mediational variable in the burnout process. In a somewhat similar, though markedly less psychodynamic vein, Harrison, and Farber (in the introductory chapter), and Heifetz and Bersani all conceptualize burnout as a process that occurs when professionals are unable to receive positive, or at least accurate, feedback from the environment regarding the effects of their efforts. Harrison, for example, sees burnout as inversely related to professionals' perceptions of competence. The probability of professionals' feeling good about their achievements, notes Harrison, may be adversely affected by a variety of factors—for example, lack of client motivation, lack of institutional support, inadequate professional skills, or excessive workload. According to Harrison, "when the practitioner seldom sees success, and particularly when failure is seen as a result of his or her efforts, burnout is likely." Similarly, Farber notes that a common characteristic of work-related stresses is their incurrence of feelings of "inconsequentiality" on the part of workers. Farber suggests that burnout, like learned helplessness, occurs when individuals feel that their actions can no longer affect desired changes in the environment and they therefore stop trying. Heifetz and Bersani use the notion of cybernetics to explain the occurrence of burnout. According to their model, "professionals' subjective experience of growth—in their clients and themselves—is strongest when it consists of the perception of milestones being approached, attained, and passed." Furthermore, the successful pursuit of these milestones is based on the presence of several key elements in the cybernetic process: for example, clearly defined goals, short-term indications of progress, and strategies for adjusting one's pursuit of goals based on incoming data. Burnout occurs, say Heifetz and Bersani, when the pursuit of professional milestones is disrupted by the lack of one or more key elements in the cybernetic process.

Several other chapters have advanced what may be termed a "deficit model" of burnout, which suggests that burnout is caused not by the presence of job stressors but rather by the absence of job motivators. In this regard, Jayaratne and Chess show that role ambiguity, role conflict, and excessive workload are not significant predictors of burnout. Instead, their study indicates that the best predictors of both burnout and job satisfaction are job challenges, financial rewards, and promotions. Eisenstat and Felner also take pains to separate the functions of job stressors and job motivators. They show that whereas job stressors are related to emotional exhaustion, job enrichers such as autonomy, skill variety, and task significance are crucial in providing motivation for human service workers. Cherniss and Krantz, too, emphasize the connection between burnout and lack of motivation: "Long hours, hard work, and the other stresses often cited as causes of burnout only lead to burnout when there is an absence of meaning in work. The burnout process thus begins not with stress but with the loss of commitment and moral purpose in work." And Fibkins, as well as Ianni and Reuss-Ianni, suggest that the critical "deficit" in the burnout process is lack of organizational support. To Fibkins, teacher burnout is "the result of the school organization's lack of responsivity to the complicated and increasingly pressurized aspects of teachers' work." Ianni and Reuss-Ianni note that while individual and sociocultural factors may influence the experience of work-related stress, they "do not seem to produce the particular syndrome seen as burnout unless they are mediated, aggravated, or complemented by some particular (usually bureaucratic) organizational structure."

Other authors caution us not to overlook the political-economic-social context within which burnout occurs. Burnout, says Sarason, is never simply a characteristic of or within an individual, "but a complex of psychological characteristics that reflect features of the larger society." Expressing a similar notion, Sakharov and Farber note the dialectical interaction between the individual and society and regard burnout as "the subjective experience of a predominantly social problem." And Aber, in describing the process of burnout among child welfare workers in Massachusetts, emphasizes the need to understand the political-economic history of these workers and their union. "Without an understanding of the history of labor-management conflict, the roots of burnout are invisible and incomprehensible." Freudenberger sums up many of these notions by commenting that "a comprehensive understanding of burnout requires a framework within which antecedent variables, of both a personal and social nature, be explored in terms of how they impact on the present of a person, and in turn change the individual's view of the future." Freudenberger argues that we must attend to the values of individuals and the systems within which they work, to the interaction between individuals and their environment, and to the nature and effects of significant transformation in society.

The necessity of attending to mediational processes (e.g., individual psychodynamics, organizational support, economic and social conditions) in understanding the etiology of burnout is one recurrent theme of this volume. Another theme that has been emphasized is that the effects of stress on professional workers can take an almost infinite variety of forms. Burnout, of course, is the most widely known stress-related syndrome affecting professional workers; increasing public and professional attention to this phenomenon has, however, obscured the fact that many professionals, although stressed as a consequence of their work, are not burned out. As several chapters point out, professionals may react in a variety of both adaptive and nonadaptive ways to the inevitable stresses they encounter. Farber, for example, notes that the stresses of psychotherapeutic work are often accepted by therapists as inevitable and even necessary components of their job. Even, however, when therapists react dysfunctionally to stress, they may do so in a "nonburned-out" manner, for example, by adopting a psychodynamic perspective regardless of the appropriateness of the situation. In addition, Mawardi points out that physician impairment is often a more encapsulated phenomenon than burnout, affecting—sometimes with quite tragic results—the delivery of optimal medical care but not causing physical, emotional, and attitudinal exhaustion.

And Freudenberger suggests that for some workers the symptoms of stress and burnout may serve a homeostatic function, that it may alert them to the necessity of monitoring and altering maladaptive personal and social systems.

If stress and burnout are not phenomena with invariant origins and symptomatology, then they also are not phenomena with easily prescribed solutions. And, as several chapters in this volume indicate, this is indeed the case. Social support, though still considered by many as the treatment of choice for burnout, is seen to be in itself a complex phenomenon that may take a multitude of forms. Social support may be provided by a series of individuals, by a formal support group, or by an ideological community. Moreover, even within these general categories, social support may take on a variety of forms. Pines, for example, indicates that when individuals provide social support for one another, they generally do so by fulfilling any one of six discrete functions: listening, emotional challenge, technical challenge, emotional support, technical support, or sharing social reality. In addition, Pines shows that the perceived importance and availability of each of these forms of social support are dependent upon an individual's cultural background, sex, and motivational pattern. Other authors have indicated the different functions of work-setting support groups. These groups may serve to facilitate personal and professional growth (Fibkins), or they may attempt to prevent burnout by generating practical solutions to work-related problems (Scully). Even ideological communities, note Cherniss and Krantz, "differ greatly in many respects, and some are clearly more effective than others in maintaining commitment and preventing burnout."

Several other authors also emphasize the variety and complexity of solutions to stress and burnout. Shinn and Mørch, for example, suggest that solutions to burnout can proceed at the individual, group, or organizational level, and that at each level, solutions can be categorized as either problem-focused (taking action on one's own or another's behalf, discussing solutions to problems with co-workers, seeking help or information elsewhere), or emotion-focused (ventilating feelings, taking vacations, diverting attention to such outside interests as reading, television, or sports). Their study shows that problem-focused solutions are more effective at the individual and group levels, but that emotion-focused solutions (e.g., providing emotional support and recognition) are more effective at the agency level. And, Eisenstat and Felner note, from the perspective of an organizational consultant, all human service agencies are not alike: "In some settings we must be attuned to reducing stress and in others to increasing motivation." Taken together, then, the chapters on treatment and prevention emphasize the need for specificity in any discussion of remediating the problems of stress and burnout. Like the question now posed in the area of psychotherapy research, we must ask those who offer solutions to the problems of stress and burnout, "What kind of intervention (or support group), offered by what kind of individual(s), aimed at what target(s) with what purpose, will have what kinds of effects on the individual, work setting, and organization?"

TOWARD A COMPREHENSIVE MODEL OF STRESS AND BURNOUT

In a retrospective look at the historical development of the field, it becomes clear that much has been accomplished in ten years. Models of burnout have progressed from a focus on intrapsychic features and discrete environmental stressors to complex conceptual formulations that emphasize the role of mediational processes and the interactive nature of individual, organizational, and social variables. Many issues, though, of both a methodological and substantive nature, remain to be investigated.

First, there is an overriding need for a common definition of burnout, for baseline data regarding the frequency of its occurrence in different occupations, and for an accepted way or ways of measuring its symptoms and intensity. Yet there is also a need for more innovative research strategies. The field's traditional dependence on survey research has several inherent problems: these instruments tend to lack the subtlety necessary for sophisticated analyses and do not readily permit idiosyncratic responses. While research based on clinical data overcomes these problems, it tends to be somewhat subjective, difficult to replicate, and limited in scope and generalizability. Some recent investigations have attempted to overcome these difficulties. For example, Evans and Bartolomé (1980) combined the two techniques in their study of middle-level managers, using semistructured clinical interviews in conjunction with formalized survey-type interviews. Their methodology may prove useful to other researchers.

Much of the present research in the field has been posited on a variety of untested assumptions. For example, we have no empirical evidence at present demonstrating a direct link between burnout and productivity, although demands for high productivity are seen as a precipitating factor in the burnout process and a decline in productivity has been reported as a symptom of burnout. Yet the relationship of burnout to productivity demands may be different for workers in different fields, and the impact of burnout on productivity may vary according to the extent to which a worker is burned out. Thus, it is possible for a helper to exhibit a number of symptoms of burnout while maintaining a fundamental commitment to work which includes an appropriate level of productivity. A psychotherapist working in a large municipal hospital, for example, may evidence all the classic symptoms of burnout in front of colleagues yet successfully "reintegrate" when in session with patients.

We also tend to assume that work-related stress and life stress outside the job affect each other in a reciprocal, linear manner. This relationship may, in fact, be curvilinear. It is possible that moderate levels of nonwork stress lead to a decathexion of the workplace and a reduction in the level of job stress. Some research exploring the relationship between personal and professional lives of workers has been done (see Evans & Bartolomé, 1980; Farber, in press; Henry, Sims, & Spray, 1973) but more work on this topic is clearly indicated.

Burnout has often been conceptualized as a single syndrome with multiple symptomatology. It may, however, by more useful to develop multiple typologies of burnout, analogous to the typologies of depression that have been proposed. Thus, just as depression can be viewed as endogenous or exogenous, or as active, passive, or reactive, burnout may be found to have similarly variant characteristics. In this regard, Gillespie (1981) characterizes burnout in protective service workers as active or passive. Active burnout is characterized by avoidant techniques and stems from organizational and social factors; passive burnout is characterized by a loss of interest and commitment and seems to stem more from internal psychological processes. Similarly, Pines and Aronson (1981) note that stress may be mutable or immutable, continuous or intermittent and that these features influence the viability of different coping mechanisms. These investigations, as well as the work of Cherniss (1980) and Lazarus and Launier (1978) typify a recent and welcome trend in the field toward specificity in the description and treatment of burnout and other stress-related disorders. On another front, recent work on "double depression" (Keller & Shapiro, 1982) may also be useful in clarifying certain aspects of burnout. Double depression refers to the situation where chronic depression is overlaid by acute depression in times of crisis. An analogous situation may well exist for work stress. Research on the effects of an acute crisis on chronic disillusionment or "low-grade" burnout would be of considerable interest and value.

Another topic that remains to be explored is the relationship between burnout and patterns of career choice. One of the postulates of the vocational counseling field is that occupational choices represent an expression of personal needs and values (see Osipow, 1973). While it is not possible to state definitively that people with character structure X choose career Y, the assumption that there is a relationship between styles of relating to the world and career choice has been empirically documented. For example, teachers as a group tend to score high on measures of nurturance and affiliation, and low on measures of achievement (Holland, 1973; Kuhlen, 1963; Gray, 1963; Super, 1970). Thus, it may be ultimately possible to predict that workers in certain fields will be particularly susceptible or resistant to specific stresses on the basis of their stance relative to the world. It may also be possible to identify patterns of both effective and noneffective coping for any given occupational group. To accept a deterministic stance that argues that certain people choose certain careers and respond in invariable ways to stress, is clearly both overly simplistic and unrealistic. However, the possibility that there may be shared characteristics within groups that affect the nature of group interaction and are related to the individual's responses to occupational stress should be considered.

Still another topic that needs to be addressed concerns the temporal aspects of the burnout syndrome. Drawing upon a medical model that may prove to be inappropriate, we have conceptualized burnout as something one "catches" and then "has" for an indefinite period of time. Edelwich and Brodsky (1980) are among the few theorists who have suggested an evolutionary sequence of burnout symptomatology (enthusiasm, stagnation, frustration, and apathy) and their model remains to be empirically tested. In general, we do not know the normative sequence of symptoms of burnout, the average duration of each symptom or cluster of symptoms, or whether, like depression, burnout abates —even without intervention—with the passage of time. In addition, we do not know whether the stages of burnout vary across individuals and, if they do, what the correlates of these divergent patterns are.

There are, undoubtedly, a great many other issues that warrant further investigation. It could not be otherwise, given the newness of the field. Perhaps though, the greatest challenge that lies ahead is the formulation of a comprehensive model of stress and burnout. The foundation for such a model might well rest on two basic assumptions: that the interactive nature of individual, work-related, and social stressors, mediated by physiological, psychological, organizational, and social variables leads to dysfunctional personal and professional effects that range from mild stress to burnout; and that the extent of these impairments is determined by the nature and relative strength of both the stressors and the mediating variables.

Clearly, there have been both positive and negative aspects to the "discovery" and "legitimization" of burnout in the last ten years. The widespread attention focused on this phenomenon has certainly provided an impetus for attending to the needs of the overstressed worker. This, of course, works to the benefit of the individual worker and, even more important, to the benefit of scores of that individual's clients. On the other hand, there is something vaguely unsettling about the rapidity and enthusiasm with which the concept has been embraced by a legion of workers. One is reminded of Jerome Frank's (1974) observation that "by calling people's attention to symptoms they might otherwise ignore and by labeling those symptoms as signs of neurosis, mental health education can create unwarranted anxiety" (p. 8). The ubiquity of the word "burnout" has perhaps led to a climate where workers *expect* that they and their colleagues will burn out; perhaps there is even some sense of shame in not conforming to this new norm. Burnout, like mental health or mental illness, will certainly not go away. It remains to be seen though, how seriously this nation will deal with the claims of the increasing number of workers who perceive themselves as burned out.

REFERENCES

Cherniss, C. *Professional burnout in human service organizations.* New York: Praeger, 1980.

Edelwich, J. & Brodsky, A. *Burnout: Stages of disillusionment in the helping professions.* New York: Human Sciences Press, 1980.

Evans, P. A. & Bartolomé, F. The relationship between professional life and private life. In Derr, C. B. (Ed.), *Work, family and career.* New York: Praeger, 1980.

Farber, B. A. The effects of psychotherapeutic practice upon psychotherapists. *Psychotherapy: Theory, Research and Practice,* in press.

Frank, J. *Persuasion and healing.* Rev. ed. New York: Shocken Books, 1974.

Gillespie, D. F. Correlates for active and passive types of burnout. *Journal of Social Service Research,* 1981, **4**(2), 1–16.

Gray, J. T. Needs and values in three occupations. *Personnel and Guidance Journal,* 1963, **42**, 238–244.

Henry, W. E., Sims, J., & Spray, S. L. *Public and private lives of psychotherapists.* San Francisco: Jossey-Bass, 1973.

Holland, J. *Making vocational choices: A theory of careers.* Englewood Cliffs, N.J.: Prentice-Hall, 1973.

Keller, M. B., & Shapiro, R. W. "Double depression": Superimposition of acute depressive episodes on chronic depressive disorders. *The American Journal of Psychiatry,* 1982, **139**, 438–442.

Kuhlen, R. G. Needs, perceived need satisfaction opportunities, and satisfaction with occupation. *Journal of Applied Psychology,* 1963, **47**, 56–64.

Lazarus, R. S. & Launier, R. Stress-related transactions between person and environment. In Pervin, L. A. & Lewis, M. (Eds.), *Perspectives in interactional psychology.* New York: Plenum Press, 1978.

Osipow, S. H. *Theories of career development.* Englewood Cliffs, N.J.: Prentice-Hall, 1973.

Pines, A. & Aronson, E., with Kafry, D. *Burnout: From tedium to personal growth.* New York: Free Press, 1981.

Super, D. E. *Work values inventory.* Boston: Houghton Mifflin, 1970.

Author Index

Subject Index

About The Editor and Contributors

Barry A. Farber, Ph.D., is Assistant Professor of Psychology and Education in the Clinical Psychology Program at Teachers College, Columbia University. He received his Bachelor's degree (1968) in psychology from Queens College, City University of New York, his Master's degree (1970) in developmental psychology from Teachers College, Columbia University, and his Ph.D. (1978) in clinical-community psychology from Yale University.

J. Lawrence Aber, Ph.D., is Assistant Professor of Psychology, Barnard College, Columbia University.

Henry A. Bersani, Jr., Ph.D., is Assistant Professor of Educational Psychology and Special Education, Miami University, Oxford, Ohio.

Cary Cherniss, Ph.D., is Associate Professor and Research Psychologist at the Institute for the Study of Developmental Disabilities, University of Illinois, Chicago.

Wayne A. Chess, Ph.D., is Professor of Social Work, School of Social Work, University of Oklahoma, Norman, Oklahoma.

Russell Eisenstat, M.A., is a doctoral candidate in the Clinical-Community Psychology program at Yale University.

Robert D. Felner, Ph.D., is Associate Professor and Director of the Clinical-Community Psychology program at Auburn University.

William L. Fibkins, Ph.D., is a community psychologist currently involved in a Counseling and Organizational Renewal Program at Shoreham-Wading River Middle School, Shoreham, Long Island, New York.

Harvey J. Fischer, Ph.D., is in the private practice of psychoanalysis and psychotherapy, Lynbrook, Long Island, New York.

Herbert J. Freudenberger, Ph.D., is in independent psychoanalytic practice in New York City, and consultant to industry.

W. David Harrison, Ph.D., ACSW, is Assistant Professor, School of Social Work, University of Tennessee, Knoxville.

Louis J. Heifetz, Ph.D., is Associate Professor of Special Education, School of Education, Syracuse University, New York.

Francis A. J. Ianni, Ph.D., is Professor, Klingenstein Fellowship Program, Teachers College, Columbia University, and Consultant in Medical Psychology, St. Luke's-Roosevelt Psychiatric Center, New York City.

Srinika Jayaratne, Ph.D., is Associate Professor of Social Work, School of Social Work, University of Michigan, Ann Arbor.

David L. Krantz, Ph.D., is Professor of Psychology, Lake Forest College, Lake Forest, Illinois.

Betty Hosmer Mawardi, Ph.D., is Associate Professor of Medical Education Research and Project Director of Career Studies at Case Western Reserve University School of Medicine, Cleveland, Ohio.

Hanne Mørch, M.A., is a doctoral candidate in psychology at New York University.

Ayala Pines, Ph.D., is Research Associate, University of California at Berkeley.

Elizabeth Reuss-Ianni, M.A., is Director, Organized Crime Research Program, Institute for Social Analysis.

Mae L. Sakharov, Ed.D., is a member of the Faculty Resource Group School of New Resources, the College of New Rochelle, New Rochelle, New York.

Seymour B. Sarason, Ph.D., is Professor of Psychology, Yale University.

Rosemarie Scully, R.N., M.S., is a staff education instructor, Johns Hopkins Medical Institutions, Baltimore, Maryland.

Marybeth Shinn, Ph.D., is Assistant Professor of Psychology, New York University.